AVID COBB

THE GOOD SHEPHERD

C. S. FORESTER

★

The Good Shepherd

London
MICHAEL JOSEPH

First published by
MICHAEL JOSEPH LTD
26 Bloomsbury Street,
*London, W.C.*1
1955

Set and printed in Great Britain by Tonbridge Printers Ltd,
Peach Hall Works, Tonbridge, Kent, in Baskerville eleven
on thirteen point, on an antique paper made by Henry Bruce
at Currie in Scotland, and bound by James Burn at Esher

With thanks to
VICE-ADMIRAL RALPH W. CHRISTIE, U.S.N. (RETIRED)
onetime Commander Submarine Southwest Pacific
and to
COMMANDER J. D. P. HODAPP, U.S.N.,
onetime Commanding Officer
U.S.S. *Hall*

THE incidents described in this book never took place. So many officers and men served, and are serving, in the United States Navy that it is likely that some of them will find their names in the following pages. No reference is intended to anyone living or dead.

I

In that hour after dawn the horizon did not seem far away. The line where the watery sky met the grey sea was not well defined; it was as if the cheerless clouds grew denser out towards that circle until at the final meeting, all the way round, there was not an abrupt transition, but a simple mingling of twin elements. So the area confined under that low sky was not a large one. Beyond the circle, in every direction, the sea extended for a thousand miles, and beneath it the water was two miles deep; neither figure was easily to be grasped by the imagination, although acceptable as an academic fact. Two long miles below lay the sea-bottom, darker than the centre of the longest and darkest tunnel ever built by man, under pressures greater than any ever built up in factory or laboratory, a world unknown and unexplored, to be visited not by men but perhaps by their dead bodies encased in and made part of the iron coffins of their crushed-in ships. And the big ships, to insignificant man so huge and so solid, sank to that sea-bottom, to the immemorial ooze in the darkness and cold, with no more ado or stir than would be caused comparatively by specks of dust falling on a ballroom floor.

On the surface the limited area enclosed by the near horizon bore many ships. The long grey rollers from the north-east swept in endless succession across the area, each demonstrating its unlimited power. To each one as it arrived the ships made obeisance, rolling far over, and then heaving up their bows, mounting towards the sky, next rolling far over the other way, bows down, sterns up, slithering down the long slope before beginning the next roll and the next pitch, the next rise and the next fall; there were many ships in many lines and many columns, and by looking at the ships the course and position of each wave could be traced, diagonally across line and column— ships here rising on the crest and there sinking in the trough until the mastheads only were visible, ships here rolling far to port and ships there rolling far to starboard, towards each other and away, as long as patience could endure to watch.

And the ships were diversified like their motions, big ships and small, samson posts and cargo booms, freighters and tankers, new ships and old. Yet they all seemed to be animated by one will, all heading doggedly to the east, their transient washes all parallel; furthermore if they were watched for any length of time it would be seen that at long irregular intervals they changed their direction, a few degrees to port or a few degrees to starboard, rear ships following their leaders. But despite these variations of course it would soon be apparent to the observer that the resultant general direction of travel of this mass of ships was eastwards, doggedly and steadily, so that with every hour that passed they had covered a few of the thousand miles that lay between them and their easterly goal, whatever it might be. The same spirit animated each ship.

Nevertheless continuous observation would also reveal

that the animating spirit was not infallible, that these ships were not faultless machines. Hardly one of those alterations of course failed to produce a crisis somewhere among those thirty-seven ships. That might have been expected by the experienced observer even if each ship had been a mere machine not subject to human direction, because every ship was different from her neighbours; each reacted slightly differently at the application of the rudder, each was influenced in a different way by the waves which met them from dead ahead, or on the bow, or on the beam, and each ship was variously influenced by the wind; with ships hardly half a mile apart in one direction, and hardly a quarter of a mile apart in the other, these small differences of behaviour soon grew into matters of intense importance.

This would have been true even if each ship had been perfect in herself, and that was far from the case. The labouring engines grinding away in each of them were not capable of quite consistent performance, nor was the fuel absolutely uniform, and as time went on tubes might clog and valves might stick, so that the propellers that the engines drove would not continue to turn at a uniform rate. And compasses might not be absolutely true. And with the consumption of fuel and stores and with the consequent change of displacement the thrust of the propellers would bring about a different result even if miraculously it was kept turning at uniform speed. All these variables might only bring about a relative change of position of a few feet in a minute, but in those close-packed columns of ships a few feet difference in one minute could bring disaster in twenty.

Above and beyond all these variables was the human variable, the greatest variable of all. Men's hands turned wheels, men's eyes watched the gauges, men's skill kept the compass needles steady on the cards. All kinds of men, of slow reactions and of fast, cautious men and reckless men, men of vast experience and men of almost none; and the differences between the men were of more importance than the differences between the ships; the latter differences might bring about disaster in twenty minutes, but the human variable—a careless order or a misheard order, a wheel turned the wrong way or a calculation brought to a wrong conclusion—could bring disaster in twenty seconds. Those alterations of course were directed by the leading ship in the centre column; the hauling down of the signal flags which blew stiffly from her halyard indicated the exact moment when the turn had to be begun, one turn of a series planned days before. It was easy enough to make a wrong turn; it was easier still to feel a slight doubt about which turn was due to be made; it was just as easy to doubt the competence of one's neighbours. A cautious man might linger a while before giving the order, waiting to see what the others were doing, and those moments of delay could bring the bows of a ship in the next column pointing right at the beam, at the centre and heart, of the ship that hesitated. A touch could be death.

Compared with the immensity of the sea on which they floated the ships were tiny, insignificant; it might seem miraculous that they should cross that immensity in the face of the forces of nature and survive with certitude at their destination. It was the intelligence and ingenuity of man which made that possible, the accumulation of knowledge and experience since the first flint was chipped and the first picture-signs written. Now it was the intelligence and ingenuity of man which were adding to the hazards. There was menace in that lowering sky and in those huge waves, yet despite that menace the ships were continuing their complex and difficult manœuvres, close-packed to within a hair's-breadth of disaster, for should they discontinue those manœuvres, should they spread out to a safe distance, they were facing worse disaster still.

A thousand miles ahead of them men were waiting for those ships to arrive, men and women and children, although they did not know of the existence of those particular ships, not their names, nor the names of the men inside them with three-quarters of an inch of iron between them and the cold immensity of the sea. If those ships, if thousands of other ships equally unknown, did not reach their destination, the men and women and children who awaited their arrival would be hungry, cold, diseased. They might be torn to pieces by explosives. They might suffer a fate even worse—a fate they had years earlier decided, coldly, would be worse; they might be subjected to a tyrant of alien thought, their liberties torn from them, and in that case—they knew it by instinct even when they were not capable of logical deduction—not only they, but the whole human race would suffer, and liberty would decline throughout the world.

On board the ships there were men imbued with the same knowledge, even if that knowledge were forgotten in the urgency of keeping station and maintaining course and speed, and even though in the same ship with them were plenty of men who did not have that knowledge, men who were there amidst those perils for other reasons or for no reason, men who desired money or drink or women or the security that money can sometimes buy, men with much to forget and half-wits with nothing to forget, men with children to feed and men with problems too difficult to face.

They were engaged upon the task of keeping the propellers turning, or of keeping the ships afloat, or of maintaining them in their stations, or of keeping them in working condition, or they were engaged in feeding the men who occupied themselves with these tasks. But while they carried out their duties, whether from motives lofty or base or non-existent, they were no more than parts of the ships they served—not machined to any measurable tolerance thanks to their human variability—and they, or their ships (not to differentiate between ships and their crews) were things to be fought for, things to be protected by one side or destroyed by the other; things to be escorted across the ocean or things to be sent down into the freezing depths.

2

THERE were nearly two thousand men in the convoy; there were over eight hundred in the four destroyers and escort vessels that guarded it. Expressing uselessly values quite immeasurable, three thousand lives and property worth fifty million dollars were in the charge of Commander George Krause, of the United States Navy, aged forty-two, height five feet nine, weight one hundred and fifty-five pounds, complexion medium, colour of eyes grey; and he was not only escort commander but captain of the destroyer *Keeling* of the Mahan class of fifteen hundred tons displacement, commissioned in 1938.

These were bald facts; and facts may mean very little. Back in the centre of the convoy was the tanker *Hendrikson*; it was of no importance that in the books of the company that owned her she was valued at a quarter of a million dollars and the oil that she carried at another quarter of a million. That meant literally nothing; but the fact that if she should arrive in England her cargo would provide an hour's steaming for the entire British Navy meant something too important to be measured at all—what money price can be put on an hour's freedom for the world? The thirsty man in the desert pays no heed to his pocketful of banknotes. Yet the fact that Commander Krause tipped the scale at a hundred and fifty-five could be of appreciable importance; it could be a measure of the speed with which he could reach the bridge in an emergency, and, once on the bridge, it might give some faint indication of his ability to withstand the physical strain of remaining there. That was something of far more importance than the book value of the *Hendrikson*; it was of more importance even to the men who owned her, although they might not believe it, never having heard of Commander George Krause of the United States Navy. And they would not have been in the least interested to hear that he was the son of a Lutheran minister, that he had been devoutly brought up, and that he was a man very familiar with the Bible. Yet these were matters of primary importance, for in war the character and personality of the leader are decisive of events much more than minor questions of material.

He was in his cabin, having come out from under the shower, and he had towelled himself dry. It was the first opportunity he had had in thirty-six hours to take a bath, and he did not expect to have another for a long time. This was the blessed moment after securing from general quarters with the coming of full daylight. He had put on his thick woollen underclothes, his shirt and his trousers, his socks and his shoes. He had just finished combing his hair, a rather perfunctory gesture, for the mouse-coloured bristles, recently cropped short, were insusceptible to treatment. He stared into the mirror to check that his shave had been all that it should be. His eyes (grey by courtesy; more hazel than grey, and with a stony quality) met those of the reflection in the mirror without recognition or sympathy, as they would meet those of a stranger— for Krause was indeed a stranger to himself, someone to be regarded impersonally if regarded at all. His body was something to be employed upon duty.

This bathing and shaving, this putting on of a clean shirt at this hour of the morning, all this dressing with the day far advanced, were a distortion of the proper order of things caused by the exigencies of war. Krause had already been on his feet for three hours. He had gone to the bridge in the darkness before general quarters had sounded, ready for the crisis that dawn might bring, and he had stood there as the blackness of the night turned slowly into the grey of dawn, with his ship and his men braced for action. With full daylight—if that melancholy greyness merited the term—the ship had secured from general quarters, and Krause could read the accumulated messages brought him by the communication officer, and he could receive brief reports from his heads of department, inspect with his own eyes, by the aid of his binoculars, the fighting ships under his command to starboard and port, and the vast mass of the convoy manœuvring far astern of him. With dawn an hour ago it might be considered that the safest moment of the day had come, and Krause could briefly retire. He could offer up his prayers on his knees. He could take his breakfast. And then he could bathe and change even though it seemed highly irregular to do so at this time and not at the beginning of a new day.

He turned away from the stranger in the mirror, satisfied that he was properly shaved, and then he stood still, with one hand on the chair-back and his eyes cast down to the deck on which he stood.

'Yesterday, today, and forever,' he said to himself, as he always did when he had passed his own inspection. That was a passage from Hebrews viii; it marked the fact that he was starting out on a fresh stage of his journey through the temporary world, to the grave and to immortality beyond it. He gave the necessary attention to that train of thought; and while his mind was so occupied his body automatically retained its balance, for the ship was rolling and pitching as only a destroyer can roll and pitch—as she had rolled and pitched without ceasing for the past several days. The deck was rising and falling beneath his feet, inclining sharply to port and starboard, forward and aft, sometimes seemingly changing its mind, with a tremor, in mid-movement, interrupting the rhythm of the rattle of the scant furnishings of the cabin under the urging of the vibration of the propellers.

Of the twenty years which had elapsed since Krause's graduation from Annapolis, thirteen had been spent at sea, and mostly in destroyers, so that his body was amply accustomed to retaining its balance in a rolling ship, even at these moments when Krause himself was thinking about the immortality of the soul and the transience of earthly things.

Krause raised his eyes and reached for the sweater that was the next garment he had planned to put on. Before his hand touched it there came a loud note from the bell on the bulkhead, and from the voice-tube issued the voice of Lieutenant Carling, who had taken over the deck when the ship secured from general quarters.

'Captain to the bridge, sir,' said Carling. 'Captain to the bridge, sir.'

There was urgency in the voice. Krause's hand changed its objective. It snatched, not the sweater, but the uniform coat dangling on its hanger. With his other hand Krause swept aside the fibre-glass curtain that screened the door-way, and in his shirt-sleeves, still holding the coat, he plunged for the bridge. Seven seconds elapsed between the time when the bell sounded its note to the time when

Krause entered the pilot-house. He did not have another second in which to look around him.

'Harry's made a contact, sir,' said Carling.

Krause sprang to the radio-telephone—the T.B.S., the 'talk between ships.'

'George to Harry. George to Harry. Go ahead.'

He swung to his left as he spoke, staring out over the heaving sea. Three and a half miles to port was the Polish destroyer *Viktor*; three and a half miles beyond her was H.M.S. *James*; she was on *Viktor*'s quarter, considerably aft; from the pilot-house she was only just visible round the corner of the superstructure, and at that distance she was often invisible, when both she and *Keeling* were down in the trough. Now she was off her course, heading northwards away from the convoy, presumably following up her contact. It was the *James* who called herself Harry in the T.B.S. code. As Krause's eyes focused on her the telephone bleated. No amount of distortion could disguise the peculiar English intonation of the voice.

'Distant contact, sir. Bearing three-five-five. Request permission to attack.'

Eleven words, one of which might possibly be omitted; but they presented a problem of enormous complexity, in which a score of factors had to be correlated—and to which a solution had to be found in as few seconds as possible. Krause's eye sought the repeater and a well-accustomed mind simplified one factor in a moment. A contact-bearing three-five-five lay, on the present leg of the zigzag, just forward of the port beam. *James*, as the wing ship of the four-destroyer escort, was three miles to port of the convoy. The U-boat—if indeed the contact indicated the presence of a U-boat, which was by no means certain—then must lie several miles from the convoy, and not far forward of the convoy's port beam. A glance at the clock; in fourteen minutes another change of course was due. This would be to starboard, turning the convoy definitely away from the U-boat. That was a point in favour of leaving the U-boat alone.

There were other factors favouring the same decision. There were only four fighting ships for the whole screen, only sufficient when all were in station to cover the whole immense front of the convoy by sonar search. Detach one —or two—and there would be practically no screen, only gaps through which other U-boats might well slip. It was a weighty factor, but there was a factor more weighty still, the question of fuel consumption—the factor that had burdened the mind of every naval officer since sail. *James* would have to work up to full speed; she would be detached far off the convoy's course. She might be searching for hours, and, whatever the result of the search, she would have to rejoin the convoy which most likely would be heading away from her during the whole search. That would mean an hour, or two, or three, at high speed with an extra consumption of some tons of fuel. There was fuel to spare, but little enough, only a small reserve. Was it advisable, at this moment, with action only just beginning, to make inroads upon that reserve? During Krause's lifetime of professional training no point had been more insisted on than that every wise officer kept a reserve in hand to employ at the crisis of a battle. It was an argument—the constant argument—in favour of caution.

But then, on the other hand, a contact had been made. It was possible—it might even just be called likely—that a U-boat might be killed. The killing of a U-boat would be a substantial success in itself. And the consequences might be more important still. If that U-boat were allowed to depart unharmed, she could surface, and by her radio she could inform German U-boat headquarters of the presence of shipping at this point in the Atlantic—shipping that could only be Allied shipping, that could only be targets for U-boat torpedoes. That was the least the U-boat might do; she might surface, and, making use of her surface speed, twice that of the convoy, she might keep the latter under observation, determine its speed and base course, and call up—if German headquarters had not already issued such orders—a wolf-pack of colleagues to intercept and to launch a mass attack. If she were destroyed, nothing of this could happen; if she were even kept down for an hour or two while the convoy made good its escape, the business of finding the convoy again would be made much more difficult for the Germans, much more prolonged, possibly made too difficult altogether.

'Still making contact, sir,' squawked the telephone.

It was twenty-four seconds since Krause had arrived on the bridge, fifteen seconds since he had been confronted with the complex problem in its entirety. It was fortunate that during hours on the bridge, during hours solitary in his cabin, Krause had thought deeply about similar problems. No possible amount of thinking could envisage every circumstance; the present case—the exact bearing of the contact, the current fuel situation, the position of the convoy, the time of day—added up to one out of thousands of possible situations. And there were other factors that Krause had envisaged as well; he was an American officer whom the chances of war had tossed into the command of an Allied convoy. A freak of seniority had put under the orders of him, who had never heard a shot fired in anger, a group of hard-bitten young captains of other nations with the experience of thirty months of war. That introduced a

number of factors of enormous importance but not suscep-
tible of exact calculation like a fuel-consumption problem
—not even as calculable as the chances of effecting a kill
after making a contact. What would the captain of the
James think of him if he refused permission to attack? What
would the seamen in the convoy think of him if other
U-boats got in through the screen so dangerously attenuated
by that permission? When the reports started to come in
would one government querulously complain to another
that he had been too rash? Or too cautious? Would officers
of one navy shake their heads pityingly, and officers of
another navy try half-heartedly to defend him? Gossip flies
rapidly in an armed service; seamen can talk even in wartime until their complaints reach the ears of congressmen
or members of parliament. Allied goodwill depended to
some extent on his decision; and upon Allied goodwill
depended ultimate victory and the freedom of the world.
Krause had envisaged these aspects of his problem, too,
but in the present case they could not affect his decision.
They merely made his decision more important, merely
added to the burden of responsibility that rested on his
shoulders.

'Permission granted,' he said.

'Aye aye, sir,' said the telephone.

The telephone squawked again instantly.

'Eagle to George,' it said. 'Request permission to assist
Harry.'

Eagle was the Polish destroyer *Viktor*, on *Keeling*'s port
beam between her and the *James*, and the voice was that
of the young British officer who rode in her to transmit
T.B.S. messages.

'Permission granted,' said Krause.

'Aye aye, sir.'

Krause saw the *Viktor* wheel about as soon as the words were spoken; her bows met a roller in a fountain of spray, and she heaved up her stern as she soared over it, still turning, working up speed to join the *James*. *Viktor* and *James* were a team that had already achieved a 'probable sinking' in a previous convoy. *James* had the new sound range-recorder and had developed a system of coaching *Viktor* in to make the kill. The two ships were buddies; Krause had known from the moment the contact had been reported to him that if he detached one it would be better to detach both, to make a kill more likely.

It was now fifty-nine seconds since the summons to Krause in his cabin; it had taken not quite a minute to reach an important decision and to transmit the orders translating that decision into action. Now it was necessary to dispose his two remaining escort ships, *Keeling* and H.M.C.S. *Dodge*, out on his starboard quarter, to the best advantage; to attempt with two ships to screen thirty-seven. The convoy covered three square miles of sea, an immense target for any torpedo fired 'into the brown,' and such a torpedo could be fired advantageously from any point of a semi-circle forty miles in circumference. The best attempt to cover that semi-circle with two ships would be a poor compromise, but the best attempt must still be made. Krause spoke into the telephone again.

'George to Dicky.'

'Sir!' squawked the telephone back to him instantly. *Dodge* must have been expecting orders.

'Take station three miles ahead of the leading ship of the starboard column of the convoy.'

Krause spoke with the measured tones necessary for the transmission of verbal orders; it called attention to the unmusical quality of his voice.

'Three miles ahead of the leading ship of the starboard column,' said the telephone back to him. 'Aye aye, sir.'

That was a Canadian voice, with a pitch and a rhythm more natural than the British. No chance of misunderstanding there. Krause looked at the repeater and then turned to the officer of the deck.

'Course zero-zero-five, Mr. Carling.'

'Aye aye, sir,' answered Carling, and then to the quartermaster, 'Left standard rudder. Steer course zero-zero-five.

'Left standard rudder,' repeated the helmsman, turning the wheel. 'Course zero-zero-five.'

That was Parker, quartermaster third class, aged twenty-two and married and no good. Carling knew that, and was watching the repeater.

'Make eighteen knots, Mr Carling,' said Krause.

'Aye aye, sir,' answered Carling, giving the order.

'Make turns for eighteen knots,' repeated the man at the annunciator.

Keeling turned in obedience to her helm; the vibration transmitted from the deck up through Krause's feet quickened, as the ship headed for her new station.

'Engine room answers one eight knots,' announced the hand at the engine-room telegraph. He was new to the ship, a transfer made when they were in Reykjavik, serving his second hitch. Two years back he had been in trouble with the civil authorities for a hit-run automobile offence while on leave. Krause could not remember his name, and must remedy that.

'Steady on course zero-zero-five,' announced Parker; there was the usual flippant note in his voice that annoyed Krause and hinted at his unreliability. Nothing to be done about it at present; only the mental note made.

'Making eighteen by pit, sir,' reported Carling.

24

'Very well.' That was the pitometer log reading. There were more orders to give.

'Mr Carling, take station three miles ahead of the leading ship of the port column of the convoy.'

'Three miles ahead of the leading ship of the port column of the convoy. Aye aye, sir.'

Krause's orders had already set *Keeling* on an economical course towards that station, and now that she was crossing ahead of it would be a good moment to check on the convoy. But he could spare a moment now to put on his coat; until now he had been in his shirt-sleeves with his coat in his hand. He slipped into it; as his arm straightened he dug the telephone talker beside him in the ribs.

'Pardon me,' said Krause.

'Quite all right, sir,' mumbled the telephone talker.

Carling had his hand on the lever that sounded the general alarm, and was looking to his captain for orders.

'No,' said Krause.

Calling the ship to general quarters would bring every single man on board to his post of duty. No one would sleep and hardly anyone would eat; the ordinary routine of the ship would cease entirely. Men grew fatigued and hungry; the fifty-odd jobs about the ship that had to be done sooner or later to keep her efficient would all be left until later because the men who should be doing them would be at their battle stations. It was not a condition that could long be maintained—it was the battle reserve, once more, to be conserved until the crucial moment.

And there was the additional point that some men, many men, tended to become slack about the execution of their duty if special demands were continually made on them without obvious reason. Krause knew this by observation during his years of experience, and he knew it academically, too, through study of the manuals, in the same way as a doctor is familiar with diseases from which he has never suffered himself. Krause had to allow for the weaknesses of the human flesh under his command, and the flightiness of the human mind. *Keeling* was already in Condition Two, with battle stations largely manned and water-tight integrity—with its concomitant interference with the routine of the ship—strictly maintained. Condition Two meant a strain on the hands, and was bad for the ship, but the length of time during which Condition Two could be endured was measurable in days, compared with the hours that Battle Stations could be endured.

The fact that *James* was running down a contact at some distance from the convoy, with *Viktor* to help her, was not sufficient justification for sounding the general alarm; it was likely that dozens more such contacts would be reported before the convoy reached home. So Krause said 'No' in reply to Carling's unvoiced enquiry. Glance, decision, and reply consumed no more than two or three seconds of time. It would have taken at least several minutes for Krause to have given verbally all the reasons for that decision; it would have taken him a minute or two at least for him to assemble them in his mind. But long habit and long experience made the reaching of decisions easy to him, and long thought had familiarized his mind beforehand with the conditions surrounding this particular emergency.

And at the same time his memory made a note of the incident, even though apparently it passed out of his mind as soon as it was disposed of. Carling's readiness to sound General Quarters was an item added to Krause's mental dossier about Carling. It would affect, to some possibly infinitesimal extent, how much Krause could trust Carling as officer of the deck. It might eventually affect the 'fitness report' which in course of time Krause would be making on Carling (assuming both of them lived long enough for that report to be made) with special bearing on the paragraph regarding Carling's 'fitness for command.' A tiny incident, one in thousands that made a complex whole.

Krause picked up his binoculars, hung them round his neck, and trained them towards the convoy. In the crowded pilot-house it was impossible to get a clear sight, and he stepped out on to the port wing of the bridge. The transition was instant and prodigious. The north-east wind, almost from dead ahead on this course, shrieked round him. As he raised the glasses to his eyes his right armpit felt the bitter cold strike into it. He should be wearing his sweater and his greatcoat; he would have been doing so if he had been left undisturbed for a minute longer in his sea-cabin.

They were passing the convoy flagship, an ancient passenger vessel with upper works lofty in comparison with the rest of the convoy. The convoy commodore whose pennant flew in her was an elderly British admiral back from retirement, undertaking a difficult, monotonous, dangerous and inglorious duty of his own free will, as of course he ought to do as long as the opportunity presented itself, even though that meant being under the orders of a young Commander of another nation. His present duty was to keep the ships of the convoy as nearly in order as possible, so as to give the escort every chance of protecting it.

Beyond the convoy flagship the rest of the convoy spread itself in irregular lines; Krause swept his binoculars round to examine them. The lines were certainly irregular, but not nearly as irregular as they had been when he had examined them at the end of the night, in the first light of dawn. Then the third column from starboard had been revealed in two halves, with the last three ships—five ships

27

in that column, four in each of the others—trailing far astern, out of the formation altogether. Now the gap had been nearly closed. Presumably No. 3 ship, the Norwegian *Kong Gustav*, had experienced an engine-room defect during the night and had fallen astern; in the radio silence and the blackout that were so strictly enforced, and with flag signals invisible in the darkness, she had been unable to inform the others of her plight, and had fallen farther and farther astern, with the ships following her conforming to her movements. Apparently the defect had been made good and *Kong Gustav* and her two followers were slowly crawling up into position again. The *Southland*, immediately astern of *Kong Gustav*—Krause had checked the name on his list soon after dawn—was smoking badly, perhaps in the effort to steam an extra half-knot to regain station, and several other ships were making more smoke than they should. Luckily, with the wind from ahead, and blowing hard, the smoke was lying low and dispersing rapidly. In calmer conditions the convoy would have been surmounted by a pillar of cloud visible fifty miles away. The Commodore had a signal-hoist flying—almost for certain it was the signal so frequently displayed in every navy—'Make less smoke.'

But conditions in the convoy could generally be described as good, with only three ships badly out of station and only a certain amount of smoke being made. There was time for a rapid glance round the *Keeling*; significant it was that Krause's first care had been for the convoy and only his second care had been for his own ship. He lowered his binoculars and turned to look forward, the wind hitting him in the face as he did so, and, along with the wind, a few drops of spray hurled aft from the heaving bows. Aloft, the 'bed-spring' of the radar antenna was making its methodical gyrations, turning round and round while the mast, with the rolling and pitching, was outlining cones, apex downward, of every conceivable dimension. The look-outs were at their posts, seven of them, all bundled-up in their arctic clothing, their eyes at the binoculars in the rests in front of them, traversing slowly to left and to right and back again, each sweeping his own special sector, but with each having to pause every few seconds to wipe from the object-glasses the spray flying back from the bows. Krause gave the look-outs a moment's inspection; Carling, with his mind preoccupied with the duty of taking the ship to her new station, would not be giving them a glance at present. They seemed to be doing their work conscientiously; sometimes—unbelievable though it might be—look-outs were found wanting in that respect, tiring of a monotonous job despite frequent relief. It was a duty that had to be carried out with the utmost pains and method, without an instant's interruption; a U-boat would never expose more than a foot or two of periscope above the surface of the sea, and never for more than half a minute at most; search had to be constant and regular to give any chance, not speaking of probability, of the transient appearance being detected. A second's glimpse of a periscope could decide the fate of the convoy. There was even the chance that the sight of torpedo wakes streaking towards the ship and instantly reported might at least save the *Keeling*.

This was as long as he dared stay out on the wing of the bridge; half his force was heading towards battle out there to port—*Viktor* had 'peeled off' to join *James* some time ago—and he must be at the T.B.S. to exert control if necessary. Young Hart was approaching the port pelorus to take the bearings for Carling in his task of taking up station. Krause gave him a nod and went back into the wheel-house. The comparative warmth of it reminded him that in that brief time outside, without sweater or P-jacket, he had been chilled through. He stepped to the telephone; it was bleating and gurgling. He was overhearing the conversations between the British officers in *James* and *Viktor*.

'Bearing three-six-oh,' said one English voice.

'Can't you get the range, old boy?' said another.

'No, damn it. Contact's too indistinct. Haven't you picked it up yet?'

'Not yet. We've swept that sector twice.'

'Come ahead slowly.'

From where Krause stood *James* was indistinguishable in the murk of the near horizon. She was only a little ship and her upper-works were not lofty. *Viktor* was bigger and higher and nearer; he could still see her, but she was already vague. With visibility so poor and the ships separating rapidly he would not have her in sight much longer although she would be prominent enough on the radar screen. Carling's voice suddenly made itself audible; he may have been speaking before but Krause, concentrating on the T.B.S., had not listened to him, as what he was saying had no bearing on the problem in hand.

'Right standard rudder. Steer course zero-seven-nine,' said Carling.

'Right standard rudder. Course zero-seven-nine,' repeated Parker.

Keeling was at her new station now, or near it, evidently. She swung round, turning her stern almost directly towards *Viktor*. The distance between the two ships would now be widening more rapidly than before. *Keeling* rolled deeply to starboard, unexpectedly; feet slipped on the pilot-house deck, hands grabbed for security. Her turn had brought her into the hollow of the next roller without the opportunity to lift to it. She lay over for a long second, levelled herself abruptly, and equally abruptly lay over to port as the roller passed under her keel, so that feet slipped in the opposite direction and Carling came sliding down upon Krause.

'Sorry, sir,' said Carling.

'All right.'

'Steady on zero-seven-nine,' announced Parker.

'Very well,' answered Carling, and then to Krause, 'Next zigzag is due in five minutes, sir.'

'Very well,' said Krause in his turn. It was one of his standing orders that he should be called five minutes before any change of course on the part of the convoy. The turn would bring the convoy's sterns exactly towards *Viktor* and *James*. It was nine minutes since *James* had peeled off; she must be more than three miles from her station now, and the distance would be increasing by a quarter or even half a mile every minute. Her maximum speed in this sea would not be more than sixteen knots. It would take her half an hour—and that half-hour one of maximum fuel consumption—to retain her station if he recalled her now. And every minute that he postponed doing so meant she would spend five extra minutes over-taking the convoy; in other words if he left her out there for five more minutes it would be a full hour before she would be back in her station. Another decision to be made.

'George to Harry,' he said into the telephone.

'I hear you, George.'

'How's that contact of yours?'

'Not very good, sir.'

Sonar notoriously could be inconsistent. There was much more than a faint chance that *James* was pursuing something that was not a submarine. Possibly even a school of fish; more likely a layer of colder or warmer water, seeing that *Viktor* was finding difficulty in getting a cross-bearing on it.

'Is it worth following it up?'

'Well, sir. I think so, sir.'

If there really were a U-boat there the German captain would be well aware that contact had been made; he would have changed course radically, and would now be fish-tailing and varying his depth; that would account at least in large part for the unsatisfactory contact. There was a new German device for leaving a big bubble behind, producing a transient sonar effect baffling to the sonar operator. There might be some new unknown device more baffling still. There might be a U-boat there.

On the other hand, if there were, and if *James* and *Viktor* were recalled, it would be some minutes before the U-boat would venture to surface; she would be doubtful as to the bearing of the convoy which would be heading directly away from her; she would certainly not make more than sixteen knots on the surface in this sea and probably less. The risk involved in leaving her to her own devices had been considerably diminished by those few minutes of pursuit. There was the matter of the effect such a decision would have on his British and Polish subordinates; they might resent being called off from a promising hunt, and sulk on a later occasion—but that reply to his last question had not been enthusiastic, even allowing for British lack of emphasis.

'You'd better call it off, Harry,' said Krause in his flat, impersonal voice.

'Aye aye, sir.' The reply was in a tone that echoed his own.

'Eagle, Harry, rejoin the convoy and take up your previous stations.'

32

'Aye aye, sir.'

There was no guessing whether the decision had caused resentment or not.

'Commodore's signalling for the change of course, sir,' reported Carling.

'Very well.'

This slow convoy did not zigzag in the fashion of fast convoys; the passage would be prolonged inordinately if it did. The alterations of course were made at long intervals, so long that it was impossible for merchant captains to maintain station on the difficult lines of bearing involved in the fast convoy system—it was hard enough for them to maintain simple column and line. Consequently every change of course meant a ponderous wheel to left or to right, only a matter of ten or fifteen degrees, but that was a major operation. One wing had to maintain speed while the other reduced speed. Leaders had to put their helms over gently, and it seemed as if the ships following would never learn the simple lesson that to follow their leaders round in a wheel to starboard it was necessary to wait and then to turn exactly where the ship ahead turned; to turn too soon meant that one found oneself on the starboard side of the leader, and threatening the ships in the column to starboard; to turn too late meant heading straight for the ships in the column to port. In either event there would be need to jockey oneself back into one's proper place in the column; not too easily.

Moreover, in this wheeling movement of the whole mass, it was necessary for the ships in the outer flank to move faster than those in the inner flank, which actually meant—seeing that those on the outer flank were already steaming as hard as they could go—that the ships in the starboard column must reduce speed. The large mimeographed booklet of instructions issued to every captain laid down standard proportionate reductions in speed for every column, but to comply with those instructions meant leafing hurriedly through the booklet and doing a rapid calculation when the right place was found. And if the correct figure were ascertained there was still the difficulty of getting an unpractised engine-room staff to make an exact reduction in speed; and there was always the difficulty that every ship responded to the rudder in a different way, with a different turning circle.

Every wheel the convoy made was in consequence followed by a period of confusion. Lines and columns tended to open out, vastly increasing the area the escort had to guard, and there were always likely to be stragglers, and experience had long proved that a ship straggling from the formation would almost certainly be sent to the bottom. Krause went out on to the starboard wing of the bridge and levelled his binoculars at the convoy. He saw the string of flags at the Commodore's halyards come down.

'Execute, sir,' reported Carling.

'Very well.'

It was Carling's duty to report that hauling down even though Krause was aware of it; it was the executive moment, the signal that the wheel was to begin. Krause heard Carling give the order for the new course, and he had to train round his binoculars as *Keeling* turned. The ship leading the starboard column six miles away lengthened as she presented her side to his gaze; the three 'islands' of her superstructure differentiated themselves in his sight now that she was nearly broadside on to him. A heavy roll on the part of *Keeling* swept the ship out of the field of his binoculars; he found himself looking at the heaving sea, and he had to retrain the glasses, balancing and swaying with the roll to keep the convoy under observation. There was confusion almost instantly. The convoy changed from an almost orderly checker-board of lines and columns into a muddle of ships dotted haphazard, ships shearing out of line, ships trying to regain station, columns doubling up with the tail crowding on the head. Krause tried to keep the whole convoy under observation, even though the farthest ships were hardly visible in the thick weather; a collision might call for instant action on his part. He could detect none, but there must be some tense moments in the heart of the convoy.

The seconds, the minutes, were passing. The front of the convoy was an indented line. To all appearances there were not the nine columns that there should have been, but ten, eleven, no, twelve. On the starboard quarter of the Commodore an intrusive ship appeared. Ships were straying, as was only to be expected, out beyond the starboard leader. If one single ship did not obey orders exactly, did not reduce speed at the correct moment, or turned too soon or too late, ten ships might be forced out of station, jostling each other. As Krause watched he saw one of the most distant ships turning until her stern was presented to him. Someone out there of necessity or from recklessness was turning in a full circle; squeezed out from his position he was about to try to nose his way into it again. And out there on that heaving expanse of water could be a U-boat, possibly one commanded by a cautious captain, hanging on the skirts of the convoy. An outlying ship like that would be a choice victim, to be torpedoed without any chance of one of the escort running down to the attack at all. Be sober, be vigilant, because your adversary the Devil as a roaring lion walketh about seeking whom he may devour.

There were flag-hoists ascending the Commodore's

35

halyards, presumably orders designed to straighten out the confusion. Inexperienced men would be trying to read them, through ancient telescopes, and with their ships heaving and swaying under their feet. Krause swung round to examine the port side column over *Keeling*'s quarter. That was in the least disorder, as might be expected; Krause looked beyond them. In the haze on the far horizon he could see a dot with a line above it. That was *Viktor*, coming up at her best speed to resume her station. *James*, with her poor sixteen knots, must be far astern of her.

As Krause turned back to re-examine the convoy a bright flash of light caught his eye, a series of flashes, from the Commodore. She was sending a searchlight signal, and her searchlight was trained straight at *Keeling*. It would be a signal for him; P-L-E- he fell behind with his reading of it, for the transmission was too fast for him. He looked up at his signallers; they were reading it without difficulty, one man noting down the letters as read to him by the other. A longish message, not one of desperate urgency then—and for moments of desperate urgency there were far more rapid means of communication. Up above they blinked back the final acknowledgment.

'Signal for you, sir,' called the signalman, stepping forward pad in hand.

'Read it.'

' "Comconvoy to Comescort. Will you please direct your corvette on the starboard side to assist in getting convoy into order, question. Would be grateful." '

'Reply "Comescort to Comconvoy. Your last. Affirmative." '

' "Comescort to Comconvoy. Your last. Affirmative." Aye aye, sir.'

Comconvoy had to word his signal like that, presumably;

he was making requests of an associate, not giving orders to a subordinate. Let thy words be few, said Ecclesiastes; the officer drafting an order had to bear that recommendation in mind, but a retread admiral addressing an escort commander had to remember the Psalms and make his words smoother than butter.

Krause went back into the pilot-house, to the T.B.S.

'George to Dicky,' he said in that flat distinct voice. The reply was instant; *Dodge* was alert enough.

'Leave your station,' he ordered. 'Go and——' he checked himself for a moment; then he remembered that it was a Canadian ship he was addressing so that the phrase he had in mind would not be misunderstood as it might be by the *James* or the *Viktor*, and he continued—'go and ride herd on the convoy on the starboard side.'

'Ride herd on the convoy. Aye aye, sir.'

'Look to the Commodore for instructions,' went on Krause, 'and get those stragglers back into line.'

'Aye aye, sir.'

'Keep your sonar searching on that flank. That's the dangerous side at present.'

'Aye aye, sir.'

I say to this man 'Go,' and he goeth; and to another 'Come' and he cometh. But what of the 'great faith' that centurion had? *Dodge* was already wheeling round to carry out her orders. Now there was more to be done. The front of the convoy had been inadequately enough screened already, and now nearly all of it was wide open to attack. So there were more orders to give, orders to set *Keeling* patrolling along the whole five-mile front of the convoy, her sonar sweeping first on one side and then on the other as she steamed back and forth in a stout-hearted attempt to detect possible enemies anywhere in the convoy's broad path, while *Dodge* moved about on the right flank of the convoy, her captain shouting himself hoarse through his bull-horn at the laggards—the words of the wise are as goads—at the same time as her sonar kept watch behind him. I was eyes to the blind, and feet was I to the lame.

Krause walked from the starboard wing of the bridge to the port side as *Keeling* made her second turn about. He wanted to keep his eye on the convoy; he wanted to use his own judgment as to when *Dodge* would have completed her task on the right flank, and as to when *Viktor* would be available to take her share of the patrol across the front. Even on the wing of the bridge, with the wind blowing, he was conscious, when he thought about it, of the monotonous ping-ping-ping of the ship's sonar as it sent out its impulses through the unresponsive water. That noise went on ceaselessly, day and night, as long as the ship was at sea, so that the ear and the mind became accustomed to it unless attention were called to it.

The Commodore's searchlight was blinking again, straight at him; another message. He glanced up at the signalman receiving it. The sharp rattle of the shutters of their light in reply told him that they had not understood a word and were asking for a repeat; he checked his irritation, for perhaps the Commodore was using some long-winded English polite form outside the man's experience. But the time the message took to transmit did not indicate that it was long.

'Signal for you, sir.'

'Read it.'

The signalman, pad in hand as before, was a little hesitant.

' "Comconvoy to Comescort," sir. "Huff-Duff——" '

There was an inquiring note in the signalman's voice there, and a second's pause.

'Yes, Huff-Duff,' said Krause, testily. That was HFDF, high-frequency direction finding; his signalman had not met the expression before.

' "Huff-Duff reports foreign transmission bearing eight-seven range from one-five to two-zero miles," sir.'

Bearing zero-eight-seven. That was nearly in the path of the convoy. Foreign transmission; that could mean only one thing here in the Atlantic; a U-boat fifteen to twenty miles away. Leviathan, that crooked serpent. This was something far more positive and certain than *James*'s possible contact. This was something calling for instant decision as ever, and that decision had to be based as ever on a score of factors.

'Reply "Comescort to Comconvoy. Will run it down." '

' "Comescort to Comconvoy. Will run it down." Aye aye, sir.'

'Wait. "Will run it down. Thank you." '

' "Will run it down. Thank you." Aye aye, sir.'

Two strides took Krause into the pilot-house.

'I'll take the conn, Mr Carling.'

'Aye aye, sir.'

'Right smartly to course zero-eight-seven.'

'Right smartly to course zero-eight-seven.'

'All engines ahead flank speed. Make turns for twenty-two knots.'

'All engines ahead flank speed. Make turns for twenty-two knots.'

'Mr Carling, sound general quarters.'

'General quarters. Aye aye, sir.'

The warning horns blared through the ship as Carling pressed down on the handle; a din fit to wake the dead, to wake the exhausted sleepers in their bunks far below, summoning every man to his post, starting a torrent of men up the ladders. Clothes would be dragged on, unfinished letters flung aside, equipment snatched up. Through the din came the report, 'Engine-room answers flank speed, sir.' *Keeling* was heeling as she turned; Heeling-Keeling was what the men called her, Heeling-Keeling, Reeling-Keeling.

'Steady on course zero-eight-seven,' said Parker.

'Very well. Mr Hart, how does the Commodore bear?'

Ensign Hart was at the pelorus in a moment.

'Two-six-six, sir,' he called.

Practically dead astern. The Huff-Duff bearing in itself would be exact enough. No need to plot a course to the estimated position of the U-boat.

Already the wheel-house was thronging with newcomers, helmeted figures, bundled-up figures, telephone talkers, messengers. There was much to be done; Krause went to the T.B.S.

'Eagle, I am running down a Huff-Duff indication bearing zero-eight-seven.'

'Oh-eight-seven. Aye aye, sir.'

'Take my place and cover the front of the convoy as quickly as you can.'

'Aye aye, sir.'

'You hear me, Harry?'

'I hear you, George.'

'Cover the left flank.'

'Cover the left flank. Aye aye, sir. We are four miles astern of the last ship, sir.'

'I know.'

It would be more than half an hour before *James* would be in her station; it would be nearly fifteen minutes before *Viktor* would be in hers. Meanwhile the convoy would be unprotected save by *Dodge* on the starboard wing. The risk run was one of the score of factors that had been balanced in Krause's mind when the Commodore's message came through. On the other hand there was this clear indication of an enemy ahead—Huff-Duff was highly reliable—and there was the poor visibility which would shroud *Keeling* while her radar could see through it. There was the need to drive the enemy under; there was the need to kill him. Even twenty miles ahead of the convoy *Keeling* would be of some protection to it.

Here was Lieutenant Watson, the navigator, reporting having taken over as officer of the deck from Carling. Krause returned his salute; it only took two sentences to inform him regarding the situation.

'Aye aye, sir.'

Watson's handsome blue eyes shone in the shadow of his helmet.

'I have the conn, Mr Watson.'

'Aye aye, sir.'

'Messenger, my helmet.'

Krause put the thing on; it was for form's sake, but at the same time the sight of the thickly-clad men about him reminded him that he was still only wearing his uniform coat and that he was already chilled through by his sojourn on the wing of the bridge.

'Go to my sea-cabin and bring me the sheepskin coat you'll find there.'

'Aye aye, sir.'

The executive officer was reporting by voice-tube from the chartroom below. Down there was an improvisation of the combat information centre already fully developed in bigger ships. At the time when *Keeling* was launched sonar was in its infancy and radar had hardly been thought of.

Lieutenant-Commander Cole was an old friend; Krause told him how matters stood.

'You're likely to get her on the radar screen any time now, Charlie.'

'Yes, sir.'

Keeling was pulsating as she tore along under nearly full power. She lurched and she shuddered as a green roller burst over her forecastle. But the huge rolling waves were just regular enough and convex enough to permit her to maintain her present high speed. Eighteen miles away or less was a surfaced U-boat; at any moment the radar antenna far above the wheel-house might pick her up; the reports had all come in that battle stations were manned. The men who had been roused from their tasks, even the men who had abandoned their routine work to seize their equipment and go to their posts, were ignorant of the reason for this sudden call. Down in the engine-room there must be plenty of men wondering why there had been the call for flank speed; the men at the guns and the men at the depth-charge racks must be warned to be ready for instant action. A second or two must be spared for that. Krause walked to the loudspeaker. The bosun's mate stationed there saw him coming, put his hand to the switch and received an approving nod. The call sounded through the ship.

'Now hear this. Now hear this.'

'This is the captain.'

Long training and long-practised self-control kept his voice even; no one could guess from that flat voice the excitement which boiled inside him, which could master him if he relaxed that self-control for an instant.

'We're running down a U-boat. Every man must be ready for instant action.'

It might almost be thought that *Keeling* quivered afresh

with excitement at the message. In the crowded pilot-house as Krause turned back from the receiver every eye was upon him. There was tenseness in the air, there was ferocity. These men were on their way to kill; they might be on their way to be killed, although for most of those present neither consideration weighed beside the mere fact that *Keeling* was heading for action, towards success or failure.

Something obtruded itself upon Krause's attention; it was the sheepskin coat he had sent for, offered him by the young messenger. Krause was about to take it.

'Captain!'

Krause was at the voice-tube in a flash.

'Target bearing zero-nine-two. Range fifteen miles.'

Charlie Cole's voice was genuinely calm. He was speaking with the unhurried care of a thoughtful parent addressing an excitable child, not that he thought of Krause as an excitable child.

'Right smartly to course zero-nine-two,' said Krause.

At the wheel now was Quartermaster First Class McAlister, a short, skinny Texan; Krause had been his division officer in the old days in the *Gamble*. McAlister would have made Chief by now had it not been for a couple of deplorable incidents in San Pedro in the early 'thirties. As he dryly repeated the order no one would imagine the fighting madman he had been with liquor in him.

'Steady on course zero-nine-two,' said McAlister, his eyes not moving from the compass repeater.

'Very well.'

Krause turned back to the voice-tube.

'What do you make of the target?'

'Dead ahead, sir. Not too clear,' said Charlie.

This Sugar Charlie radar was a poor job. Krause had

heard of Sugar George, the new radar; he had never seen one, but he wished passionately that *Keeling* had been equipped with one.

'Small,' said Charlie Cole. 'Low in the water.'

A U-boat for certain, and *Keeling* was rushing down upon her at twenty-two knots. We have made a covenant with death, and with hell are we at agreement. Comconvoy's radio operator must be wonderfully good to have estimated the distance so accurately merely by the strength of the signals.

'Bearing's changing a little,' said Charlie. 'Bearing zero-nine-three. No, zero-nine-three and a half. Range fourteen miles. She must be on a nearly reciprocal course.'

The range had decreased by a mile in one minute and sixteen seconds. As Charlie said, she must be heading nearly straight towards *Keeling*, coming to meet her. Hell from beneath is moved for Thee to meet Thee at Thy coming. In five more miles, in seven minutes—less than seven minutes now—she would be within range of the five-inch. But *Keeling* had only two guns that could bear dead ahead. It would be better not to open fire at extreme range. With a high sea running, the range rapidly changing, and a radar that might or might not be accurately lined up, instant hits with a two-shell salvo were unlikely. Better to wait; better to hold on in the hope that *Keeling* might come rushing out of the murk to find her adversary in plain sight at easier range.

'Range thirteen miles,' said Charlie. 'Bearing zero-nine-four.'

'Right smartly,' said Krause, 'to course zero-nine-eight.'

The U-boat was apparently holding a steady course. This turn to starboard would intercept her, and if the target were to reveal itself it would be fine on the port bow instead of right ahead; only a small additional turn would then be necessary to bring the after guns to bear as well.

'Steady on course zero-nine-eight,' said McAlister.

'Very well.'

'Stop that noise,' barked Watson, his voice suddenly cutting through the tension. He was glowering at a telephone-talker, a nineteen-year-old apprentice seaman, who had been whistling through his teeth into the receiver before his mouth. From the telephone-talker's guilty start it was obvious that he had been quite unconscious of what he was doing. But Watson's sharp order had been as startling as a pistol shot in the tense atmosphere of the crowded pilot-house.

'Range twelve miles,' said Charlie. 'Bearing zero-nine-four.'

Krause turned to the telephone-talker.

'Captain to gunnery officer. "Do not open fire without orders from me unless enemy is in sight." '

The talker pressed the button of his mouthpiece and repeated the words, with Krause listening carefully. That was not a good order, but it was the only one that would meet the present situation, and he could rely upon Fippler to understand it.

'Gunnery officer replies "aye aye, sir," ' said the talker.

'Very well.'

That boy was one of the new draft, fresh out of boot-camp, and yet it was his duty to pass messages upon which the fate of a battle might depend. But in a destroyer there were few stations which carried no responsibility, and the ship had to fight even with seventy-five recruits on board. With two years of high school to his credit the boy had at least the educational requirements for his station. And only experience would tell if he had the others; if he would stand at his post amid dead and wounded, amid fire and destruction, and still pass on orders without tripping over a word.

'Range twenty thousand,' said the talker. 'Bearing zero-nine-four.'

This marked an important moment. Calling the range in thousands of yards instead of in miles was the proof that the enemy was almost within range; eighteen thousand yards was the maximum for the five-inch. Krause could see the guns training round ready to open fire on the instant. Charlie was speaking on the circuit to gunnery control and captain. And the bearing had not altered either; *Keeling* was on a collision course with the U-boat. The climax was approaching. What was the visibility? Seven miles? Twelve thousand yards? Apparently about that. But that estimate was not to be relied upon; there might be a clear patch, there might be a thick patch. At any moment the U-boat might come into sight over there, where the guns were pointing. Then the shells would be sent winging to the target. It must be hit, shattered, before the U-boat crew could get below at the sight of the destroyer rushing down upon them, before they could dive, before they could armour themselves with a yard of water as impenetrable to *Keeling*'s shells as a yard of steel, and armour themselves with invisibility as well. Hide thyself as it were for a little moment, until the indignation be overpast.

'Range one-nine-oh-double oh. Bearing steady on zero-nine-four,' said the talker.

A constant bearing. U-boat and destroyer were nearing each other as fast as was possible. Krause could look round the crowded pilot-house, at the tense faces shadowed by the helmets. The silence and the immobility showed that discipline was good. Forward of the bridge he could see the crew of one of the starboard 40-mm. guns, staring out

46

in the direction the five-inch were pointing. The tremendous spray that *Keeling* was flinging aft from her bows must be driving against them but they were not taking shelter. They certainly were keen.

'Range one-eight-five-double oh. Bearing steady on zero-nine-four.'

The silence was, of course, even more impressive, because the pinging of the sonar had ceased, for the first time for thirty-six hours. Sound ranging was quite ineffective with the ship making twenty-two knots.

'Range one-eight-oh-double oh. Bearing steady on zero-nine-four.'

He could open fire now. The five-inch were straining upwards, their muzzles pointing far above the grey horizon. A word and they would hurl their shells, upwards and outwards, there was the chance that one of them might crash into the U-boat's hull. One shell would be enough. The opportunity was his. So was the responsibility for refusing to take advantage of it.

'Range one-seven-five-double oh. Bearing steady on zero-nine-four.'

On the U-boat's bridge would be an officer and one or two men. The shell would come through the murk instantaneously for them; one moment they would be alive and the next moment they would be dead, ignorant of what had happened. In the control-room below the Germans would be stunned, wounded, flung dying against the bulkheads; in the other compartments the crew would hear the crash, would feel the shock, would stagger as the boat staggered, would see with horrified eyes the water rushing in upon them, in those few seconds before death overtook them as their boat went down, spouting great bubbles of air forced out by the inrushing water.

'Range one-seven-oh-double oh. Bearing steady on zero-nine-four.'

On the other hand, the salvo might plunge into the sea half a mile from the U-boat. The columns of water thrown up would be clear warning. Before another salvo could be fired the U-boat would be gliding down below the surface, invisible, unattainable, deadly. Better to make sure of it. This was only a Sugar Charlie radar.

'Range one-six-five-double oh. Bearing steady on zero-nine-four.'

Any moment now. Any moment. Were the look-outs doing their duty?

'Target disappeared,' said the talker.

Krause stared at him; for a couple of seconds he was uncomprehending. But the boy met his gaze without flinching. He was clearly aware of what he had said, and showed no disposition to amend it. Krause sprang to the voice-tube.

'What's this, Charlie?'

'Afraid he's dived, sir. It looked like it the way the pip faded out.'

'Radar's not on the blink?'

'No, sir. Never known it so good before.'

'Very well.'

Krause turned back from the voice-tube. The crowd in the pilot-house were looking at each other under their helmet brims. By their attitudes, heavily clothed though they were, their disappointment was clearly conveyed. They seemed to sag in their bundled clothing. Now every eye was on him. For two and a half minutes it had been in his power to open fire on a U-boat on the surface; every officer in the United States Navy craved for an opportunity like that, and he had made no use of it. But this was no time for regret; this was not the moment to be self-conscious under the gaze of eyes that might or might not be accusing. There was too much to be done. More decisions had to be taken.

He looked up at the clock. *Keeling* must be about seven miles ahead of her station in the convoy screen. *Viktor* would be there by now, with her own sonar trying to search five miles of front. The convoy might now be in order, with *Dodge* on the starboard flank free to pay all her attention to anti-submarine duty; *James* would be fast coming up on the other flank. Meanwhile *Keeling* was still hurtling forward, away from them, at twenty-two knots. And the enemy? What was the enemy doing? Why had he dived? Watson, the ranking officer on the bridge, ventured to voice his opinion.

'He couldn't have seen us, sir. Not if we couldn't see him.'

'Maybe not,' said Krause.

Keeling's look-outs were perched high up; if the U-boat had been visible to them only *Keeling*'s upper works would have been visible to the U-boat. But visibility was a chancy phenomenon. It was possible, barely possible, that in the one direction visibility had been better than in the other, that the U-boat had sighted them without being sighted herself. She would have dived promptly enough in that case.

But there could be other theories almost without limit. The U-boat might be newly fitted with radar—that was a development that must be expected sooner or later, and this might be the time. Naval Intelligence could debate that point when the reports came in. Or she might have been informed of the course and position of the convoy and have merely gone down to periscope depth as soon as she was squarely in its path—her course up to the moment of disappearing had been apparently laid to intercept the convoy. That was a good tactical possibility, perhaps the likeliest. There were others, though. It might be merely a routine dive. She might merely be exercising her crew at diving stations. Or more trivial yet. It might be the U-boat crew's dinner time and the cook may have reported that he could not prepare a hot meal with the boat tossed on the sea that was running, and that might have decided the captain to take her down into the calm below the surface. Any explanation was possible; it would be best to retain an open mind on the subject, to remember that about eight miles ahead there was a U-boat under the surface, and to come to a prompt decision regarding what should be done next.

First and foremost it was necessary to get *Keeling* as close to the U-boat, within sonar range. So flank speed should be maintained at present. The point where the U-boat had dived was known; she could be proceeding outwards from that point at two knots, four knots, eight knots. In the plot down below circles would be drawn spreading out from that point like ripples round the spot where a stone drops into a pond. The U-boat would be known to be within the largest circle. In ten minutes she could travel a mile easily, and a circle with a radius of a mile would be over three square miles in area. To search three square miles thoroughly would take an hour, and in an hour the maximum circle would expand to enclose a hundred square miles.

It was most unlikely that the U-boat would linger near the point where she dived. She would head somewhere, in some direction, along one of the three hundred and sixty degrees radiating out from her centre. Yet it seemed the most reasonable assumption that below the surface she would continue the course she had been following on the surface. Even a German submarine, cruising in the North

Atlantic in search of prey, did not wander about entirely aimlessly. She would make a wide sweep in one direction and then a wide sweep in another. If she had dived for some trivial reason she would probably maintain her course; if she had dived to attack the convoy she would probably maintain her course, too, seeing that was the course that would bring her square into its path. If she was on any other course it would be hopeless to seek her with a a single ship; hopeless, that was the right word, not difficult, or arduous, or formidable, or nearly impossible.

Then was it worth while to make the attempt to regain contact? It would be something over ten minutes before *Keeling* would cross the U-boat's path if both ships maintained course, but as the convoy was almost following them *Keeling* could conduct a search and regain station in the screen without being away much more than that time. The alternative was to head straight back and in the regular position in the screen to hope that the U-boat came into contact as she crept into ambush. Defence or offence? Move or counter-move? It was the eternal military problem. The attack was worth trying; it was worth making a search; so Krause coldly decided, standing there in the crowded pilot-house with every eye on him. He that seeketh findeth.

'Give me a course to intercept if the target maintains course at six knots,' he said into the voice-tube.

'Aye aye, sir.'

It would hardly be different from the present course; on the surface the U-boat must have been making about twelve. He could have produced a close approximation in his head. The tube called him.

'Course zero-nine-six,' it said.

A trifling variation, but would make a difference of a full mile in ten minutes at this speed. He turned and gave the order to the quartermaster, and then turned back to the tube.

'Warn me when we are within two miles,' he said.

'Aye aye, sir.'

'Steady on course zero-nine-six,' said McAlister.

'Very well.'

About nine minutes to go; it would be best if the ship's company were told of the situation. He addressed himself to the loudspeaker again.

'The U-boat has dived,' he said into the unresponsive instrument. 'He appears to have dived, at least. We are going on looking for him.'

A more sensitive man than Krause, a man with the telepathic perception of the orator, might have been aware of the atmosphere of disappointment that pervaded the ship as he stepped away from the instrument. He looked at the clock again and strode out on to the wing of the bridge. The wind there was tremendous, what with *Keeling*'s twenty-two knots practically added to the north-easterly wind. There was dense spray flying, too, freezing cold. As he looked aft he could see the unfortunate men stationed at the depth-charge racks cowering for shelter; it was well that the routine even of battle stations allowed them regular relief. He raised his glasses. He could just make out in the murk, very vaguely, *Viktor*'s peculiar foremast, a speck of more solid grey in the general greyness. With *Keeling* leaping and rolling as she was, and with the spray flying, it was impossible to make out more detail than that, and although he swept the rest of the horizon astern with the glasses he could see nothing else at all. Radar would tell him instantly where the convoy was, but that was not what he wanted. He wanted to see with his own eyes what would be the condition of the battlefield if battle there should be, if miraculous good fortune should lead to a U-boat being located between *Keeling* and *Viktor*. He turned and swept the horizon ahead; the same grey murk, the same vague junction of sky and water. But should a U-boat surface within range of the 40-mm. guns her bridge would be visible enough to look-outs and gun crews and gunnery officer.

He came back into the pilot-house with his eyes on the clock. The messenger sprang forward, still holding out the sheepskin coat he had sent for long before. Long before? Not so long, measured in minutes. He put his arms into it and the weight of the coat pressed his clothes against his body. His body was cold but the clothes were colder still, chilled down to freezing-point by the forty-knot wind that had blown between its fibres. He shuddered uncontrollably at the contact. He could hardly bear it. Hands, limbs, and body were frozen; he found his teeth chattering. It had been folly to go out on the open bridge without being fully bundled up; he had not even put on his sweater under his uniform coat. If he had caught young Ensign Hart doing anything as foolish he would have bawled him out. Even now he was not properly clad; sweater, gloves, and scarf were all missing.

He mastered the chattering of his teeth and hugged the coat to him in the comparative warmth of the pilot-house so as to make the chilly contact as brief as possible, for warmth to creep back from his revivifying body into the thick woollen underclothing against his skin. He would send for the rest of his clothes in a moment. The voice-tube summoned him.

'Two miles, sir.'

'Very well.' He swung round, too cold to use the full formula. 'Standard speed.'

'Standard speed,' repeated the hand at the annunciator. 'Engine-room answers "Standard speed." '

That was self-evident at once. The churning vibration died away magically, to be replaced by a more measured beat that seemed by contrast almost gentle, and *Keeling* ceased to crash, shatteringly, into the waves that met her bow. She had time to lift and to incline to them, to heave herself up the long grey slopes and to corkscrew herself over them, so that again by contrast her motion seemed almost moderate.

'Get the sonar going,' ordered Krause, and the words were hardly out of his mouth before the first ping made itself heard through the ship, succeeded before it had died away by another ping, and by another after that, and another, so that the ear, already long accustomed to the monotonous sound, would soon have omitted to record it, were it not that on this occasion everyone in the pilot-house was listening to it intently, wondering if it would reveal an enemy. That monotonous ping, each ping an impulse, feeling out through the dark water in search of a foe creeping along in the depths; it searched slowly to the left, and slowly to the right, searching and searching. This was the hearing ear of Proverbs Twelve, taking over the task of radar's seeing eye.

Did the last ping sound different? Apparently not, for there was no report from sonar. Down below was Radio-man First Class Tom Ellis. He was a graduate of the Key West Sound School and had been in the ship since the outbreak of war; presumably efficient when he came, he had spent the intervening months listening to pings, eternally listening, from watch to watch during all the time *Keeling* had been at sea. That was not to say he was more efficient than when he left the Sound School; it might mean the reverse. At Key West he had gone through a few hurried exercises. He had listened to the echo from a friendly submarine, had noted the variations of pitch as the submarine altered course under water, had taken the bearing and estimated the range; he had been hurried through a couple of lessons on enemy counter measures, and then he had been sent off to sea to listen to echoes. And never since had he heard one; the vibrations he had sent out had never bounced back to his listening ear from a submarine, friendly or hostile; he had no refresher exercise, and most certainly he had never played the deadly game of hide and seek with an enemy. It was humanly possible that now he would not recognize an echo if he heard one; it was certainly likely that he would not draw the instant deductions from the nature of the echo that were necessary if an attack were to be successful. A depth-charge dropped within ten yards of its target meant a probable victory; a depth-charge dropped twenty yards away meant a certain failure. The difference between ten and twenty yards could be accounted for by the difference between the prompt reactions of a practised operator and the tardy reactions of an unpractised one.

And that still left out of consideration the question of nerve; there was no way of knowing as yet whether Ellis was nervous or cool, which was not the same thing as being cowardly or brave. A man could grow flustered merely at the thought of failure, without even thinking as far as the possible censure of his division officer or his captain. Fingers became thumbs, quick wits became slow, in certain men, merely because much depended on accurate manipulation or rapid thinking. Ellis down there could hardly fail to be aware that success or failure hinged upon his sole efforts, upon the delicacy with which he turned his dial, the deductions he had to make from a variation in the quality of the echo. That could make him stupid or clumsy or both. The fact that failure might mean a torpedo into *Keeling*'s side which would blow Ellis and his instruments into fragments, was not so important, Krause knew. Plain cowardice was far rarer than idiocy, just as plain courage was more common than nerve. Krause thought about Ellis as he knew him, sandy-haired, a most ordinary type of young man, except perhaps for the slightest hint of a cast in his right eye. He had addressed him personally a dozen times at most. Those few sentences exchanged at inspections and brief interviews could tell him nothing about the man upon whom now everything depended, the young seaman standing at attention, the young seaman indistinguishable in a line of others at quarters.

The seconds were creeping on as *Keeling* rolled and pitched and staggered her way forward over the waves; Krause stood balancing on the heaving decks in the silence of the pilot-house—silent despite the din of wind and water outside. It was a surprise when the talker spoke.

'Sonar reports contact, sir.'

The talker was a short, stocky man with a misshapen nose; the large helmet, apparently over-large to accommodate his ear-phones, gave him a gnome-like appearance.

'Very well.'

Everyone in the pilot-house was doubly tense at the news. Watson took a step forward; other men fidgeted. No need to harass Ellis with questions; on the contrary, it might fluster him. Ellis must be presumed to know what was wanted of him until the contrary should be proved.

'Contact bearing zero-nine-one,' said the talker. Ellis was passing the first test, then.

'Range indefinite.'

'Very well.'

56

Krause could not bring himself to say more than those words. He shared the tenseness of the others; he could feel the beating of his heart and the sudden dryness of his throat. He looked over at Watson and jerked his thumb; he knew that hand would tremble if he allowed it to; this was buck-fever, unmistakably. Watson sprang to the repeater with the order to McAlister, staring down at the compass repeater.

'Contact bearing dead ahead, sir,' said the talker. 'Range still indefinite.'

'Very well.'

This talker was good at his job. Each word was uttered expressionless and distinct. It was like a schoolboy repeating a recitation learned by heart without any understanding at all. Emotion in a talker was a most undesirable quality.

'Contact bearing dead ahead, sir,' said the talker again. 'Range two thousand.'

'Very well.'

They were bearing straight down at the U-boat, then. Krause had his watch in his hand; it was an effort to read the sweeping second-hand.

'Range nineteen hundred yards.'

A hundred yards in fourteen seconds? With *Keeling* going twelve knots? There was something quite impossible about that figure. That was just her time to go a hundred yards, and the U-boat would hardly be lying still. Any other figure than that would be more promising. Those range estimates depended entirely on the accuracy of Ellis's ear. They could be completely wrong.

'Range eighteen hundred yards.'

'Very well.'

'No contact, sir. Contact lost.'

'Very well.'

It was to be guessed that the talker was repeating exactly word for word what Ellis down below was saying into his mouthpiece. On that evidence it was to be assumed that Ellis was not flustered, at least not as yet.

'Captain to sonar. "Search on the starboard bow." '

The talker released his button. 'Sonar answers "Aye aye, sir." '

'Very well.'

What was the contact that had been made? Some will-o'-the-wisp effect of a cold layer? A *pillenwerfer* bubble released by a U-boat? It may have been a real contact broken off by some intervening condition. But it was important that they had made contact almost exactly at the point where contact was to be expected if the deductions he had made from the radar indication were correct. Then the U-boat had been on a course at a slight angle to *Keeling*'s, crossing from port to starboard. The likeliest possibility was that she was still maintaining that course after letting off a *pillenwerfer*; but there was also the chance that she had been moving very slowly across *Keeling*'s bows—slowly enough for the reported range to have remained constant for a time—and had then taken sudden evasive action, going deep and turning; turning in which direction? The sonar pinged on monotonously; minutes were passing, precious minutes. Five minutes meant that *Keeling* was at the last indicated position; it also meant that the U-boat was half a mile or more from it. It might mean, too, that she was aiming a torpedo for *Keeling*'s vitals.

'Sonar reports contact, sir. Port beam, range indefinite.'

So he had been wrong in thinking she had continued her course to his starboard side; but there were no seconds to spare to think about it.

'Left full rudder.'

'Left full rudder,' repeated McAlister.

The desire to increase speed was passionate within him; he wanted to hurl *Keeling* down along the bearing of the new contact, but that was inadvisable. Already at this snail's crawl he was going as fast as the sonar would tolerate.

'Report all bearings as relative,' he ordered.

'Contact bearing port five-zero, sir.'

'Very well.'

Keeling was still turning; she had not come round far enough, when the echo returned, to be pointing straight in the direction of the previous one.

'Contact starboard zero-five. Range twelve hundred yards.'

Excellent. *Keeling*'s speed might be a snail's crawl, but that of the submerged U-boat was slower still.

'Contact starboard one-zero. Range twelve hundred yards.'

The U-boat was turning too. Her turning circle submerged would be considerably smaller than *Keeling*'s.

'Right full rudder.'

'Right full rudder.'

Speed above versus manœuvrability below. But with the rudder hard over *Keeling* would lose speed; two opponents evenly matched. Green water crashed over *Keeling*'s low waist as she heeled on the sharp turn.

'Contact starboard one-zero. Range steady at twelve hundred yards.'

'Very well.'

Turning exactly together. This high sea was reducing *Keeling*'s manœuvrability; a moment's smooth would give her the chance to come round more sharply, if only one would come.

'Range eleven hundred yards.'

They were cutting down on the U-boat.

'Bearing?' snapped Krause, to regret the question instantly. The talker could only repeat what was coming to him through his ear-phones.

'Bearing starboard one-zero.'

'Very well.'

Bearing constant, range growing less. *Keeling*'s greater speed was prevailing over the U-boat's smaller turning circle. In time—in time—*Keeling* would cut across the U-boat's track, would pass over her, would destroy her.

'Contact bearing starboard zero-five. Range one thousand.'

Closer! More nearly ahead! *Keeling* must be answering her helm better. Victory was nearer than he had thought. *Keeling* was shearing through white water now. She was crossing her own wake, having turned in a full circle.

'Contact bearing port zero-five. Range eleven hundred yards. Opening, sir.'

'Left full rudder!' roared Krause.

The U-boat had fooled him. At the moment of the previous report she had been turning in the opposite direction. Now she was off on a different track entirely, with *Keeling* still swinging away from her. She had regained her lost hundred yards and would regain more before *Keeling* could come round again. McAlister was spinning the wheel round savagely. *Keeling* lay far over, took in another green sea, and staggered.

'Contact bearing port one-zero. Range twelve hundred.'

The U-boat might be getting clear away. She had made the best use of her superior manœuvrability, and she had taken full advantage of the necessary time interval intervening between a change of course on her part and the news of it reaching her enemy's captain. The information reaching *Keeling* was limited and slow; the deductions to be drawn from it could be faulty—we know in part, and we prophesy in part; the U-boat captain was aware of *Keeling*'s limitations.

'Contact bearing port one-five. Range indefinite.'

'Very well.'

Most assuredly had the U-boat fooled him. She had gained some considerable distance on him and widened her bearing. Three minutes ago he had been congratulating himself upon closing on her. Now he felt fear in case she should get clear away. But *Keeling* was swinging fast.

'Contact bearing port one-five. Range indefinite.'

'Very well.'

With left full rudder *Keeling* was chasing her tail again in the opposite direction. An ignorant observer might think the analogy to a kitten's behaviour a close one, if he were not aware of the life-and-death battle she was waging against an invisible opponent.

'Contact bearing port one-five. Range twelve hundred yards.'

So that was the measure of what he had lost. If he were fooled a couple more times like this he might well find himself on an opposite course to the U-boat, and the latter would get clear away before he could turn again. The talker was sneezing, explosively, once and then twice. Now everyone was looking at him. The whole battle could hinge upon his mastering the convulsion; the sneeze of one single seaman might change the fate of empires. He straightened himself and pressed his telephone button.

'Repeat.'

Everyone waited until he spoke again.

'Contact bearing port one-three. Range eleven hundred yards.'

So *Keeling* was regaining the lost ground.

'You going to do that again?' demanded Krause.

'No, sir. Don't think so, sir.'

The talker had brought his handkerchief out from his bundled clothing, but was not attempting to use it with his instrument clamped before his face. If he was going to have further fits of sneezing it would be best to relieve him. He decided to risk it.

'Contact bearing port one-one. Range one thousand.'

'Very well.'

The U-boat had met with a limitation too. Having gained in distance from *Keeling* she was out on a wider arc so that *Keeling* could turn within her, closing up until equilibrium was again established, for U-boat and destroyer to circle about each other again, like planet and satellite. The equilibrium could only be broken by an extra piece of good fortune on the part of the U-boat enabling her to break off contact altogether—or an extra piece of good management on the part of *Keeling* enabling her to close with her antagonist. And the time factor might incline to either party; if the struggle were sufficiently prolonged the U-boat would find her batteries and her air exhausted— but if the struggle were sufficiently prolonged *Keeling* might find herself so far from her post of duty with the convoy that she would have to turn away and rejoin. A game of catch, a game of hide and seek; but a game with table stakes played for keeps.

'Contact bearing port one-one. Range one thousand.'

'Very well.'

Destroyer and submarine were circling about each other. As long as this particular situation prevailed, *Keeling* had the edge. Time was on her side; the U-boat's batteries would not last for ever, and the chances were more in favour of *Keeling* closing the gap through unusual conditions than that the U-boat could simply out-run and out-turn her. As with the last time they had circled, it was up to the U-boat to do something about the situation.

'Contact bearing port one-one. Range steady at one thousand.'

'Very well.'

Krause took a sudden decision.

'Right full rudder.'

A fifth of a second's hesitation in McAlister's reply; the tiniest sharp note of surprise or protest in his tone. It was as if *Keeling* were breaking off the battle. McAlister was spinning the wheel round clockwise; *Keeling* lurched, rolled, shipped a hundred tons of water as her circular momentum was abruptly nullified and then reversed.

Two children running round a table, one in pursuit of the other. It was the oldest stratagem in the world for the pursuer to reverse direction, and run the other way round, for the pursued to run straight into his arms; it was up to the pursued to anticipate that turn and turn himself at the same moment. In this pursuit of U-boat by destroyer it was not possible for the destroyer to attempt the same manœuvre; the destroyer turned far too slowly and far too wide; reversing her turn would take her far out of sonar range; it would be, as McAlister thought, an abandonment of the pursuit. But that was not all the story. In this pursuit it was up to the U-boat to do something different, for if she maintained her circling course indefinitely she would certainly be caught in the end.

There was really only one change she could make, to turn suddenly and head in another direction, in the opposite direction for choice. She had practised that trick once already with considerable success. She turned faster than the destroyer in any case; and she had the advantage of gaining time. There were the seconds it took for Ellis to note the change in the bearing. There were the seconds it took for that change to be reported to the bridge. There were the seconds it took for new helm orders to be given, and then there were the long, long seconds it took for *Keeling* to alter course. The U-boat could start her turn at her own selected moment, in response to a single order from her captain. It would be half a minute before the destroyer could begin to imitate her, and half a minute on practically reciprocating courses meant a divergence of some hundreds of yards, an enormous gain. The U-boat had only to repeat the manœuvre successfully a few times to be out of sonar range and safe.

But what if the destroyer anticipated the manœuvre, and turned a second or two before the U-boat did? Then for those seconds, or longer, until the U-boat realized what the destroyer was doing—and she would be under much the same handicap regarding the translation of information in action as the destroyer had been labouring under— the U-boat would be running straight into the destroyer's arms, like the child running round the table. A childish stratagem indeed, simplicity itself, like most of the stratagems of war; but, like most of the stratagems of war, more easily thought of than executed. Not only quickness of thought was necessary for the execution, but resolution, determination. It was necessary to make up one's mind and carry the plan through, to balance risk against gain and to be neither deterred by the one nor dazzled by the other. At the moment when Krause gave the order for right rudder *Keeling* had the U-boat well within sonar range, she was in hot pursuit, and even if she took no radical new action she had a slight chance of closing on her enemy. The turn meant risking all this. If the U-boat simply continued her course while *Keeling* wheeled away loss of all sonar contact would ensue practically for certain. The U-boat would be free to carry out any attack on the approaching convoy that her captain might decide upon. That was the stake that Krause was laying on the table, apparently. But it was not as great as it appeared, for there was the consideration that if he went on circling after the U-boat, turning, tardily, after she turned, he would gradually be left behind, would gradually find himself on a wider and wider bearing and would eventually be shaken off. He was not staking a certainty against a possibility, but one possibility against another.

There was a further consideration that might have influenced Krause; it might have influenced him but it did not. He was handling his ship, so to speak, under the eyes of the battle-hardened crews of the Polish destroyer and the British and Canadian corvettes. They had fought a dozen actions and he had never fought one. They would be keenly interested in the standard of the performance the Yank would put up, especially as mere chance had put them under his command, especially as he had called them off from one pursuit already. They might be amused, they might be contemptuous, they might be spiteful. Some temperaments might have given some consideration to this side of the matter. It is a fact that Krause gave it none.

To analyse in this fashion all the tactical elements of the situation, and then the moral factors which led to Krause's uttering the order for right rudder, would take a keen mind several minutes, and Krause's decision had been reached in no more than one or two seconds without any conscious analysis at all, as the child running round the table suddenly reverses his course without stopping to think. A fencer's parry changes into riposte in the tenth of a second, in the fiftieth of a second; that comparison might have additional force because (although it was not often remembered now) eighteen years before, and fourteen years before, Krause had been on the Olympic fencing team.

Keeling wallowed as she made her turn, shipping green water.

'Contact bearing indefinite,' said the caller.

'Very well.'

In the confusion of the water that was not to be wondered at. *Keeling* was coming round.

'Ease the rudder. Meet her,' ordered Krause.

Keeling had now completed her turn. McAlister repeated the order, and *Keeling* steadied herself.

'Contact bearing port zero-two. Range eight hundred yards,' said the talker.

'Very well.'

The manœuvre had met with success. *Keeling*'s turn had anticipated the U-boat's. She had her enemy almost dead ahead of her now, and she had closed in by two hundred invaluable yards.

'Steady as you go,' said Krause.

The U-boat might still be turning, probably was; if so it was better to let her continue across *Keeling*'s bows, losing more distance.

'Contact bearing dead ahead. Up Doppler,' said the talker.

The U-boat had continued her turn, then, coming still closer into *Keeling*'s power. The Doppler effect indicated that she and *Keeling* were right in line, on the same course; in other words *Keeling* was on the U-boat's tail and overhauling her at their difference in speed, six knots or so, and less than half a mile behind. Four minutes of this and they

66

would be right over her. There was the temptation to let loose all *Keeling*'s forty thousand horse-power, so as to leap the intervening distance, but that temptation must be resisted because of the deafening effect any increase in speed would have on the sonar.

'Contact bearing starboard zero-one. Range seven hundred. Up Doppler.'

They were overhauling her rapidly. The Doppler effect and the smallness of the change in bearing indicated that she was not turning at the moment Ellis got the last echo. The U-boat captain down there, having swung his boat out of the circle, had had to wait to hear from his own echo-ranging apparatus; perhaps he had not trusted the first report; perhaps he was waiting to see if *Keeling* were turning farther still; perhaps he was taking a second or two to make up his mind as to what to do next, and he was losing time, time and distance. He had turned straight out of the circle, not completely reversing his course, and he must have been astonished to find his adversary's bows pointed straight at him when he steadied on the course he hoped would carry him to safety. Now he must manœuvre again; three more minutes steady on this course and he was lost. He could turn to starboard or he could turn to port. Anticipate him once more and he would be close overside. His last turn had been to starboard; were his reactions such that he would instinctively turn to port this time, or would he be more cunning and repeat his previous turn? Krause had two seconds to think this all out, much longer than, when blade to blade, the fencer has to decide whether his adversary is going to lunge or feint.

'Right standard rudder.'

'Right standard rudder.'

At the moment of the reply the talker reported.

'Contact bearing starboard zero-two. Range six hundred yards.'

Only six hundred yards between them; not too wide a turn, then.

'Ease the rudder.'

'Ease the rudder.'

And this was the moment to catch the eye of Lieutenant Nourse, torpedo officer and assistant gunnery officer standing in the starboard after-corner of the wheel-house.

'Stand by for medium pattern.'

'Aye aye, sir.'

Nourse spoke into his mouth-piece. Krause gulped with excitement. The moment might be very close. It was always true, handling ships at sea, that time seemed to move faster and faster as the crisis approached. Two minutes ago action seemed far off. Now *Keeling* might be dropping her depth-charges at any second.

'Contact bearing port one-one. Range six hundred.'

That change in bearing was due to *Keeling*'s turn, uncompleted at the moment when Ellis got his echo. The next report would be the vital one. Nourse was standing tense, waiting. The crews of 'K' guns and of the depth-charge racks would be crouching ready to go. As Krause looked back from Nourse to the talker his gaze met momentarily that of a strange pair of eyes; he looked back again. It was Dawson, communications officer, clip-board in hand, come up to the bridge from his station below. That meant that some message—which must be radio—had come in too secret for anyone to see save Krause and Dawson. Secret and therefore important. But it could not be as important for the next few seconds as the business in hand. Krause waved Dawson aside as the talker spoke again.

'Contact bearing port one-one. Range five hundred yards.'

A constant bearing, and the range closing. He had anticipated the U-boat's turn. *Keeling* and the U-boat were heading straight for a mutual rendezvous, a rendezvous where death might make a third. Another glance at Nourse; a clenching of hands.

'Contact dead ahead. Range close!'

The gnome-like talker's equanimity was gone; his voice rose an octave and cracked.

'Fire!' bellowed Krause, and he shot out his hand, index finger pointing at Nourse, and Nourse spoke the order into his mouth-piece. This was the second when Nourse and Krause were trying to kill fifty men.

'Fire one!' said Nourse. 'Fire two! Fire three!'

The sudden alteration of bearing of the contact could mean nothing else than that the U-boat captain, finding himself headed off once more, finding the two vessels rushing together, had put his helm hard over again, turning straight for his antagonist, aiming to surprise him by passing on opposite courses and making the danger moment as brief as possible. That 'range close' meant three hundred yards or so—the smallest range at which sonar could function. The U-boat might at this very time be passing right under the destroyer, right under Krause's very feet. The depth-charges rumbling down off the racks, sinking ponderously through the opaque sea, might then be too late, would explode harmlessly astern of the U-boat. But the U-boat might still be just forward of *Keeling*, heading aft, and in that case the depth-charges would burst all about her if the depth setting were anything like correct, and would smash in her fragile hull. Yet she might not be passing directly below; she might be a hundred yards to port or to starboard. The double bark of the 'K' guns at that moment told how further depth-charges were being flung out on either side of the ship in anticipation of this possibility. They might catch her. One of the four depth-charges dropped might burst close enough. It was like firing a sawed-off shotgun into a pitch-dark room to try to hit a dodging man inside. It was as brutal.

Krause strode out on to the wing of the bridge as the 'K' gun at the fantail went off. The ugly cylinder it had flung into the air hung in his sight for an instant before it dropped with a splash into the sea. And as it fell the sea far behind in *Keeling*'s wake opened up into a vast, creamy crater, from the centre of which rose a tower of white foam; as it rose Krause heard the enormous but muffled boom of the underwater explosion. And the tower of foam was still hanging, about to drop, when another crater opened, and another tower rose up out of the sea, and another on one side, and another on the other. He maketh the deep to boil like a pot, as Job said. It looked as if nothing could possibly live in the long ellipse of tortured water, but nothing showed at all. No dripping hull emerged, no huge bubbles, no oil. The odds were ten to one at least against a single depth-charge pattern scoring a hit. It would have been fortunate indeed if *Keeling*'s first pattern—if Krause's first attempt to kill a man—had been successful.

Indeed that was so; Krause felt a dreadful pang of conscience as he jumped into the pilot-house. He should not have been out here at all. It was five seconds since the last explosion, five seconds during which the U-boat could travel a full hundred yards towards safety. Buck-fever again; and simple neglect of duty.

'Right full rudder,' he ordered as he entered.

'Right full rudder.'

The quartermaster repeated the order that Krause gave.
'Get a course from the plot back to the firing point.'

'Aye aye, sir.'

'Steady on reverse of present heading,' ordered Krause.

'Sonar reports apparatus temporarily not functioning,
sir,' said the talker.

'Very well.'

Sonar, as delicate as a human ear, was deafened for a
time by underwater explosions. *Keeling* was coming round
in a tight circle, but not nearly fast enough for Krause's
impatience. It always took several minutes for her to come
all the way round, with the U-boat—if she were uninjured
—making off as fast as her propellers would drive her. She
could well be a mile away—more—by the time *Keeling*
had her bows pointed at her again, so far away that sonar
would not be able to tell him that she had achieved this
state of affairs. And Dawson was thrusting the clip-board at
him again. He had actually forgotten about Dawson's arrival
on the bridge with a message, three minutes ago. He took
the board and read the central words of the message first.

HUFF-DUFF INDICATES ENEMY CONCENTRATION—here followed a latitude and a longitude—SUGGEST RADICAL CHANGE
OF COURSE SOUTHWARD.

Those figures for latitude and longitude had a suspiciously
familiar appearance, and it was the work of only a moment
to confirm those suspicions. Within a mile or two either
way that was exactly where *Keeling* found herself at this
moment. They were right in among the U-boat wolf-pack.
It was an Admiralty message, addressed to him as Comescort, and it was two hours old. That was the speediest
transmission that could be expected; the Admiralty staff,
with its charts and its plotting-board, must have hoped
hopelessly for good fortune when it sent out that warning.

Miraculously speedy transmission, and the convoy steaming an hour or two late, and there would have been time to wheel the convoy away from the wolf-pack. As it was? Quite impossible. The convoy, well closed up by now, he hoped, was lumbering forward with its dead-weight momentum. It would only take a few seconds to transmit orders to the Commodore, but it would take minutes to convey those orders to every ship in the convoy, and to make sure they were understood. And the wheel round would lead to a repetition of the previous disorder and straggling—worse, probably, seeing that it was quite unscheduled.

'Back on reverse course, sir,' reported Watson.

'Very well. Start pinging.'

And even if the convoy should execute the wheel round perfectly, it would be of no avail in the midst of a wolf-pack which would be fully aware of it. It would only mean delay, not merely unprofitable but dangerous.

'Sonar reports no contact, sir.'

'Very well.'

Wednesday. Afternoon Watch—1200–1600

The only thing to do was to fight a way through, to beat off the wolf-pack and lumber on ponderously across the Atlantic. He had at least had his warning; but seeing that convoy and escort habitually were as careful as if there was always a wolf-pack within touch the warning was of no particular force. There was no purpose, for that matter, in passing on the warning to his subordinates and to the Commodore. It could not affect their actions, and the fewer people who were aware how accurately the Admiralty was able to pin-point U-boat concentrations the better.

'Sonar reports no contact, sir.'

'Very well.'

The plan then was to fight his way through, to plod doggedly onward, smashing a path through the U-boat cordon for his lumbering convoy. And this message which he still held in his hand? These few words from the outside world which seemed so impossibly far away from his narrow horizon? They must remain unanswered; there must be no violation of radio silence for a mere negative end. He must fight his battle while the staffs in London and Washington, in Bermuda and Reykjavik, remained in ignorance. Every man shall bear his own burden, and this was his—that was a text from Galatians; he could remember learning it, so many years ago—and all he had to do was his duty; no one needed an audience for that. He was alone with his responsibility in this crowded pilot-house, at the head of the crowded convoy. God setteth the solitary in families.

'Sonar reports no contact, sir, for thirty degrees on both bows.'

'Very well.'

He turned from the one problem straight back to the other.

'Come right handsomely.'

'Come right handsomely.'

'Call out your heading, Quartermaster.'

'Aye aye, sir. Passing one-three-zero. Passing one-four-zero. Passing one-five-zero. Passing one-six-zero. Passing one-seven-zero.'

'Meet her. Steady as you go.'

'Meet her. Steady as you go. Heading one-seven-two, sir.'

Krause handed back the clip-board.

'Thank you, Mr Dawson.'

He returned Dawson's salute punctiliously, but he did not notice Dawson any more. He was quite unaware of Dawson's glance or of the rapid play of expression on Dawson's young chubby face. Surprise succeeded by admiration, and that by something of pity. Only Dawson beside his captain knew what weighty news there had been in the message he bore. Dawson alone could feel admiration for the man who could receive that news with no more than a 'thank you' and go straight on with what he was doing. Krause would not have understood even if he had noticed. There was nothing spectacular to him about a man doing his duty. His eyes were sweeping the horizon before Dawson had turned away.

Contact was certainly lost, and they had searched for thirty degrees on either side of the course the U-boat had been following at the moment of the last contact. Now he had started on a new sector, to starboard and not to port, with no observational data at all on which to base his choice. But a turn to starboard would be towards the convoy, now just visible in the distance. If the U-boat had gone off to port she was heading away from the convoy's path, to where she would be temporarily harmless. The course he had just ordered would carry *Keeling* back towards her station in the screen, and it would search out the area in which the U-boat would be most dangerous.

'Steady on course one-seven-two, sir,' said Watson.

'Very well.'

'Sonar reports no contact, sir.'

'Very well.'

They were heading for the centre of the convoy now. *Viktor* was in plain sight on their starboard bow, patrolling ahead of the convoy, but *James* on the left flank was still invisible. Krause began to consider the matter of securing from general quarters; he must not forget that he was using up the battle reserve of his men's energy and attention.

'Sonar reports distant contact, sir!' said the talker, his voice several tones higher with excitement. 'Port two-zero. Range indefinite.'

The slackening tension in the pilot-house tightened up again.

'Right standard rudder to course one-nine-two.'

'Right standard rudder to course one-nine-two.'

Keeling came round; Krause was looking at *Viktor* again through his glasses. It was a question whether he should use *Viktor* to make a thrust or retain her where she was to make a parry.

'Sonar reports distant contact one-nine-zero. Range indefinite.'

Another brief order, another minute turn. There was the temptation to niggle at Ellis with questions and orders, to ask him if he could not do better than that 'range indefinite.' But his knowledge of Ellis had vastly increased during the last few minutes; Krause guessed that he needed no prodding to do his best, and there was the danger that prodding might disturb his vitally-important equanimity.

A wild yell from the look-out forward of the bridge; a piercing yell.

'Periscope! Periscope! Dead ahead!'

Krause was on the wing of the bridge in a flash, before the last word was uttered, glasses to his eyes.

'How far?'

'Gone now, sir. 'Bout a mile, I guess, sir.'

'Gone? You sure you saw it?'

'Positive, sir. Dead ahead, sir.'

75

'A periscope or a feather?'

'Periscope, sir. Certain. Couldn't mistake it. Six feet of it, sir.'

'Very well. Thank you. Keep looking.'

'Aye aye, sir.'

It seemed very likely that the look-out had seen what he said he saw. The U-boat would know, after the dropping of the depth-charges, that she was a long way from her pursuer. She would be aware of the proximity of the convoy and of the screen, and it would be desperately important for her to get the bearings of her enemies. She would put up her periscope for a sweep round; that was so likely that it could be considered certain. And with this sea running she would show plenty of periscope, too. The six feet the look-out reported was not at all an unlikely figure. That grim object cutting through the tossing water was something a man one year enlisted could be sure about if he caught even a glimpse of it. Even the briefness of the glimpse—just long enough for one complete sweep round —was confirmation. Krause walked back to the radio-telephone.

The excitement in the pilot-house was intense. Even Krause, with his hard lack of sympathy, could feel it beating round him like waves about the foot of a cliff; he was excited as well, but he was too preoccupied with the need for quick decision to pay attention in any case. He spoke into the T.B.S.

'George to Eagle. George to Eagle. Do you hear me?'

'Eagle to George,' bleated the T.B.S. 'I hear you. Strength four.'

'I have a contact dead ahead of me, bearing one-nine-zero.'

'Bearing one-nine-zero, sir.'

'Range about a mile.'

'Range about a mile, sir.'

'I sighted his periscope there a minute ago.'

'Yes, sir.'

'Leave your station and give us a hand.'

'Come and give a hand. Aye aye, sir.'

Viktor could cover the five miles between her and the U-boat in fifteen minutes, if she set her mind to it.

'Sonar reports contact dead ahead, sir. Range indefinite.'

'Very well.'

As long as the contact was right ahead he could be sure he was closing up on it as fast as he could. With the glasses to his eyes he swept the horizon again. The convoy seemed to be in fair order from what he could see of it. He went to the T.B.S. again.

'George to Harry. George to Dicky. Do you hear me?'

He heard the bleated answers.

'I am seven miles from the convoy bearing zero-eight-five from it. I've called Eagle to join me in chasing a contact.'

'Yes, sir.'

'Yes, sir.'

'You must screen the convoy.'

'Wilco.'

'Aye aye, sir.'

The talker at Krause's elbow broke into the conversation.

'Sonar reports no contact, sir.'

'Very well.' He spoke those words over his shoulder before continuing his orders. 'Harry, patrol all the port half, front and flank.'

'Port half. Aye aye, sir.'

'Dicky, take the starboard half.'

'Aye aye, sir.'

'Over.'

'Sonar reports no contact, sir,' said the talker again.

'Very well.'

It might be thought there was irony in those two words. Having called *Viktor* from her screening duties, having stretched the defences of the convoy to the utmost, he was greeted with the news that contact had been lost. But he could only hold on and hope that it might be recovered. He felt he could at least trust Ellis to go on trying. *Viktor* was much more plainly in view now, coming up fast and heading to cross *Keeling*'s course some distance ahead.

'Captain to sonar. "A friendly destroyer will be crossing our bows in approximately seven minutes." '

The talker was repeating the message as Krause went to the T.B.S. again.

'George to Eagle. George to Eagle.'

'Eagle to George. I hear you.'

'Contact lost at present.'

'Aye aye, sir.'

The talker was speaking now.

'Sonar answers——' The talker broke off as a new message came in to his ear-phones. 'Faint contact. One-nine-four.'

'Very well.' No time to spare to be pleased. 'George to Eagle. Contact again five degrees on our starboard bow. I am turning to follow it.'

'Aye aye, sir.'

No doubt the U-boat was fish-tailing and changing her depth in the effort to shake off her pursuer. She would not have heard *Viktor* approaching yet.

'Eagle to George.'

'George to Eagle. Go ahead,' said Krause.

'I am reducing speed to one-two knots.'

'One-two knots. Very well.'

When *Viktor* had slowed down her sonar would be able to come into action; and it would make her approach somewhat harder for the U-boat to detect. *Viktor* had come up as fast as she could. She was an old hand at the anti-submarine game.

'Sonar reports no contact, sir.'

'Very well.'

Viktor was four miles off, Krause estimated, broad on the starboard bow. That peculiar foremast was clear in every detail. The two ships were converging. The bridge was silent, save for the sound of the sea and the monotonous pinging of the sonar.

'Sonar reports no contact, sir.'

'Very well.'

Keeling must have advanced nearly a mile since the last contact. If the U-boat had made a radical change of course at that time the bearing would by now be changing very fast.

'Two-zero-five!' exclaimed the talker. Everyone on the bridge tensed again. Krause was about to speak on the T.B.S. when he realized what he had heard. A sour note; he glanced at the talker.

'That's not what you were taught,' he snapped. 'Mind what you're saying. Repeat.'

'Sonar reports contact two-zero-five, sir,' said the talker, abashed.

'Very well.'

There must be no buck-fever on the bridge of the *Keeling*; better to waste a second now than have confusion arising later.

'Take the conn, Mr Watson,' said Krause harshly; he had two ships to direct. He himself was calm as he addressed the T.B.S.; it was an advantage to be of an unsympathetic temperament. Then other people's excitement pushed one into indifference. 'George to Eagle. Contact again on my starboard bow. I am turning towards it.'

'Eagle to George. Aye aye, sir.'

He fancied he could detect an alteration of course on *Viktor*'s part, but he could not be certain at that distance and with the relative bearing altering. But there was no need to issue orders to *Viktor*. That Polish captain knew his job. No need to tell a terrier at a rat-hole what to do.

'Sonar reports contact bearing two-one-zero, sir. Range one mile.'

'Very well.'

'Steady on new course, sir!' reported Watson at that very moment.

'Very well. Carry on, Mr Watson. George to Eagle. Contact is still crossing my bows from port to starboard, distance one mile.'

'Eagle to George. Aye aye, sir.'

Krause had spoken with the dead flat intonation he relied upon to be intelligible, with distinct pauses between words. The English officer in *Viktor* was answering as coldly, as far as Krause could tell from his peculiar accent and the distortion of the radio-phone. Now he could see *Viktor* surging right round, in an eight-point turn or more, so that she was presenting her starboard bow slightly to his gaze. The terrier was running to cut off the rat's retreat.

'Sonar reports contact bearing two-one-zero, sir. Range two thousand yards.'

'Very well.'

The old situation was repeating itself, the U-boat circling and *Keeling* circling after her; but this time there was *Viktor* to intercept.

'Eagle to George.' Just as he was about to speak. 'Contact, sir. On my starboard bow. Range indefinite.'

'Very well. On my starboard bow too. Range one mile.'

The rat was running into the terrier's jaws. The two ships were approaching fast, and between them was the U-boat.

'Sonar reports contact dead ahead, sir.'

'Very well.'

That made it seem as if the U-boat had begun to swing in the opposite direction, out of the circle. There was no knowing if she was yet aware of *Viktor*'s presence, but it seemed as if she must be. *Viktor* was swinging to starboard already. Her sonar must be good.

'Eagle to George. Eagle to George. Contact close on my port bow. Converging.'

'George to Eagle. I hear you.'

Once more that phenomenon of the varying speed of time. With the ships close together seconds were speeding by; even during the brief exchange of messages the situation had tightened considerably.

'Eagle to George. Submit I attack.'

'George to Eagle. Carry on. Permission granted.'

'Sonar reports contact dead ahead, sir,' said the talker. 'Range indefinite. Interference from the other ship.'

'Very well. George to Eagle. Contact dead ahead of me.'

He must hold this course for a moment or two longer to enable *Viktor* to get a cross-bearing. Then he must alter course to avoid collision. Which way? Which way would the hunted U-boat turn to avoid *Viktor*'s attack? Which way should he head to intercept her if she survived it? *Viktor* was turning to starboard a trifle farther. When *Keeling* had made her attack, the U-boat—as far as he knew—had turned right under her on an opposite course.

It was the best thing she could do; it would be her best move again. 'Come right fifteen degrees, Mr Watson.'

'Aye aye, sir. Right rudder to course——'

'Eagle to George. Depth-charges away.'

Keeling was turning. Fine on her port bow rose the first column of water; farther and farther round rose the others, in *Viktor*'s wake. The sound of the explosions was audible and muffled.

'Sonar reports contact obscured, sir.'

'Very well. Captain to sonar. "Search on the port bow."'

That tremendous temptation again to call for flank speed, and chance muffling the sonar; the temptation must be put aside. Blessed is the man that endureth temptation; for when he is tried, he shall receive the crown of life. On this course they would pass clear by a wide margin of the area of tortured water which *Viktor* had depth-charged. *Viktor* was turning hard to starboard, coming back to the attack.

'Sonar reports close contact bearing one-eight-two.'

'Follow it up, Mr Watson!' Watson gave the order as Krause spoke into the T.B.S. 'George to Eagle. George to Eagle. Keep clear. I am going to attack.'

'Aye aye, sir.'

'I am setting for medium pattern. Set yours for deep.'

'Deep pattern. Aye aye, sir.'

'Medium pattern, Mr Nourse.'

'Aye aye, sir.'

'Sonar reports close contact dead ahead, sir. Strong up Doppler.'

'Very well. George to Eagle. I think contact is on reciprocal course to mine.'

'Eagle to George. Reciprocal course. Aye aye, sir.'

'Sonar reports contact lost, sir.'

'Very well. Mr Nourse!'

Three hundred yards at a combined speed of say eighteen knots; thirty seconds. Deduct fifteen for an ash-can to sink to medium depth. A ten-second spread before and after.

'Fire one!' said Nourse.

Viktor was close, her bows pointed straight at *Keeling*; she had wheeled right round and was aiming to cross close behind *Keeling*'s stern. If this were a peace-time manœuvre that Polish captain would be bawled out for endangering both ships. The 'K' guns were going off on either side, their coughing explosions coinciding with the loud hollow boom of the first depth-charge. Wait fifteen more seconds.

'Come right, Mr Watson.'

No delay this time, no wasting of valuable moments idly watching depth-charge explosions before beginning to circle back again. Now with *Keeling* beginning her turn he could step out on to the wing of the bridge. The last up-flung column of water was falling back to the foaming sea. *Viktor* was beginning her run at the edge of the area *Keeling* had searched with her charges; Krause saw the first of *Viktor*'s depth-charges drop.

'Meet her, Mr Watson! Steady as you go!'

Better not to come too close for a moment, better to hover on the outskirts where *Keeling*'s sonar would be less seriously deafened, and where he would be free to turn in either direction at the first new contact. The sea exploded again, the huge columns rising towards the grey sky. Krause was watching *Viktor* closely; with the dropping of her last depth-charge she was turning to starboard too. The last charge flung up its column of water. Now was the time to continue the circle.

'Come right, Mr Watson!'

The two destroyers were circling about each other. It

was to be hoped that the U-boat was within the area enclosed by the intersection of the two circles. Krause's eyes were still on *Viktor*; he was standing at the end of the bridge when the starboard side look-out yelled, not two yards from him.

'There he is! Sub. on the starboard beam!'

Krause saw it. A thousand yards away the long, conical bow of a U-boat was rearing out of the tortured water. It levelled off as a wave burst round it in a smother of spray. It lowered and lengthened. A gun came into sight. A rounded bridge. The sub. shook itself as though in torment —as indeed it was. *Keeling*'s guns went off, like doors being slammed intolerably loudly. Wang-o. Wang-o. Wang-o. The look-out was screaming with excitement. It was hard to focus the glasses on the thing. A wave seemed to run along it, and it was gone.

Krause sprang back into the pilot-house.

'Right rudder, Mr Watson.'

'Rudder's hard over, sir,' said Watson. *Keeling* had been turning at the moment of sighting.

A talker was trying to make a report. At first he jumbled his words with excitement, but he managed to steady himself.

'Gunnery control reports sub. sighted broad on starboard bow, range one thousand. Fifteen rounds fired. No hits observed.'

'Very well.'

Lieutenant Fippler's first attempt to kill a man had ended in failure.

'Did you get the bearing, Mr Watson?'

'Only approximately, sir. We were turning at the time.'

Speak every man truth with his neighbour. Far better to be honest than to pretend to knowledge one did not have.

'We're coming to course one-nine-five, sir,' added Watson.

'Better make it one-eight-five.'

'Aye aye, sir.'

The U-boat when sighted had been nearly on the same course as *Keeling*. Even if she turned instantly on submerging she would need time and distance to effect the turn. Better head to intercept. And would she turn to starboard or port? Hard to guess. Would she go deep or stay close under the surface? That might be easier to guess.

'Sonar reports contact bearing one-eight-zero. Range approximately four hundred yards.'

'Very well. Come left ten degrees, Mr Watson. Deep setting, Mr Nourse.'

The submarine's instinct after involuntarily surfacing would be to go deep; and the crew would have the controls jammed over hard already to combat the involuntary movement. And in the thirty seconds between submergence and the explosion of the next charge she would have plenty of time to reach extreme depth. He had to watch *Viktor*; she was still turning, but she would be late this time in crossing *Keeling*'s wake.

'Fire one,' said Nourse into his mouthpiece, and Krause checked himself as he was about to move to the T.B.S. No need to tell *Viktor* he was attacking. That was self-evident.

'Fire two,' said Nourse. ' "K" guns, fire.'

It would take longer this time for the depth-charges with their deep setting to explode. A longer time for them to sink to the additional depth, and a more irregular spread with their somewhat random downward fall. Streamlined depth-charges would be more effective than clumsy cylinders; they were already in production and Krause wished he had them.

85

The boom of the exploding charges was distinctly lower in pitch, distinctly more muffled, at this greater depth. Krause heard the last one; he could stand still now during this interval. Buck-fever was not so evident.

'Come right, Mr Watson.'

'Aye aye, sir.'

There had been a momentary temptation to turn to port instead of to starboard, to change the pattern of the manœuvre in the hope of surprising the U-boat, but it could not be done this time; too much chance of meeting *Viktor* bow to bow. He trained his glasses back over the starboard quarter, looking out over the stained and foaming sea. No sign of anything. The T.B.S. calling him.

'Eagle to George! Eagle to George!'

The Englishman in *Viktor* seemed unwontedly excited.

'George to Eagle. Go ahead.'

'You've got him, sir! Got him!' There was a moment's pause again; when the Englishman spoke next he was calmer, almost languid, but with a crude hardness about his nonchalance. 'You've got him, sir. We've just heard him crunch.'

Viktor had heard the crunch; they had heard the breaking up noises as the U-boat crumpled under the overwhelming pressure like a piece of paper crushed in the hand. Krause stood silent at the T.B.S. He was a hard man, but his silence was partly due to the thought that two minutes ago, far below the *Keeling*, fifty men had died a horrible death; quick, but horrible. But in most part his silence was due to the unworded realization that this was a peak in his career; he had achieved the thing for which he had been trained as a fighting man for more than twenty years. He had killed his man; he had destroyed an enemy ship. He was like a student momentarily numbed at hearing he has won a prize. Yet the other realization was present equally unworded and even less conscious; fifty dead men graced his triumph. It was a little as though in a fencing match his foil had slipped past the opposing guard and, instead of bending harmlessly against his opponent's jacket, had proved to be unbuttoned and sharp and had gone through his opponent's body.

'Do you hear me, George?' bleated the T.B.S.

Krause's brief numbness vanished at the sound, and he was the trained fighting man again, with rapid decisions to make and an enormous responsibility on his shoulders, a man with a duty to do.

'I hear you, Eagle,' he said. His dead, flat tone disguised the last traces of the emotional disturbance that had shaken him. He was quite normal by the time he had uttered the words. He was searching in his mind for the most appropriate thing to say to the representative of an allied power.

'That's fine,' he said, and as that did not seem adequate he added, 'Magnificent.'

That was an outlandish word. He tried again, a little desperately; the careful wording of some of the British messages he had received welled up in his memory and came to his rescue.

'My heartiest congratulations to your captain,' he said. 'And please give him my best thanks for his wonderful co-operation.'

'Aye aye, sir.' A pause. 'Any orders, sir?'

Orders. Decisions. There were no seconds to waste even in the moment of victory, not with the convoy inadequately screened and a wolf-pack prowling about it.

'Yes,' he said. 'Resume your position in the screen as quick as possible.'

'Aye aye, sir.'

Krause was about to leave the T.B.S. when it demanded his attention again.

'Eagle to George,' it said. 'Eagle to George. Submit I search for proof of sinking.'

That must be the Polish captain's reaction when the British liaison officer had reported Krause's orders to him. Proof was of some importance. Certainty of the U-boat's destruction would be of help to the staffs in Washington and London writing their appreciations of the situation. And the Admiralty at least, if not the Navy Department, were very insistent upon positive proof before giving credit for a victory; there were jokes that nothing less than the U-boat captain's pants would satisfy them. His own professional standing, his naval career, depended to some extent on his claim to a success being allowed. But the convoy was almost unguarded.

'No,' he said heavily. 'Resume your place in the screen. Over.'

The last word was the decisive one. He could turn away from the T.B.S.

'Mr Watson, take station in the screen, three miles ahead of the leading ship of the second column from the right.'

'Aye aye, sir.'

There was a faintly-puzzled note in Watson's voice; everyone in the pilot-house was looking at Krause. They had heard something of what he had said on the T.B.S., and this new order seemed to confirm their suspicions—their hopes—but they could not be sure. Krause's tone had not been enthusiastic.

'Sonar reports no contact, sir,' said the talker, and Krause realized he had heard that same report several times lately without attending to it.

'Very well,' he said to the talker and then faced the crowd on the bridge. 'We got him. We got him. The Pole heard him crunch after that last pattern.'

The faces in the shadow of the helmets broke into smiles. Nourse uttered a half-suppressed cheer. Delight was so obvious and spontaneous that even Krause relaxed into a grin. He felt the marked contrast between this and a stilted international relationship.

'That's only number one,' he said. 'We want lots more.'

'Sonar reports no contact, sir,' said the talker.

'Very well.'

The whole ship must be told of the victory, and there must be a special word for Ellis. He went to the loud-speaker and waited while the bosun's mate called the attention of the ship's company.

'This is the captain. We got him. *Viktor* heard him crunch. He's had it. This was an all-hands job. Well done to you all. Now we're heading back into screening position. There's still a long way to go.'

He came back from the loudspeaker.

'Sonar reports no contact, sir,' said the talker.

Ellis was still doing his duty.

'Captain to sonar. "Discontinue negative reports unless fresh contact is made." Wait. I'll speak to him myself.'

He spoke on the circuit to the sonar.

'Ellis? This is the captain.'

'Yes, sir.'

'You heard we got him?'

'Yes, sir.'

'You've been a big help. I'm glad I can depend on you.'

'Thank you, sir.'

'You can discontinue negative reports now.'

'Aye aye, sir.'

The light-hearted atmosphere was still apparent on the bridge. But now all the look-outs were reporting at once. Krause hurried on to the starboard wing of the bridge.

'Oil, sir! Oil!' said the look-out, stabbing overside with a mittened hand. Krause looked over; dead fish, white bellies showing, and, as well, a long streak of oil; but not very much. The dirty slick patch was not fifty yards across if three times that amount long. He walked through the pilot-house and out on to the port wing. No oil at all was showing there. Back on the starboard wing they were already leaving the patch behind. As it lifted on a roller it barely extended from crest to trough. Krause tried to visualize a wrecked U-boat sinking down into the fathom-less depths, gliding down as it were on a long slope, very likely. Her fuel tanks being kept full might take a long time to rupture; then there would be a considerable interval before the escaping oil came welling up to the surface. Krause knew from reports he had read that it might be as much as an hour all told. This little patch would be what was present in a nearly-empty tank at the moment of disaster. And badly battered U-boats often left a slick of oil behind even though they were still capable of manœuvre. Naval Intelligence suggested that they some-times purposely let oil escape to disarm pursuit. But his first decision still appeared the correct one to him; it was not worth while to leave a valuable destroyer circling the spot, maybe for an hour, to make sure of the evidence. He could forget the presence of this oil for now. No. He could make some use of it in a minute or two, when he had more time. First he must put an end to the drain on his battle reserve.

'You sure got that sub., sir,' said the starboard-side look-out.

'Oh, yes, sure,' said Krause. The man was not being impertinent. In this moment of victory Krause could let pass the lapse from strict etiquette, especially with so much more on his mind; but he had to think of the safety of the ship. 'Keep your mind on your duty, there.'

He returned to the pilot-house and spoke into the voice-tube to the executive officer.

'Secure from general quarters, Charlie,' he said. 'Set Condition Two, and see if you can manage for some hot chow for the men off watch.'

'Aye aye, sir,' said Charlie.

The loudspeaker blared the order through the ship. Now half the men would be able to eat, to rest, to warm up. Krause looked at the clock; circumstances were different from his preceding glances when he was counting minutes. Now he was perceptibly shocked to note the passage of time. It was past thirteen hundred; over four hours since he had been called from his cabin, and nearly three of general quarters. He should not have brought the men to battle stations at all. He was not much better than Carling. But that was water over the dam; no time for regrets at present.

'Get me a signal-pad and pencil,' he said to the messenger beside him; the crowd in the pilot-house was changing with the setting of the watch.

He tried to write, and the pencil fell from his hand as he applied it to the paper. His fingers were stiff with cold, numb and completely without sensation. Although he had put on his sheepskin coat he still had not put on the sweater and scarf and gloves he should have worn. His hands were freezing, and all the rest of him was bitterly cold.

'Write it for me,' he snapped at the messenger, irritated with himself. ' "*Keeling* to *Viktor*." No'—he was watching over the messenger's shoulder—'Spell that with a "K." No, not "CK." Just V-I-K. "Have sighted oil patch confirming destruction of U-boat. Stop. Many thanks for your brilliant"—two "L's" in "brilliant," damn it—"co-operation" C-O-O-P. That's right. Take that to the signal bridge.'

When the messenger came back he would send him for his gloves and scarf. Meanwhile he must have another look round at the situation. He went out on to the bridge again. There were fresh look-outs at their posts; relieved men were still leaving the gun positions and making their way along the deck, ducking the fountains of spray and timing their dashes from point to point as the ship rolled. *Keeling* was approaching the front of the convoy; the British corvette on the left flank was rolling hideously in the heavy sea. The leading line of the convoy was fairly straight; as far as he could see the rest of the convoy was fairly well closed up. Out on the right was the Canadian corvette; it was nearly time to give the order for normal screening stations. Above him came the sharp rattle of the shutters of the lamp as his message was transmitted to *Viktor*. He looked aft and saw her ploughing along half a mile astern, rolling deeply in the trough, her odd foremast leaning far over towards the sea, first on one side and then on the other. She was nearly up to station, and he must give that order. He might just as well not have come out here into the cold, for all the good he had done, but it was a commanding officer's duty to keep an eye on his command—and he would not have known any peace of mind until he had done so, duty or not duty. He was just able to relax his hands sufficiently to let the glasses fall from them on to his chest, and he went stiffly back into the pilot-house, to the T.B.S.

'George to escort. Do you hear me?'

He waited for the acknowledgments, Eagle to George, and Harry to George, and Dicky to George. Those code names were an excellent choice. Four distinct vowel sounds, impossible to confuse even with serious distortion. He gave the order in his flat voice.

'Take up normal daylight screening stations.'

The acknowledgments came in one by one, and he replaced the hand set.

'Signal bridge reports your signal acknowledged by *Viktor*, sir,' said the messenger.

'Very well.'

He was about to send for his extra clothing, but Nystrom, the new officer of the deck who had just taken over, demanded his attention.

'Permission to secure boilers two and four, sir?' said Nystrom.

'Damn it, man, you know the routine to be followed when securing from general quarters. That's for the officer of the deck to decide without troubling me.'

'Sorry, sir. But seeing you were here, sir——'

Nystrom's blue pop-eyes registered his distress. He was a young man frightened of responsibility, sensitive to reproach, and slow of thought. The Annapolis standards were not what they were, decided Krause, the graduate of twenty years' service.

'Carry on with your duty, Mr Nystrom.'

'Aye aye, sir.'

Dodge was turning away, a mile ahead of *Keeling*, to take up her station on the right flank. It was almost time for *Keeling* to turn ahead of the second column from the right. He looked aft; *Viktor* was already on station, with *James* moving out to the left flank. He decided to watch Nystrom take the ship into station.

'Leading ship of the second column bears two-five-five, sir,' reported Silvestrini from the pelorus.

'Very well,' said Nystrom.

Ensign Silvestrini was a pert, little fellow newly graduated from officers' school. Previously he had been majoring in modern language at an Eastern university.

'Left standard rudder. Steer course zero-nine-two,' said Nystrom, and the helmsman repeated the order.

Keeling came steadily round to take up her station. Everything was well and in order. Krause decided not to send for his clothes. He wanted to get down to the head in any case, and at the same time the thought of a cup of coffee came up into his mind. Instantly he was yearning for it, hot, stimulating, comforting. One cup? Two cups. He was moderately hungry too; the thought of a sandwich along with the cups of coffee made a sudden appeal to him too. And a few minutes' warmth, and the leisure to dress himself properly. It all seemed like an astonishingly good idea to him. Here was Watson with the noon position, unreported until now with the ship at battle stations. Krause acknowledged the report; the noon position was no news to him, closely coinciding as it did with the Admiralty's predicted position for the assembling of a wolf-pack. But by the time he had glanced at it Ipsen the Chief Engineer was waiting with the fuel report for noon. That called for closer attention, and a word or two with Ipsen about the fuel situation, and even those few words were a trifle distracted, for Krause while he talked, was aware out of the tail of his eye that *Dodge* was blinking a message to the ship. The message was at his elbow as he returned Ipsen's salute. It was *Dodge*'s noon fuel report. That had to be studied too, with some care; *Dodge* was fortunate in having a considerable reserve in hand. There were two more messages waiting for him by the time he had completed his study of it. Here was *Viktor*'s fuel report, and then *James*'s. Krause pulled a long face as he studied the *James* report. A minimum of fast steaming for *James* in future. He dictated a carefully worded reply.

'Comescort to *James*. "Use utmost efforts to conserve fuel." '

Now it was Charlie Cole, up from the chartroom, with a smile on his face and words of congratulation about the sinking of the U-boat. It was pleasant to exchange those few sentences with Charlie. But then Charlie came a little closer, and dropped his voice to a confidential tone, so as not to be heard by the others on the bridge.

'There's Flusser to be dealt with, sir,' said Charlie.

'Hell,' said Krause. His use of that word was proof of his irritation at the delay.

Yesterday, Flusser had punched a petty officer on the nose and was under arrest for this gravest of crimes. In a ship of war with general quarters being repeatedly sounded the presence of a criminal in a cell is a continual nuisance. And Navy Regs. demanded that his case be considered as promptly as possible.

'It's more than twenty-four hours, sir,' prompted Charlie.

'Hell,' said Krause again. 'Oh, all right. I've got to get down to the head. I've got to have a sandwich. Then——'

That was the moment when a talker suddenly made his announcement.

'After look-out reports two white rockets from the convoy, sir.'

It was a surprise, worse than that time when the French fencer's riposte had gone clear past Krause's foil during the Olympic Games at Antwerp and he had felt the touch of the button on his breast just when he himself had been about to make the decisive lunge. It was two full seconds before Krause reacted, even though his brain had been instantly aware that two white rockets meant a torpedoing. For those two seconds he stared at the talker, but then he ran out on to the wing of the bridge, glasses to his eyes. It was hard to see anything; *Keeling* was three miles ahead of the leading ships and five miles ahead of the rearmost. He hailed the after look-out.

'What do you see?'

'Two white rockets, sir.'

'Where?'

'Back there, sir. 'Bout the last ship in our line.'

'Signal from the Commodore, sir.' This came from the signal bridge. 'General alarm.'

'Very well.'

Keeling rose high on a wave; now he could see that the third ship in the second column was out of position; the ship following her was swerving to avoid her. If he sent back the Canadian corvette she would be left behind, and with her small excess of speed it would be long before she rejoined the convoy. A destroyer was needed; there was only the choice between *Keeling* and *Viktor*, and *Keeling* was the nearer. He went back into the pilot-house.

'I'll take the conn, Mr Nystrom.'

'Aye aye, sir.'

'Right full rudder. Steer course one-eight-zero.'

The helmsman repeated the order as Krause went to the T.B.S.

'George to Eagle. George to Dicky. I am going to the rear of the convoy. Close up to protect the van.'

'Aye aye, sir.'

'Wilco.'

96

Keeling had turned as he spoke. She was on a collision course now towards *Dodge*.

'Right standard rudder. Steer course two-seven-five.'

'Right standard rudder. Course two-seven-five, sir.'

Round she came again, turning on her heel into the gap between *Dodge* and the convoy.

'All engines ahead full speed.'

Keeling leaped forward as the man at the annunciator reported.

'Engine-room answers all engines ahead full, sir.'

'Steady on course two-seven-five, sir.'

A glance was enough to make sure that they would just shave the starboard line of ships. On opposite courses they passed the leading ship at a hundred yards' distance. She was wallowing ponderously along, meeting the seas on her bow more submissively than a ship of war. She was battered and dingy, with rust showing along her sides. There were one or two heads in sight as they went by, and somebody waved an arm. They seemed to pass her in a flash. Another ship succeeded her, and another after that, each one plodding steadily forward; they were leaving behind them a sister, hard hit, probably mortally wounded, but all they could do was to hold their course fatalistically. Through the gap between third and fourth Krause caught sight of the upper works of a ship already far astern of the convoy. The glimpse of the smoke-stack and foremast that he caught of her told him that she was *Cadena*, the designated rescue ship of the convoy; the fourth ship passed on and he could see again. Nothing beside *Cadena*, some three miles on the starboard bow. No; there were two boats visible as they rose on the crest. And what was *that*, heaving up on the crest? A long dark straight line, like a log floating on a river, bigger than any log ever seen by man. It rose again in a wide smother of spray; a ship nearly bottom up; that long, dark line was the turn of her bilge. She was three-quarters over and nine-tenths submerged, still floating.

'All engines ahead standard speed.'

'All engines ahead standard speed.'

'Engine-room answers "All engines ahead standard speed," sir.'

'Resume sonar search.'

Both life-boats were alongside *Cadena* now; she was rolling in the trough to give them a lee, and she had her scramble-nets down. Against her dark starboard side, which was just coming into Krause's view as *Keeling* headed across her bows, Krause could just see through his glasses the specks which were men climbing her side.

'Torpedo to port!'

That was a scream from the port-side look-out.

'Right rudder.'

That was Krause's instant order, given while the glasses were still at his eyes; the parry to the thrust, coming with the instinct more quick than thought. More likely a shot from slight astern than from slightly ahead. Left rudder, towards the danger, might take *Keeling* across the torpedo's course. Right rudder by a small balance of the odds was the safer, after that so recent reduction in speed. Krause sprang out on to the port wing of the bridge.

'There, sir!' shouted the look-out, pointing over the quarter. That transient white wake along the face of a lifting roller; a torpedo track, most likely. Krause estimated its direction, balancing it against *Keeling's* course before her turn. Most likely it would have missed in any case passing close ahead. That would be because of the reduction in speed; the torpedo must have been launched a few seconds before he gave that order. If a spread had been fired this would be the right-most torpedo.

With the numbing wind blowing round him Krause's mind went on with its hasty calculations. Then the U-boat was likely *there*, where *Keeling*'s stern was now pointing. Then —each step of the deduction was necessarily vaguer, with an accumulating uncertainty, but some plan must be made, and quickly, and acted upon—then the U-boat had approached the convoy from the flank, just outside *Dodge*'s sonar sweep, had fired into the mass of the convoy; her shot had passed between the ships of the outer column to hit this sinking ship of the second column. Then the U-boat had headed in to take a shot at *Cadena* lingering behind. *Keeling* had come down—possibly unexpectedly—between the U-boat and her target, and the U-boat had fired a spread at *Keeling* to eliminate her from the scene—she would have time to use gunfire against *Cadena* then. He must keep between the U-boat and *Cadena*, screening while he shepherded *Cadena* back into the convoy. It would be as well to make his own movements as erratic and unpredictable as possible.

'Left standard rudder!' he ordered, hastening back into the pilot-house.

'Left standard rudder, sir,' answered the quartermaster, and *Keeling* began the second loop of an 'S.'

A long feather of steam blew away from *Cadena*'s upper works; he caught his breath with silly apprehension for a moment. It stopped and then started again; it was *Cadena*'s steam-whistle—the sound of the first blast was just reaching him across the wind. Four puffs.

'F for fox from the merchant ship, sir.'

'Very well.'

The typewritten signal-code hanging on the board told him that this meant 'Rescue completed.'

'Still coming left, sir,' said Nystrom.

'Very well.'

By completing this circle he would bring *Keeling* into a suitable screening position.

'Messenger! Write this. Comescort to *Cadena*. C-A-D-E-N-A. "Rejoin convoy at best speed. Modified zigzag." Take that to the signal bridge. And tell them not to send too fast.'

'Signal bridge. Aye aye, sir.'

It was in the blood of all signalmen to send messages as rapidly as they could, and it was always a source of gratification to them if they could burn up the recipient. In this case the recipient was a merchant seaman, unpractised in reading messages; and it was important. His glance darted round the horizon, at *Cadena*, at the convoy, at the guessed at bearing of the hidden U-boat.

'Ease the rudder,' he said.

'Ease the rudder.'

'Sonar reports distant contact port beam, sir.'

Port beam? Another U-boat? Krause looked out. No. That was the hull of the sinking ship.

'Steady as you go,' he snapped at the helmsman.

The sinking ship was still three-quarters over. But now she was farther down by the stern; a considerable length of her bottom-up bow was protruding at a small angle from the surface of the sea, and the rest of her was invisible. Against the bow waves were breaking as though against a rock.

'Steady on course zero-nine-five,' reported the helmsman.

'Very well.'

'Sonar reports heavy breaking up noises, sir.'

'Captain to sonar. "The noises you hear come from a sinking ship. Search elsewhere." '

The bows of the wreck were rising higher. Those breaking-up noises which sonar reported told of cargo and engines and boilers tumbling aft down the slope. Now she was heaving over, bows still raised high. Her upper works came bursting out through the surface of the sea, water cascading from them. Right over, and then back again, like a creature struggling in torment.

A message from the signal bridge.

'*Cadena* to Comescort. "Speed eleven point five knots." '

'Very well.'

Better than could be expected. But—his next glance at the convoy was a little disquieting. Six miles, he judged, by now. It would be well over two hours before *Cadena* was back in station again. One last glance back at the sinking ship. She hung vertical now, with a bare twenty feet of her bow straight up above the sea. She would soon be gone; two miles from her the two abandoned lifeboats rose and fell on the rollers, marking where the fortunate crew had climbed up *Cadena*'s side; fortunate, but he realized he did not know how many men had died when the torpedo struck. There were some fragments of wreckage floating on the surface, too, the miserable trophies of a Nazi victory.

'Right ten degrees rudder,' he said sharply to the helmsman; there was pressing work to be done, and not a moment to spare to think about the sunken ship, or about the report he would have to make regarding the loss. With a U-boat within torpedo range he must not keep *Keeling* on the same course for very long at one time.

'Ease the rudder. Steady as you go.'

He would like *Cadena* to zigzag widely as well, but that

would make the interval before she rejoined interminable. He was between her and the enemy—or so he hoped—and his menacing presence would keep the U-boat far enough away to make it a very long shot if the U-boat commander was trying to get a torpedo into her.

'Steady on course one-zero-six,' reported the helmsman.

'Very well.'

With this overcast sky it would be quite dark by five o'clock. *Cadena* would have a hard job inserting herself into the ranks of the convoy then. The spray on the pilot-house windows was making it hard to see out. He shifted his position to take advantage of one of the two spinning discs of glass set in the windows, the centrifugal force of whose motion kept two circular areas clear enough to see through. The disc was not spinning; it was stationary, and as hard to see through as the rest of the glass.

'Mr Nystrom!'

'Sir!'

'Get this thing working again. Call the electrical officer.'

'Aye aye, sir.'

The other disc was still turning, but very slowly, too slowly to clear itself. Visibility through the glass was so bad that it would be better to go out on to the wing of the bridge. Out into the windy cold. But that was the T.B.S. demanding his attention.

'Harry to George! Harry to George!'

'George to Harry. Go ahead.'

'Pips on the radar screen, sir, bearing oh-nine-one. Range one-oh miles, sir. Two pips. Look like subs.'

'Very well.'

Two submarines right ahead, nearly in the track of the convoy.

'Orders, sir?'

'Dicky to George!' This was *Dodge* breaking into the circuit.

'George to Dicky. Go ahead.'

'We've got a pip, too. Bearing oh-nine-eight. Range one-four miles. Looks like a sub., too, sir.'

'Very well.'

James on one wing, *Dodge* on the other, reporting submarines ahead. Another close on his starboard bow, submerged. Wheresoever the carcass is there will the eagles be gathered together. Should he send his subordinates forward to the attack? With night approaching? With *James* having to be economical of fuel? It might be best.

'Eagle to George! Eagle to George!'

'George to Eagle. Go ahead.'

'We've got Harry's pips, sir, bearing oh-eight-five. But we've got another, bearing oh-nine-oh, range one-three miles.'

That was not *Dodge*'s pip. Four submarines ahead of the convoy. One at least close astern of it.

'Very well.'

'Harry to George. Range is closing fast. Range nine miles for one pip. Bearing oh-nine-oh. Other pip bearing oh-nine-two. Range nine miles.'

'Very well.'

It was time to think about his own ship.

'Left standard rudder!' he called over his shoulder to the helmsman and then addressed himself to the instrument again.

'George to escort. Keep your stations. Open fire when within range.'

Then back to the helmsman.

'Meet her! Steady as you go.'

Keeling was on a fresh zigzag. While he was speaking

on the T.B.S. he must not forget that a U-boat was manœuvring for a shot at him.

'Steady on course zero-nine-four, sir.'

'Very well.'

The T.B.S. was conveying the escort's acknowledgments of his orders.

'Good luck, you fellows,' he said.

In the face of those numbers he could not send the escort forward to the attack. It would open too many gaps in a screen already far too weak.

Rudel, the electrical officer, was awaiting his attention; an electrician's mate and his striker stood behind him. A glance showed the discs were still not spinning.

'Haven't you got them working yet?' demanded Krause. Rudel saluted.

'It's not an electrical failure, sir. They're frozen.'

'The spray's freezing all over the glass, sir,' supplemented Nystrom. It was growing almost impossible to see out of the pilot-house.

'Then get to work on it,' snapped Krause.

He debated within himself; that was not an easy assignment for Nystrom. And Nystrom was not a brilliant officer.

'Put two men to work with buckets and swabs,' said Krause. 'Warm water. Not boiling. Yes, and have that water salty—as salty as you can get it.'

'Aye aye, sir.'

'Very well, Mr Rudel.'

He returned Rudel's salute, looking round him as he did so, forward at the distant convoy, to port at *Cadena*, to starboard where—perhaps—a U-boat was looking at him. The glass front of the pilot-house was already too spotted with ice to afford reasonable visibility, and he went out on to the starboard wing of the bridge.

'Left standard rudder!' he ordered, and watched the ship come round.

'Meet her! Steady as you go!'

It was essential to keep *Keeling* zigzagging, and quite irregularly.

'Steady on course zero-eight-zero, sir.'

'Very well.'

He was converging now slightly on *Cadena*. The hands he laid upon the rail in front of him were numb, almost without sensation, but not quite numb enough for something different to be called to his notice. The forward curve of the rail was slick and smooth with a thin coating of ice. That and the wind which blew round him decided him to send for his additional clothing. Until then he had literally not had a moment in which to do so. Now this was an interval of leisure; leisure with a U-boat within torpedo range of him.

'Messenger!'

Wink. Wink. Wink. Far ahead in the convoy a message was being flashed back, just visible in the gathering gloom. The Commodore, most likely—for certain.

'Yes, sir.'

It was the bridge messenger; in those few seconds he had forgotten him.

'Go down to my cabin. I want the fur gloves you'll see there. And I want the sweater and scarf. Wait. I want the hood, too. You'll have to look for it in the second drawer down. Gloves, sweater, scarf, hood.'

'Aye aye, sir.'

The rattle of the lamp-shutters above him told him the signalmen were acknowledging the Commodore's signal. He looked over at *Cadena*; he was drawing ahead of her and was well on her bow. The messenger from the signal bridge came clattering down.

COMCONVOY TO COMESCORT. NUMEROUS FOREIGN LAN-
GUAGE TRANSMISSIONS TEN TO ONE-FIVE MILES AHEAD
VARIOUS BEARINGS.

'Very well.'

The U-boats out ahead were talking to each other,
setting their plans. Or perhaps they were reporting to
L'Orient where—what was that name? Doenitz—where
Doenitz would co-ordinate their efforts. He was cold.

'T.B.S., sir!' said Nystrom. 'Eagle.'

As he went in to speak he decided that it would be better
to order a new course now rather than wait until his conversation was finished.

'Alter course ten degrees to starboard, Mr Nystrom.'

'Aye aye, sir.'

'George to Eagle. Go ahead.'

'Pips are all on the move, sir. Three to port, bearing
oh-eight-five for two of them and oh-eight-one. Range
constant at one-oh miles. Two to starboard, bearing oh-
nine-eight and one-oh-four. Range one-one miles. They're
keeping their distance ahead of us. And they're transmitting, sir. Signals all the time. And we think we got another
pip, too, sir. Five minutes ago. Dead ahead range five
miles. It faded out almost as soon as we saw it, but we're
pretty certain of it.'

'What's your visibility there?'

'Just about five miles, sir. Look-outs saw nothing.'

'Very well. Retain your stations. Over.'

U-boats ahead making no attempt at concealment.

'Steady on course one-zero-four, sir,' reported Nystrom.

'Very well.'

And one—one at least—closer in, below the surface. An
ambush, posted there ready for action whether the escort
advanced to the attack or plodded forward in the screen.

A momentary appearance, perhaps to transmit a message or perhaps involuntary, breaking surface while rising to periscope depth. It occurred to him to give a warning to *Viktor*, but he discarded the idea. No need to tell those Polish fellows to keep alert. Those U-boats on the surface must be waiting for darkness to attack. The pestilence that walketh in darkness.

Here was Charlie Cole, saluting.

'Ship's icing up, sir. I've been round. Footing's bad aft by the tubes.'

'Depth-charges free?'

'Yes, sir. I've given orders for the steam-hoses.'

Trust Charlie to attend to these matters. With depth-charges frozen to the racks and unable to roll—it had been known to happen—*Keeling* would lose nine-tenths of her usefulness as an escort.

'Thank you,' said Krause.

'Thank you, sir,' said Charlie, saluting again with his usual exactness.

The messenger was standing by with his arms full of clothes.

'Fine!' said Krause. He began to unbutton the sheep-skin coat. That was the moment for the voice-tube from the chart-house below to call him. The bell was still vibrating as Krause sprang to the tube.

'Pip bearing two-zero-seven. Range eleven thousand.'

That was well abaft the starboard beam. It must be the U-boat from which he had been screening *Cadena*. Finding herself being left behind she had surfaced. A second or two more for thought in this new situation. Turn end on and attack? Could he be sure it was not a ruse to draw him away? Yes. There had so far been no pips on this sector. If there were two U-boats they could not have concerted any plan.

'Right standard rudder. Steer course two-zero-seven.'

'Right standard rudder. Steer course two-zero-seven.'

'Captain to gunnery control. "Prepare to open fire on radar direction." '

The talker repeated the order.

'Gunnery control answers "Aye aye, sir." '

'Steady on course two-zero-seven.'

'Very well.'

'Target bearing two-zero-eight. Range approximately one-oh-five-double oh.'

That was Charlie Cole's voice. He must have dashed down below the moment he heard the pip reported. It was a comfort to know he had taken charge down there.

'What do you mean by "approximately," Charlie?'

'Screen's fuzzy, sir, and it's jumping a little.'

This accursed Sugar Charlie radar!

'Lieutenant Rudel to report to the chartroom immediately,' said Krause to the bosun's mate at the loudspeaker. Perhaps Rudel could persuade the thing to give a little more definition.

'Bearing's changing, sir. Two-zero-nine. Two-one-zero, approximately, sir. And I think the range is closing now. Range one-oh-four-double oh.'

Krause's mind, accustomed to dealing with problems of vessels on all sorts of bearings, plotted out the present situation. The U-boat on the surface was hightailing it from *Cadena*'s starboard quarter round to her port quarter, doing an 'end around.' With this sea running she could not do more than twelve knots, most likely. Fourteen, possibly. No, not very possibly. She was six miles almost astern of *Cadena* who was going at eleven and half. She was ten miles astern of the convoy. She was out of harm's way, then, for two, three, perhaps four hours. He could make that interval longer still at small cost.

'Right ten degrees rudder. Steer course two-two-zero,' he ordered, and then addressed himself to Charlie again. 'I'm leading him.'

As the hunter aims his gun at a point ahead of the flying duck, so he was aiming *Keeling* at a point ahead of the moving U-boat.

'Steady on course two-two-zero,' said the quartermaster.

'Very well.'

'Bearing approximately two-one-two,' said Charlie. 'Range one-oh-three-double oh as near as I can make it out.'

The morning's problem was presenting itself again; the U-boat was within easy range of *Keeling*'s five-inch. But was it worth while opening fire on an invisible foe located merely by a dancing spot on a radar screen? Not with a better opportunity possible in the near future.

'I think the bearing's staying constant, sir,' said Charlie. 'Two-one-two. Yes, and the range is closing. One-oh-two-double oh. One-oh-one-double oh.'

Keeling and U-boat were approaching each other on converging courses, a hundred yards nearer at every minute.

'Range ten thousand,' said Charlie.

Ten thousand yards; six miles. Visibility in this darkening afternoon was—he stared at the horizon—five miles? Four miles? Whether he opened fire with radar direction or with the U-boat in sight he would only be granted the short time it would take the U-boat to submerge in which to score a hit. Direct observation was far surer.

'Range nine-eight-double oh,' said Charlie. 'Bearing two-one-two.'

'Captain to gunnery control. "Hold fire until target is in sight."'

The messenger with his arms full of clothes was still standing by.

'Spread those on the radiator,' said Krause with a gesture. He was so cold now that he could yearn to be warm even with a surfaced U-boat on a converging course.

'Bearing's changing, sir,' said Charlie. 'Changing fast. Two-zero-five. Two-zero-three. Range nine-three-double oh. Nine-two-double oh.'

The U-boat had altered course to starboard. She must have decided that she had gone far enough with her 'end around' and that now she had the opportunity to close in on *Cadena*.

'Left standard rudder. Steer course one-eight-zero,' said Krause.

He was turning to meet her in full career. The U-boat had been long submerged before she had come up to the surface and was—it was a heartening thought to a man encompassed by enemies—far more ignorant of the situation that he was.

'Bearing changing,' said Charlie. 'Range nine thousand —no, eight-eight-double oh.'

Not long before they would sight each other then.

'Steady on course one-eight-zero,' said the quartermaster.

'Very well.'

'Target bears two-zero-one. Range eight-six-double oh. Eight-five-double oh.'

The guns were training round to starboard. At any moment now the U-boat might appear out of the murk on the starboard bow.

'Bearing two-zero-two. Range eight-three-double oh.'

Much less than five miles. Then it happened. A yell from a look-out. Krause had his glasses in his numbed hands, on the point of raising them. Wang-o, wang-o, wang-o went the guns. He did not have the glasses trained in quite the right direction; it was the splashes of the shells that guided him. Then he saw it, the square grey silhouette of a U-boat's bridge tiny in the distance, pillars of water a little to one side of it; the pillars moved in on it—wang-o, wang-o, wang-o. The pillars of water were all about it, hiding it; not for more than a second or two did he have it in sight. Then the ear-shattering din ended and there was nothing to be seen as the grey water rose into the field of his binoculars and sank again with the heave of the ship. All over. He had achieved his surprise. He had seen his shells beating all about his astonished enemy, but not once had he seen—he compelled himself to be realistic about it— had he seen the flash and the momentary glow that would mark a hit.

'Gunnery control to captain. "Fire opened on target bearing one-nine-nine," ' said the talker. ' "Range eight thousand. Twenty-seven rounds fired. No hits observed." '

No hits.

'Very well.'

Another decision to be made, with every second valuable, whether it was a question of dealing with one enemy four miles away in one direction or half a dozen twenty miles away in the other.

'Left standard rudder,' he ordered. 'Steer course one-zero-zero.'

He was turning away from the enemy. He could see a glance or two exchanged among those in the pilot-house who could realize the implications of the order. He was tempted, by the use of a cutting phrase or two, captain to subordinates, to make them wipe that look off their faces, but of course he did nothing of the sort. He would not use his rank for such a purpose. He would not attempt to justify himself, either.

He could have run down towards where the U-boat had disappeared. In a quarter of an hour he would have been in the vicinity, conducting a sonar search. He might have made a contact, but it was ten to one, fifty to one, against it, with the convoy drawing away from him all the time that he would be conducting an hour-long search. And ahead of the convoy his three other ships were about to go into battle against heavy odds. He must hasten to their aid without wasting a moment. The U-boat he had fired upon had gone under. It might well be a long time before she would venture to surface again after this experience with an enemy who had dashed so unexpectedly out of the haze with guns firing. The U-boat was far astern of the convoy already; she would be farther astern still by the time she surfaced. Even with exact knowledge of the convoy's position and speed and course it would take her the best part of the approaching night to overtake. He had forced her into uselessness for some hours. Better to head at once for certain action than to linger here trying to wring some unlikely further success out of a situation now unpromising. Even if—even if his shells had scored an unobserved hit. A U-boat's superstructure was both tough and capable of receiving damage without crippling her underwater performance. It was the slimmest, the most unlikely of chances that she would be just under the surface, unable to dive deeper, perhaps leaking oil to reveal her position. It was not worth taking into account; he had made the right decision.

'Steady on course one-zero-zero,' said the quartermaster.

The time it had taken *Keeling* to make the turn was the

measure of the time Krause's instincts and training had taken to leap to the conclusions a logical speech would have consumed minutes over.

'Very well.'

'Captain, sir,' said Charlie up the voice-tube.

'Yes?'

'Lieutenant Rudel is here. Can he speak to you?'

'Very well.'

'Captain,' said Rudel's voice, 'I can try to line up this radar better. I don't believe I can improve on it much, though. If at all, sir.'

'Can't you do better than that?' snapped Krause.

'I made a written report on it four days ago, sir,' replied Rudel.

'So you did,' admitted Krause.

'I'd have to shut it down to work on it, sir.'

'How long for?'

'Two hours perhaps, sir. And I don't guarantee results even then, sir, as I said.'

'Very well, Mr Rudel. Leave it as it is.'

Better a radar out of kilter than no radar at all. The night cometh when no man can work. There was much to do still.

The need to go down to the head was overpowering, and this seemed a favourable opportunity, the first since he had been called from his cabin. No; there was one other thing to do first. He was leaving *Cadena* to make her way back into the convoy by herself. She must not think she was being deserted; she did not have his knowledge of the tactical situation and must be reassured.

'Messenger! Write this. Comescort to *Cadena*. "Sub. now seven miles astern. Good-bye and good luck." Take that to the signal-bridge. Mr Nystrom, take the conn.'

He dashed down below, even in his present need still revolving that message in his mind. It was a grim situation when a message to the effect that a hostile submarine was seven miles away was meant to be heartening. But *Cadena* might have the sense to understand all that he implied. She would undoubtedly leave off zigzagging and sprint for the convoy for all she was worth.

'Signal-bridge reports *Cadena* acknowledges message, sir,' said the messenger in greeting to him as he emerged on the bridge again.

'Very well.'

There were his additional clothes, lying on the radiator. It was stimulating even to see them. He took off his sheep-skin coat—it was so long ago since he had unbuttoned the first button with this in mind—and his uniform coat. The act of picking up his sweater called his attention to the fact that he was still wearing his helmet. All the other men in the ship had discarded theirs the moment he had secured from battle stations, several hours back. But he himself had not had one single second in which to do the same. He had been running around wearing it all this time, like a kid in his big brother's uniform.

'Hang this up,' he snapped at the messenger, tearing the thing off and handing it over.

But it was instantly mollifying to put that sweater on over his shirt. The sweater was hot from the radiator, wonderful. So was the scarf that he wound round his neck. He put his uniform coat on over this miraculous warmth. The hood was warm too, embosoming his freezing head and ears. He made fast the clip under his chin with a sense of gratitude to a generous world. Then the sheepskin coat again. He pressed his icy hands on the radiator for as long as he could bear it—not long—and then drew on the gloriously warm fur gloves. It was fantastic how two minutes could alter one's whole outlook for the better—or for the worse.

Wednesday. Dog Watches—1600–2000

Nystrom was standing beside him awaiting his attention.

'Report having been relieved, sir,' he said, saluting. 'Course one-zero-zero. Standard speed twelve knots. We are making twelve knots, sir.'

'Very well.'

So it was four o'clock. Past four, and the watch had been relieved. The men coming off duty had been at their stations since the time when he had been foolish enough to sound general quarters. But now they could relax and rest, and he could build up the battle reserve he had so recklessly drawn upon. There was a long period of strain ahead and he must not draw upon that reserve except in the most desperate crisis. He must fight, as he had fought just now, in Condition Two; half the ship would be off duty then, able to take what rest they could with guns firing and depth-charges exploding. Plenty of them would sleep through it, so his extensive experience of the American sailor told him.

Charlie Cole, as he expected, was here on the bridge when the watch was relieved.

'Be sure the third and fourth sections get hot food, Commander.'

'Aye aye, sir.'

There was approval in the executive officer's eye at the sight of his captain at least hooded and gauntleted and wrapped up, but there was no leisure for the exchange of further words, not with *Keeling* heading back towards action again. Yes, and they were not doing as well as they should. Another lapse. When they had turned away from the submarine he had forgotten, clean forgotten, to order an increase in speed. Even the 'twelve knots' in Nystrom's report had not reminded him. He had wasted perhaps as much as five minutes in transferring *Keeling* from one scene of action to the other.

Harbutt was the officer of the deck, the youngest of all the watch-standing officers, fresh-faced and pink-complexioned. His childlike eyes looked innocently out from his hood like a baby's. He hardly looked old enough to entrust with a row-boat on the lake in Central Park.

'Mr Harbutt!'

'Sir!'

'Increase speed. Try her with twenty-four knots.'

'Twenty-four knots. Aye aye, sir.'

Doubling the speed meant multiplying by four the rate at which they were overtaking the convoy. He could not judge yet whether their present course would take them clear of the right flank.

'Twenty-four knots by pit, sir.'

'Very well.'

The increase in speed was obvious in the way *Keeling* was meeting the seas. Like the rushing of mighty waters. From within the pilot-house he could feel and hear, rather than see, how she was taking it. Well enough.

'Messenger!'

'Yes, sir.'

'Bring me a cup of coffee. A pot of coffee. A big pot of coffee. And a sandwich. Tell the mess-boy I want one of my specials.'

'Aye aye, sir.'

116

There was just light enough to see the rearmost ships of the convoy, still plodding along. Now the T.B.S. calling him again. He had to unclip the hood and let it dangle round his face to get the ear-phone to his ear.

'Dicky to George! Dicky to George!'

'George to Dicky. Go ahead.'

'Asdic contact, sir. Distant contact, on our port bow.'

'Go after it then. I'm coming up behind you.'

'Eagle to George. Shall I join in, sir?'

Viktor and *Dodge* were three miles apart with the contact between them, nearer *Dodge* than *Viktor*. It would open a gap to call *Viktor* over. But the U-boat was only three miles ahead of the convoy. She only had to keep alive for twenty minutes to be in among it. If only he was up ahead where he could bring the weight of *Keeling* to bear!

'Very well, Eagle. Carry on. Good luck to you.'

He was in a fever of impatience.

'Mr Harbutt, try her with another couple of knots. See if she can take it.'

'Aye aye, sir.'

They were close under the quarter of the last ship of the starboard column now, and overtaking her fast. Krause stepped out on to the port wing of the bridge to look at the convoy. *Keeling* took a deep roll as he did so, and his feet shot from under him. He saved himself from a bad fall by grabbing the rail, tried to stand, and lost his footing again as *Keeling* rolled the other way. This time his gloved hands almost lost their grip of the rail, and it was only by a convulsive effort that he caught himself again. The deck was glazed with ice as well as the rail. It called for the most elaborate precaution to stand at all. A wave smashed over *Keeling*'s port bow, clear over, rolling aft to burst in a leaping wall of water against the five-inch gun houses, a solid lump flying aft to hit him in the face as he stood. *Keeling* wallowed deeply and flung herself up the face of the next sea with a lunatic's strength. By the time Krause had recovered his balance and his breath they had passed the rearmost ship and were closing up on the next ahead. It was so dark now that the ship farther on still, a bare half-mile from where he stood, was only visible as a thickening in the gloom. And it would soon be much darker than that. *Keeling* took another green wave on her bow, shuddering under the blow. Krause half slid, half walked back into the pilot-house.

'Slow her a bit, Mr Harbutt. She won't take it.'

'Aye aye, sir.'

There was just light enough to see the Filipino mess-boy in his white coat. In his hands was a tray covered with a white napkin, as he had been taught to serve meals, and as he always would serve them, with U-boats on the horizon or not. He had obviously just tried to put the tray down on the pilot-house chart-table, and had as obviously been shooed away by the indignant quartermaster in jealous charge of the chart and instruments there. Now he stood unhappily holding it, surging with the heel of the ship— Krause knew exactly how, under the napkin, the cream— they still brought him up cream although they ought by now to know he never used it—and coffee were slopped over the tray-cloth. And worse might happen at any moment. The tray soared up and swooped down in the half-darkness as *Keeling* rose over a wave. Krause suddenly felt he could not bear the thought of that precious load falling to the deck. He grabbed at pot and cup, balanced himself, and poured the cup half-full. He balanced again, pot in one hand, cup in the other. In that second there was nothing in the whole world that he wanted as much as that coffee. His mouth was dry even though his face was still wet. He sipped thirstily at the scalding stuff, sipped again, and drained the cup. He could feel the comforting fire of it all the way down his throat. He smacked his lips like a savage, poured himself another half-cup, and, watching his moment, set the pot on the tray.

'Put that tray on the deck and don't take your eye off it,' he said.

'Aye aye, sir.'

He drank again. It was only nine hours since he had breakfasted, but he did not think a man could possibly feel so thirsty or so hungry. The thought of pouring unlimited coffee into himself, and then of eating to ease his savage hunger filled him with exultation.

'Look-out reports gunfire on the port bow, sir,' said the talker.

Krause sprang to the T.B.S. He had been inattentive for three minutes. Eagle and Dicky were in rapid communication, the sentences snapping back and forth, straining at the leash of the trained manner; the English nonchalance was bursting at the seams.

'Bearing two-seven-oh from me.'

'I've got him on the screen.'

'I'm firing star-shell. Stand by.'

Gunfire. Star-shell. That meant a surfaced U-boat. And bearing two-seven-oh. That meant the U-boat was between the screen and the convoy, dashing in to charge. The darkness forward of the port beam was suddenly changed as the star-shell burst high in the sky, the brilliant white light dangling from its parachute. Wave tops caught the light. Close on the port beam the leading ship of the starboard column of the convoy was silhouetted against it. *Keeling* was back in the battle again.

'George to Dicky! George to Dicky! I'm turning across the convoy's bows. Look out for me.'

'Wilco.'

'I'll take her, Mr Harbutt.'

'Aye aye, sir.'

'Left full rudder. Meet her. Steady as you go.'

'Steady on course——'

Krause did not trouble to listen to the figure given. He was content to be able to see that *Keeling* was shaving as near as he dared across the shadowy bows of the advancing convoy. The star-shell was extinguished. Reduce speed and start pinging? No time to spare for that; no need, with a sub. on the surface. He rang the voice-tube bell, but as the same moment action began.

'Sub. bearing broad on starboard bow. Range three-five-double oh.'

'Captain to gunnery control. "Do not fire without orders." '

Then down the voice-tube.

'See that we keep just clear of the convoy.'

He went to the T.B.S., and almost fell over the Filipino mess-boy still standing guard over the tray.

'Get below!'

Into the T.B.S.

'George to Dicky. George to Dicky. Star-shell again.'

Out on the starboard wing of the bridge he braced himself against the treacherous ice that glazed everything.

'Sub. bearing zero-four-two. Range three-two-double oh.'

Bearing changing as well as range. Somewhere in the darkness just ahead the U-boat was crossing *Keeling*'s bows, heading for the convoy. *Keeling* dipped and plunged in the high sea. Then it came, the streak of gold against the dark sky, and the miracle of light hanging in the heavens, lighting the sea, the wave tops, the ships; dazzling white, as bright as moonlight. And there, on *Keeling*'s starboard bow, not two miles ahead, the slinking grey shape hurrying over the silvered water, the grey wolf running at full stretch for the flock.

'Gunnery control. "Open fire!" '

It would be a surprise for the U-boat; until the guns should open she would have no idea of the presence of the destroyer flying along across the convoy's bows to intercept her. The guns went off with a blinding flash and a shattering crash. Krause clapped one gauntleted hand across his eyes while he kept his balance with the other on the slippery rail. Even though the range was so short it was rapidly changing; so was the bearing; and the sea was running high. But there was a chance that a hit might be scored. The burst of firing ended, and Krause looked again; he was one of the few men in the ship not blinded by the flashes. There was the grey shape; it was far nearer both to *Keeling* and to the convoy, and it was different—there was a noticeable white bow wave in evidence. The U-boat had altered course directly for the convoy. The star-shell was still burning in the sky with hardly diminished light—the British certainly had the most efficient star-shell Krause had ever seen. Flash and crash again, blinding and shattering. The starboard side 40 mm. were firing now as well, beating out a loud tonk-tonk-tonk against the frantic wang-o, wang-o, wang-o of the five-inch. Krause left his hand over his eyes and groped into the pilot-house.

'Target altering course,' said a talker through the din.

The guns ceased firing as the blinded gunners lost their target. Krause took his hand from his eyes and peered forward.

121

'Ship dead ahead! Ship dead ahead!'

It was a yell from down below, which would have been audible even without the voice-tube.

'Left rudder! Hard over!' shouted Krause.

He had seen that frightful thing at the same moment. The leading ship of one of the columns was far ahead of station, a full cable's length at least. The dark looming shape was across their bows.

Keeling leaned far over as she turned with the rudder hard against the port stop at high speed; talkers and officers staggered and struggled for their balance. *Keeling* turned abruptly; the whole ship seemed to groan with the strain put upon her.

'Left hard rudder,' came the voice of the helmsman in the darkness.

The dark shape ahead was coming nearer and nearer even though *Keeling* was swinging.

'Look-out reports ship dead ahead,' said a talker; the late warning was ludicrous in the tension of the moment. *Keeling* slithered on a wave, but she was round, the merchant ship's looming, upper works close beside the bridge. Somebody was shouting from there at the top of his lungs, clearly audible. There was still danger that *Keeling*'s starboard quarter might crash into her even though her bows had turned.

'Meet her! Right full rudder! Meet her!'

The ship receded abruptly out of their field of vision; *Keeling* was now flying down the lane between two columns of ships. There were the huge lumps of the dark vessels close on either side.

'All engines ahead standard speed.'

The message was passed down.

'Engine-room answers "All engines ahead standard

speed, sir," ' and the tension seemed to ease in the pilot-house as *Keeling*'s vibration died away.

There was the tiny glow of the repeater, the faint light showing through the letters of the annunciator. *Keeling* was churning in the seas tossed up by the convoy; it seemed as if in the sudden silence they could hear the bow waves of the labouring ships on either side. But not for more than two seconds did this quiet time endure. A rocket soared and burst on their starboard side. There were machine-guns firing. On their starboard quarter a great sheet of red flame suddenly shot to the sky, and the sound of a frightful explosion shook the pilot-house. The U-boat they had so nearly intercepted was in the next lane of the convoy to them, dealing out destruction. Pin-point jabs of orange fire on their starboard bow, growing suddenly shorter and brighter. A sudden violent irregular clatter all about them, a harsh, metallic twanging and a more musical sound of falling glass. Someone in the last ship of the column had sighted them and opened fire with a fifty-calibre machine-gun, unable in the darkness and excitement to distinguish between a destroyer and a U-boat. The burst had swept clean across the front of the pilot-house just above Krause's head, smashing the glass. They could feel the cold air pouring in upon them. The first shots *Keeling* had ever received in battle—the first bullets ever to endanger Krause's life —had been fired by the hand of a friend. But no time for any thought about the matter.

'Anyone hurt?' asked Krause automatically, but he did not stay for an answer.

The dark shape of the ship had vanished; they were in the clear now—and what was that far out on the starboard beam, illuminated by the flames of the burning wreck?

'Right full rudder!'

A U-boat's superstructure, heaving up on a sea.

'Right full rudder.'

She had come down the next lane in the convoy neck and neck with *Keeling*.

'Meet her! Steady as you go.'

A wave heaved up and the U-boat was gone. She must have been in instant diving trim—or had he not seen her at all? He was sure he had; a thousand yards ahead of where *Keeling*'s bows were pointing at this moment. He strained his eyes at the clock.

'Prepare to fire medium pattern!' snapped Krause over his shoulder.

A voice behind him spoke orders into a mouth-piece— Pond, Lieutenant J. G., the make-learn assistant gunnery officer on duty.

'Commence sonar search.'

The U-boat under water would head for the sheltering noises of the convoy.

'Right standard rudder. Ease the rudder. Steady.'

'Sonar reports heavy interference, sir.'

Naturally, with thirty ships' propellers all beating together. A thousand yards at twelve knots. Allow something for the U-boat's travel. Three minutes altogether—a desperately long time from the point of view of a man having to reach the predicted position of a U-boat; desperately short with so much to bear in mind.

'Mr Pond!'

'Fire one!' said Pond. 'Fire two!'

Krause turned round to look at him, saw that Nourse was standing at Pond's shoulder. Well and good. The 'K' guns barked. Looking aft, Krause saw the sea in *Keeling*'s wake suddenly lit up from below with the bursting of the first depth-charge; the deep on fire, and again with the next depth-charge, and again, over a huge area, as the charges thrown by the 'K' guns burst, thirty fathoms deep, at the same time as the next charges from the racks. The flame below the surface lingered on the retina; now it was gone. The foaming sea reflected faintly the red glare of the burning ship.

'Right standard rudder. We'll fire another pattern as we go back, Mr Pond.'

'Aye aye, sir.'

'Ease the rudder. Steady as you go.'

The burning ship was a valuable point of reference in determining *Keeling*'s position and course. He would depth-charge the area between that beaten by the last charges and the receding convoy. It was the most likely area, but it could be wrong by a mile.

'Mr Pond!'

'Fire one,' said Pond. 'Fire two.'

They were heading directly towards the burning ship; she grew larger and brighter as he looked at her, while the depth-charges thundered and flashed behind him. Flames were spouting from her, reaching far upward, and so thick about her that he could make no attempt at identifying her. Then a tremendous flash, reaching up to the clouds above, an explosion-wave which he could feel where he stood, and then the frightful crash of the explosion. And then nothing; darkness; silence, eyes blinded and ears deafened to everything until sensation came slowly back, with first the ears reporting the sound of *Keeling* cleaving through the sea and then the eyes dimly becoming conscious of the foam-flecked surface all about them. Silence in the pilot-house, broken only by someone's nervous cough.

'Ship ahead, sir,' said the voice-tube. 'Bearing one-seven-five, distance one mile.'

That would be *Cadena* doing rescue work. On that bearing they would pass her close on *Keeling*'s port bow. She would not long have resumed her place in the convoy before having to drop back again on this fresh mission.

'How's the convoy?'

'Three ships well astern of the rest, sir. Nearest one bearing one-six-zero, distance two miles.'

It was remarkable—it was good news—that no more than three ships were out of station besides *Cadena*, seeing that a U-boat and a destroyer had both passed clean through the convoy and a ship had been torpedoed in the heart of it.

A cry from the sea—a scream; a human voice screeching for aid at the highest agonized pitch of anxiety and terror. The very fact that it came from some distance, faint and yet so clearly recognizable, accentuated the urgency of it.

'Object close on the port bow!' reported the port side look-out.

It was something dark on the dark surface of the water, and from it came that wild cry again. Survivors—one survivor at least—floating on wreckage or a life-raft; lucky men who had flung themselves overboard before being caught in the flames, and who had found the life-raft floating there—probably they had thrown it over first— and who had with further good fortune been left behind as the ship drifted on with her residual way so that the explosion did not kill them. Lucky men? It would only be a matter of minutes before they froze to death. Call *Cadena*'s attention to them? *Cadena* was a mile away, and the only way to inform her would be to approach her and hail her with the bull-horn. The chances were she would never find that tiny object; and would he be justified in bringing her back another mile, with a sub. within torpedo range? No; *Cadena* was worth more than one or two or half a dozen lives even if they could be certainly saved. Save them himself? In the name of Christian charity? There was no Christian charity in the North Atlantic. It would be imperilling his ship. *Keeling* and her crew were worth a thousand merchant seamen's lives—two thousand perhaps. Yet—how great was the risk? A life or two were intrinsically worth something. If he left them, if he passed by on the other side, his whole ship's company would know about it sooner or later. What effect would it have on them? Not a good one. And international amity? Saving those lives would be something to cement Allied solidarity. If he saved them, the news would spread little by little in circles where Allied solidarity was precious.

'Right full rudder,' he said, and then down the voice-tube. 'Give me a course to bring me back here.'

The order had come quickly; as the fencer's quivering foil circles to meet the disengage and the lunge. And a hundred peace-time 'man overboard' exercises had at least imbued his mind with the difficulties of the undertaking and the necessarily instant action that must be taken.

'All engines ahead one-third speed. Make turns for six knots.'

'Six knots, sir. Engine-room answers "six knots."'

'Who's the junior O.D.?'

'I am, sir,' said a voice out of the darkness. 'Wallace, sir.'

'Get down to the port side quick. Get the lines ready. Put a couple of volunteers into bowlines ready to lower them overside.'

'Aye aye, sir.'

'Hail me the minute you've got 'em out.'

'Aye aye, sir.'

Seamanship now; with the rudder hard over *Keeling*'s speed was lessening fast. Charlie Cole's voice up the tube coached him into position; but with the dark object spotted again he had to swing farther still to bring it on his port side to give it a lee; he had to time his next order exactly as the wind against *Keeling*'s broadside started moving her down, and the wind acting against her lofty forecastle would swing her; he had to allow for that, too. In a 'man overboard' exercise they would have a search-light running, boats ready to lower, a life-buoy flare to indicate the spot.

'All engines back two-thirds.'

'All engines back two-thirds. Engine-room answers "all engines back two-thirds," sir.'

'All engines stop.'

'All engines stop. Engine-room answers "all engines stopped," sir.'

Several difficult seconds now, with *Keeling* rolling dead in the water; her sonar still pinging, the sound of the sea on her starboard side, the sound of the wind about them almost drowning the small noises that reached them from the port side. Silence in the pilot-house. Then Wallace's voice from below:

'All aboard, sir! We got 'em!'

'All clear overside?'

'All clear, sir. Ready to go ahead.'

'All engines ahead standard speed.'

'All engines ahead standard speed. Engine-room answers "ahead standard speed," sir.'

'Left rudder. Meet her.'

That was a necessary order to carry the stern of the ship clear from the abandoned life-raft as they left it behind.

Keeling came to life again; the unnatural windy stillness was over. Down the voice-tube.

'Where's *Cadena*?'

'Bearing one-eight-seven, distance two thousand.'

'Right standard rudder. Steer course one-nine-zero.'

Cadena must still be searching for survivors; with that distance and bearing she could not have been heading after the convoy while *Keeling* had made her circle.

'Objects on the port bow!'

'Objects on the starboard bow!'

Wreckage, bits of planking, gratings, hatch-covers, blown from the exploding wreck. No voices. Wallace looming up in the darkness beside him.

'We got four men, sir. Sent 'em in to the doctor. Two of 'em were burned, but I don't know how bad. Couldn't see 'em, sir.'

'Very well.'

Perhaps it was very well that young Wallace had not seen the burned men. Krause had seen one or two in his life and never wanted to see another. He must remember that Wallace had done a clean, quick job.

There was the loom of *Cadena* on the port bow, half a mile away; careful observation necessary to determine which way she was heading; careful helm orders to come alongside within voice range. Krause went to the loud-hailer.

'*Cadena*!'

A faint reply, just audible; the quality indicated a speaking-trumpet.

'Comescort. *Keeling*. We got four survivors.'

'We didn't get any,' said the speaking-trumpet.

'Head after the convoy now. Course eight-seven. Look out for stragglers ahead.'

'O.K.'

'Left standard rudder. Steer course zero-zero-zero,' said Krause to the helmsman.

Due north was a course as good as any. Somewhere in that direction might be the sub. he had pursued and depth-charged, more likely there than anywhere else, which did not mean very much. He could sweep in that direction as he headed for the flank of the convoy; he had that much time in which to make up his mind whether to continue to patrol astern of the convoy or go on round ahead of it again.

'Gunnery control reporting, sir,' said a talker in the darkness, and then into his mouth-piece, 'Repeat, please.'

A few seconds delay before the talker spoke again.

'Gunnery control reports that they believed they made one or two hits firing on the sub. the second time, sir.'

One or two hits; they had not prevented the sub. from dashing into the convoy, from firing at least one torpedo, and from submerging when he was about to attack her again. Unless she had sunk when he thought her sub-merging? No; that would be too good to be true. A five-inch shell could go clean through the fragile superstructure of a sub. before exploding, and without impairing her diving qualities in the least.

'Who is that reporting?'

'Mr Kahn, sir.'

'Very well. Acknowledge the message.'

Kahn might be right. He might be honestly mistaken. He might be a pushful optimist. It was to his credit that he had waited for a quiet moment before making a report of little present importance. Krause regretfully decided that he did not know enough about young Kahn to be able to form an opinion of his judgment and reliability.

'How does the convoy bear?' he asked the chartroom.

'Last ship of the left column on our starboard beam

bearing zero-eight-five, distance three miles, sir. Five-five-double oh.'

'Very well.'

He would sweep back once more across the rear of the convoy.

'Right standard rudder. Steer course one-seven-zero.'

That dark figure newly arrived on the bridge and watching the repeater must be Watson. Now he was stooping over the chart-table. Now he kicked something which returned a metallic jangling. Of course—that was the tray with his sandwich and coffee, lying forgotten on the deck! Krause knew instant, raging hunger and thirst again, hunger and then thirst, but the thirst was more acute even if he was only conscious of it secondarily.

'That's my tray,' said Krause. 'Let's have it.'

Watson picked it up and put it on the sacred table.

'I bet it's cold, sir,' said Watson. 'Let me send for some more.'

'Messenger. Bring me another pot of coffee. Bring it yourself, not the mess-boy.'

'Aye aye, sir.'

But he could not wait for that, not now he had been reminded of his hunger and thirst. His hands found the coffee pot, still half-full. He had not the least idea where the cup had gone, but that did not matter. He put the pot to his lips, stone cold, and drank and drank. He felt coffee grounds in his mouth and swallowed them too. He was wildly hungry; his gauntleted hands felt something that must be the sandwich. He raised it with both hands and bit ravenously. It was as cold as if it had come out of a refrigerator; it was both stale and soggy, but he bit off a huge mouthful and chewed with gusto. Between the slices of bread lay a thick slab of corned beef liberally daubed with mayonnaise, and on the beef lay thick rings of raw onion. Only the onion had any life in it at all now; the mayonnaise had soaked into the inner surfaces of the bread, and his second bite told him that the under slice was wet with slopped cream, and his third bite told him that the upper slice had a wet patch most likely caused by a drop or two of spray coming in through the broken windows. But none of that mattered. The onion rings crunched between his teeth even though the doughy bread adhered in a sticky mass against his palate. He bit and chewed and swallowed in the darkness. At the fourth bite his lips came in contact with a peculiarly unpleasant sensation, against the fur glove in which he held the sandwich, and the fifth bite recorded the additional flavour of the glove.

'Pips astern of us!' said the voice-tube. 'Bearing zero-zero-five, range two thousand.'

'Left full rudder. Steer course zero-zero-five,' said Krause, the rim of the sandwich still in his left hand.

That must be the sub. they had put down earlier. A desperately persistent fellow. He had been under gunfire; he had been depth-charged, but now he had surfaced and presumably was speeding to overtake the convoy again.

'Steady on course zero-zero-five,' said the helmsman.

'Target's heading east,' said the voice-tube. 'Course zero-eight-five as near as I can make it as yet. Bearing zero-zero-six. Zero-zero-seven.'

'Right smartly to course zero-one-zero,' said Krause.

A tactical problem almost identical with what had gone before. To head off the U-boat. To open fire or not? Better to reserve his fire until he was as near as he could be. His first salvo would be the signal for the U-boat to submerge. In this pitch-black night there was more than a chance that he might creep up on him without being seen.

'Captain to gunnery control. "Do not open fire." '

He went out on to the wing of the bridge. In the silence and the windy darkness it was strange to shout at the top of his voice, ridiculous though it was to be afraid that the U-boat a mile away would hear him.

'There's a sub. on the surface ahead. Keep your eyes skinned.'

An incautious step nearly lost him his footing again on the ice-glazed deck, and after he had grabbed at the rail he realized that he had crushed the remnants of his half-eaten sandwich into the furry palm of his glove. That must be a horrible mess; he almost blessed the darkness for concealing it from him. He tried to wipe it on the rail.

'Target bearing zero-zero-eight. Range one-eight-double oh.'

They were closing in on the U-boat.

'T.B.S., sir,' said Wallace.

Dicky and Harry and Eagle were all talking. They had contacts in plenty, fighting a pitched battle ahead of the convoy, while here he was astern again. Yet while he had this contact he could not go to their aid. Would they think the less of him? He did not mind on his own account, but he was fearful for the well-being of the entity that was the escort.

'Screen's pretty fuzzy, sir,' said Charlie Cole's voice up the tube—Charlie had found his way back to the chart-house at a crucial moment as usual. 'But the bearing's pretty nearly constant, I think. Zero-zero-eight—zero-zero-seven. Range one-six-double oh. One-five-double oh.'

It would be *Keeling*'s bow wave that would be first detected by the U-boat's look-outs. They would see it faint white in the darkness; they would look again. Krause drove his imagination to work on the picture of what they would do next. They would see the bow wave before they would see the ship. They would be able to make a rough guess at her course before they could make out her upper works. That would tell them very nearly all they needed to know; a straggler from the convoy would be holding a course nearly east and not nearly north. And the speed—the twelve knots he was making—would tell them the rest. *Keeling* would be identified as an enemy, the Klaxon horns would sound, and the U-boat would submerge before even *Keeling*'s upper works had been seen or the U-boat's listening devices had identified the distinctive beat of her propellers. If he altered course farther to the eastward and reduced speed to eight knots? That might well deceive the enemy while the converging courses brought them closer together. It was with a shock that he pulled himself up at that point. That would also invite a torpedo; in the eagerness of the hunt he was actually forgetting that his quarry carried deadly weapons. He rubbed his nose reflectively and remembered too late about the crushed sandwich. He could feel cold mayonnaise on his nose.

'Sonar reports contact, sir. Zero-zero-five. Range indefinite.'

'Very well.'

That was an enormous, an immense, gain.

'D'you get that difference in bearing, Charlie?'

'Yes, sir,' said Charlie.

There was a chance of lining-up the radar with the more accurate sonar.

'Range one-three-double oh. Bearing zero-zero-seven approximately.'

The fact that the U-boat had permitted an approach as close as this was an indication that her detection devices were not as acute as *Keeling*'s. Or that her crew was not as

134

alert. Or that her captain was bold. Something more for Naval Intelligence to work out when his report came in.

'Pip gone, sir!' said Charlie. 'Yes. Pip disappeared.'

The U-boat had at last taken the alarm, then.

'Sonar reports contact bearing zero-zero-five. Range twelve hundred yards.'

They still held the sub. in the sonar beam, then. Krause took the telephone and spoke on the battle circuit.

'Captain speaking. Who's on the sonar?'

'Bushnell, sir. And Mannon.'

Radio men second class, trained by Ellis.

'Ellis off watch?'

'Yes, sir.'

'Very well.'

It was a temptation to call for Ellis and put him to work at the sonar. But better not. A long battle still lay ahead, and Ellis's fitness was part of that battle reserve which he must not draw upon yet.

'Sonar reports strong contact. Bearing zero-zero-zero. Range one thousand.'

The old game of hide and seek again, of catch round the table. To lay *Keeling* on a course that would intercept the U-boat.

'Come left smartly to course zero-zero-zero,' ordered Krause.

He could only keep his bows directly on the contact until further reports gave him an indication of the U-boat's course.

'Steady on course zero-zero-zero.'

'Very well.'

'Sonar reports contact dead ahead. Range eight hundred yards.'

Keeling was right on the sub.'s tail, then. The sub. must

turn soon; no guessing whether it would be to port or to starboard as yet.

'Sonar reports contact dead ahead. Range seven hundred yards. Six hundred yards.'

'He's stationary, sir,' said an unexpected voice in the background. That must be Pond.

'Thank you. I was thinking so myself.'

'Sonar reports contact dead ahead. Range five hundred yards.'

Was the sub. contriving to hang motionless on a cold stratum of water? That was possible. But it was more likely that——

'Sonar reports no contact, sir.'

His growing suspicions hardened into certainty. It was a *pillenwerfer* they had been pursuing. They had been chasing bubbles while the U-boat was escaping. It could not be a question of being too close to the target for the sonar to record; the last report had placed them well outside that limit.

'Sonar reports no contact, sir.'

Failure. He had been completely fooled. No, not quite completely, thanks to fortuitous circumstances. If the *pillenwerfer* had lasted a little longer, continuing to emit its bubbles for another five minutes, he might well have gone on and depth-charged it, and circled back to depth-charge it again, wasting ammunition and time on a phantom. His suspicions until the contact disappeared had not been strong enough to save him from doing that.

'Right standard rudder. Steer course zero-eight-zero,' he snapped, and then, down the voice-tube. 'Where's the convoy?'

'Nearest ship bearing zero-eight-nine, distance four miles.'

'Very well.'

'Steady on course zero-eight-zero.'

'Very well.'

He must close up on the left column of the convoy and sweep once more close across its rear.

'Report when we're one mile distant.'

'Aye aye, sir.'

There was movement all about the ship now, shadowy figures entered the pilot-house. The watch was changing, twenty hundred. The hours fled by when filled with action and concentrated thought. A thousand years in Thy sight are but as yesterday when it is past, and as a watch in the night. A figure beside him speaking with Harbutt's voice and giving an almost invisible salute.

Wednesday. First Watch—2000–2400

'Report having been relieved, sir. Course zero-eight-zero. Standard speed, twelve knots. Ship in Condition Two. No unexecuted orders.'

'Who has the deck?'

'Carling, sir.'

'Very well. Get some sleep while you can, Mr Harbutt.'

'Aye aye, sir.'

'Mr Carling!'

'Sir!'

It was necessary to inform Carling of the tactical situation in case he had not been able to form a clear mental picture from the information he would be given in the chartroom on his way to the bridge; it was necessary to inform him of the presumed position and course of the U-boat, and of the plan to intercept her again. He might have to hand over the conn to Carling at any moment if other matters were to demand too much of his attention. He might fall down in a fit, or further stray bullets might this time find a human target, leaving Carling in control temporarily.

'Do you understand?' asked Krause; he had made his sentences as short and as clear as he could.

'Yes, sir.'

There was nothing positive in Carling's tone, all the same. Nor was there any bloodthirsty eagerness. It was possible that Carling was at this moment regretting his choice of a profession. Well, there were good officers and bad. It was a relief to find Charlie Cole reporting to him next.

'Sections Three and Four have the watch, sir. They've all been fed, and Sections One and Two are getting their chow now.'

'Thank you, Commander. And will you see that they get some rest after that?'

'Aye aye, sir. And what about yourself, sir?'

'I'm not tired yet. Can't leave the bridge at present. But I want those men fresh for the twelve to four.'

And Sections One and Two would have their next period off watch after this one curtailed by general quarters before dawn; they must get all the sleep possible now.

'I'll see about it, sir. But a lot of them won't settle down unless I make 'em.'

'You'll make 'em, Charlie.'

'I'll try, sir.'

'And get a nap yourself.'

'I'll try, sir.'

'Very well, thank you, Commander.'

'Thank you, sir.'

138

Krause peered at the clock. More than fifteen minutes since they had turned away from the *pillenwerfer*; that spot was now more than three miles behind them, but they would not have closed the convoy by more than a mile as yet. There was time, and urgent need, to get down to the head again. Now that the idea had occurred to him he could not wait a moment.

'Mr Carling, take the conn.'

'Aye aye, sir.'

He put on the red spectacles and hurried down the ladder, and brushed through the spun-glass curtain. With his eyes fully accustomed to the darkness he did not have to wait a long time to recover his vision when he returned. He groped his way in. He was no sooner there than he heard the bell, and the voice-tube.

'Captain, sir! Radar pip, sir!'

Carling's voice came through the tube urgent and loud enough for him to hear it where he was. Delay was unavoidable; it must have been a full minute before he was back in the pilot-house again. His first action was to call down to the chartroom.

'Captain here.'

'Pip bearing two-one-nine. Range eight thousand.'

'Very well. Mr Carling, I'll take the conn. What's the course?'

'Zero-eight-zero, sir.'

'Right full rudder. Steer course one-seven-zero. Turn towards the target another time, Mr Carling.'

'Aye aye, sir.'

Carling had wasted all that time keeping *Keeling* on a course almost certainly divergent from the sub.'s. He should never have gone below leaving Carling with the conn.

'Steady on course one-seven-zero.'

'Very well.'

'Pip bearing two-one-eight—two-one-seven. Range seven-eight-double oh.'

Closing fast, but the bearing changing. The U-boat was crossing *Keeling*'s bows heading once more to overtake the convoy, as he had expected. She must have altered course about twelve points to starboard after dropping the *pillen-werfer* and have surfaced again when she thought all was clear. She was four miles away. At their last meeting he had been on the sub.'s starboard bow. A slight alteration of course and he could intercept her again in the same fashion on her port bow. But she had sighted him in time to submerge in safety. It might be better to sneak up from behind her. She might not maintain as efficient a look-out aft as ahead. Dangerous to allow her to get between him and the convoy, but it might bring results. She was four miles away at present.

'Pip bearing two-one-six. Range seven-five-double oh.'

Krause shut his eyes to consider a problem of trigonometry. Even in the dark that was a help to concentration. He listened to the next bearing and range being called. Down below they would work out the problem for him, but only if he could explain exactly what was in his mind. That would take time, and he still might be misunderstood. With the next bearing and range his mind was made up. He was allowing her to get just a little too far ahead of the safety area. He opened his eyes and gave the order.

'Left smartly to course one-six-five.'

That was McAlister at the wheel—his trick had come round again. It was satisfactory that he had a reliable helmsman even if he had an OOD who was doubtful.

'I'm going to try to sneak up behind her, Mr Carling,' he said.

140

'Y-yes, sir.'

It was a fact, strange but true, that Carling was not quite clear about the tactical situation, although there was nothing complex about it; it should be perfectly clear to anyone who had been on the bridge for the last half-hour. It could not be the complexity; Krause began to realize that Carling's vagueness was the result of nerves. He was too excited, or too agitated, or—possibly—too frightened to think clearly. Men of that sort existed, Krause knew. He remembered his own buck-fever of the morning. His own hand had trembled with excitement, and more than once he had been guilty of sins of omission. Carling might grow hardened; but that desire to sound general quarters this morning—perhaps that might have been evidence of anxiety on Carling's part to rid himself of the responsibility of being officer of the deck. But there was no more time to waste on Carling. Luckily his mind had been recording the reported range and bearings as they came in.

'Target's course and speed?' he asked down the voice-tube.

'Course zero-eight-five, speed eleven knots. That's only approximate, sir.'

Approximate or not, it agreed with his own estimate.

'Where do I cross her wake on this course?'

'A mile astern of her. More. Less than two miles, sir.'

'Very well.'

That was what he was aiming at. The range was steadily closing although the bearing was not constant. Now, once more, gun or depth-charge? Gun flashes were blinding. Should he stake his vision at the crucial moment against the chances of a hit? At close range? But with a high sea running and with the range changing as rapidly as he could manage it? He decided against the gun.

'Torpedo officer on duty.'

'Yes, sir.'

Young Sand, J. G. He was having woman trouble at home, but he was a steady enough officer to all appearances.

'Stand by to fire a close pattern. We'll be going at high speed over the target, so make it real close. And a shallow setting.'

'Close pattern. Shallow setting. Aye aye, sir.'

In giving that last order he was taking a further chance. It did not take a sub. long to go deep, and a sub. surprised on the surface would almost certainly go deep as fast as she could be driven down. He was counting on her not having time to dive far. With a deep setting the charges would explode harmlessly far below her, if his plan was successful. He wanted them to burst close alongside her.

He spoke into the telephone.

'Engineer officer on duty.'

It was Ipsen who answered. So he was not resting.

'Captain. Stand by to give us twenty-four knots as soon as you get the signal, Chief.'

'Twenty-four knots. Aye aye, sir. Sea's running pretty high, sir.'

'Yes. It'll only be for two or three minutes. Just time to work her up, and then we'll come down to standard again.'

'Aye aye, sir.'

Now for the look-outs. He turned to the talker.

'Captain to look-outs. "I hope to sight a sub. on the surface nearly dead ahead soon after our next turn. Keep on your toes." '

The talker repeated the message with Krause listening.

'Look-outs answer "aye aye, sir." '

'Sonar on stand-by.'

There was always a chance that the U-boat might pick up *Keeling*'s sonar impulses. For the next minute or two *Keeling* would be unguarded; that was a risk to be taken, but it would not be for long. Soon the increased speed would both protect her and render the sonar ineffective. The silence that fell as soon as the pinging stopped was uncanny.

'Target bearing zero-eight-seven. Range two-four-double oh.'

'Left full rudder. Steer course zero-eight-five.'

That would allow for the advance during the turn.

'Target bearing zero-eight-five. Range two-five-double oh.'

Dead ahead.

'All engines ahead flank speed. Make turns for twenty-four knots.'

'All engines ahead flank speed. Engine-room answers twenty-four knots, sir.'

'Very well.'

This was the moment. A vast increase in vibration as *Keeling* began to pick up speed. He went out on to the starboard wing of the bridge into the howling darkness. He was overtaking the sub. at thirteen knots. Four or five minutes before he would sight her. Then it would be say two and a half minutes before he was on top of her. Ample time for a sub. in diving trim to submerge. But he hoped it would be less than that as he might not be detected immediately, overtaking from right aft. There would not be much time for the sub. to go deep or far.

'Target bearing zero-eight-five. Range two-three-double oh. Two-two-double oh.'

Keeling was picking up speed. He heard the crash, and felt the shudder, as she hit a sea with her port bow. Spray flew at him viciously. She leaped frantically. If the props came out of water he might strip a turbine.

'Range two thousand. One-nine-double oh.'

He could not judge of the visibility; it was only a guess that it was half a mile.

'One-eight-double oh. One-seven-double oh.'

He gulped. No; it was only a wave top, not the thing he was looking for. With his feet slipping on the treacherous deck, and the grip of his gloved hands insecure on the icy rail, he made himself lean forward with his arms over the pelorus, locking it in his armpits, even though he wanted instinctively to stand upright as if to extend his limited horizon.

'One-one-double oh. One thousand.'

Keeling lurched wildly; he could hear the sea boiling over the main deck below.

'Sub. ahead! Zero-zero-five! Zero-zero-five!'

He saw it on a wave-top, something solid in the inky night.

'Right rudder! Meet her!'

He saw it again.

'Left rudder! Meet her! Steady as you go!'

The bow was pointing right at it as *Keeling* hurtled down a wave-face and it rose on another ahead. He saw it again. Four hundred yards at four hundred yards a minute. Gone? He could not be sure at first. Sand was beside him; twice Sand slipped on the heaving deck but he was holding on with his arm locked round a stanchion.

'Fire one! Fire two! "K" guns, fire!'

'All engines ahead standard speed. Right standard rudder.'

Astern the depth-charges were exploding in the tossing black sea like lightning in a thunder cloud.

'Engine-room answers "All engines ahead standard speed," sir.'

'Very well. Quartermaster, call out your heading.'

'Passing one-one-zero. Passing one-two-zero. Passing one-three-zero.'

Keeling, leaning over to the helm, was rolling confusedly with the changing course and the dwindling speed.

'Passing one-six-zero. Passing one-seven-zero.'

'Deep setting, Mr Sand. Wide pattern.'

'Deep setting, wide pattern. Aye aye, sir.'

'Stand by.'

'Aye aye, sir.'

'Passing two-one-zero. Passing two-two-zero.'

Keeling was turning to complete the circle, to depth-charge the strip next to the one she had already attacked.

'Resume sonar search.'

'Passing one-four-zero. Passing one-five-zero.'

'Sonar reports indications confused, sir.'

'Very well.'

The speed was probably still too high in any case, and there was *Keeling's* eddying wake to be considered, and the circling whirlpools of the depth-charges.

'Passing one-eight-zero. Passing one-nine-zero.'

She had the sea on her quarter now, and heaved up her stern with a sickly motion, corkscrewing over a sea.

'Passing two-zero-zero. Passing two-one-zero.'

Was anything happening out there in the black night? A shattered U-boat breaking surface? Or 'crunching' far below it? Despairing survivors struggling in the water? All perfectly possible but not likely.

'Passing two-two-zero.'

'Sonar reports indications still confused, sir.'

'Very well.'

'Passing two-three-zero.'

Krause was carrying in his mind the diagram of *Keeling*'s turning circle; he planned to parallel his former course and bomb the strip next to it; there was no knowing, and almost no guessing, what the U-boat's reaction had been after she had dived and had been depth-charged; she could have turned in any direction and she could have gone to any depth within her limit—but the chances were she had dived as deep as she would dare.

'Standing by for deep pattern, sir.'

'Very well. Steady upon course two-six-seven.'

'Course two-six-seven, sir.'

'Very well.'

There was nothing whatever to be seen round about.

'Steady on course two-six-seven, sir.'

'Very well.'

Wait for it. They that wait upon the Lord shall renew their strength.

'Sonar reports indications confused.'

'Very well.'

Hopeless perhaps to expect water and sonar to get back to normal as quickly as *Keeling* could complete the circle. Now must be the time.

'Now, Mr Sand.'

'Fire one!' said Sand. 'Fire two!'

Thunder and lightning again under water astern. White pillars of water just visible rising in their wake. Wait one minute after the last explosion.

'Left standard rudder. Steer course zero-eight-seven.'

Back again for another parallel sweep.

'Deep pattern again, Mr Sand.'

'Aye aye, sir.'

'Sonar reports indications confused.'

'Very well.'

'Steady on course eight-seven, sir.'

'Very well. Mr Sand, let 'em have it.'

Another ellipse of explosions, beside the previous ones. Krause had gone through the course at the anti-submarine school at Casco Bay; he had read, with painful concentration, innumerable classified pamphlets digesting all the British experience acquired in two and a half years of war against submarines. Mathematicians had devoted their talents and their ingenuity to working out the odds for and against scoring a hit on a submerged U-boat. The most sensitive instruments had been devised, and the most powerful weapons developed. But no one had thought of a way yet to reach a U-boat captain's mind, of making a certainty out of the simple guess as to whether he would turn to starboard or port, go deep or stay shallow. And there was no machinery to supply a destroyer captain with patience and pertinacity and judgment.

'Right standard rudder. Steer course two-six-seven. One more deep pattern, Mr Sand.'

'Aye aye, sir.'

'Steady on course two-six-seven, sir.'

'Very well. Mr Sand!'

'Fire one,' said Sand.

With the firing of this pattern it remained to conduct a final sweep. Helm orders to carry *Keeling* back diagonally over the bombed area, out to the northward, back to the eastward, round again to the south-westward, with the sonar's impulses seeking out through the depths in an effort to make contact again. And nothing to report— negative, negative, the ship wheeling hither and thither in the darkness, apparently aimlessly now in comparison with her previous orderly runs.

'Sir!' Sand was on the wing of the bridge with him, looking out into the darkness, with the wind blowing lustily about them, piercing cold. 'Sir—do you smell anything?'

'Smell?' said Krause.

'Yes, sir.'

Krause sniffed reflectively, sniffed again, pulling cold air into his nose from the hurtling wind. Not easy in those conditions to be sure of smelling anything, especially as, now that he was being really searching about it, he could not help being conscious of the raw onion he had eaten last watch. But it could not be that that Sand was referring to.

'It's gone now, sir,' said Sand. 'No. There it is again. May I ask Mr Carling, sir?'

'If you like.'

'Mr Carling, can you smell anything?'

Carling came out and sniffed beside them.

'Oil?' he said, tentatively.

'That's what I thought,' said Sand. 'Don't you smell it, sir?'

Oil! That would be an indication that the sub. had at least been hard hit. And if there were much of it, a great lake of oil welling up from below and spreading over a mile of sea, it would be practically proof of destruction. Krause sniffed again. He could not be sure—or more definitely he was nearly sure he could smell nothing.

'Can't say that I do,' said Krause.

'Look-out, there!' hailed Sand. 'D'you smell any oil?'

'Not now, sir. Thought I smelt some a while back.'

'You see, sir?' said Sand.

They looked out at the dark water below, hardly visible from the heaving bridge. It was quite impossible to tell in the darkness if there were oil on the surface.

'I wouldn't say there was,' said Krause.

The pleasure it would give him to be sure that there was oil made him particularly sceptical, although—Krause not being given to self-analysis—he was unaware of it and made no allowance for that particular reaction. But the very high standards of proof demanded by the Admiralty undoubtedly influenced him.

'I don't think I can smell it now, sir,' said Sand. 'But we've come a long way since I thought I smelt it first.'

'No,' said Krause. His tone was quite expressionless because he was set on keeping all emotion out of the argument. 'I don't think there was anything worth mentioning.'

'Very well, sir,' said Sand.

Literally (in Krause's opinion) it was not worth mentioning; it would find no place in his report when it came to be written. He was not of the type to try and claim credit for himself on insufficient evidence. Prove all things, hold fast that which is good. Yet the possibility was a deciding factor.

'Let's go,' said Krause.

Balancing one chance against another it seemed likely that there was no more profit to be gained in staying astern of the convoy. The sub. *might* be sunk; certainly she was below the surface and likely to stay there for some time, and probably was sufficiently far astern to be out of harm's way for a much longer time. This was certainly the moment to return to the head of the convoy and take part in the struggle the other three ships were waging. Krause's 'Let's go' was not a suggestion put forward for comment; it was the announcement of a decision, as his officers knew with out a moment's thought.

'Take the conn, Mr Carling,' said Krause. 'I want to

head round the left flank of the convoy at our best practicable speed.'

'Aye aye, sir,' said Carling, and, after a moment's thought, 'Zigzagging, sir?'

'No,' said Krause.

He had wanted to blaze out at Carling. It was nonsense to talk about zigzagging when *Keeling* would be going twenty knots or more in the darkness, but the very fact that Carling should ask the nonsensical question was a proof that he was not fully master of himself. A sharp reprimand now would very likely unnerve him completely. On the other hand, to put him in charge of a quite simple manœuvre which he could carry out with complete success might re-establish his self-command and help to make him a good officer in time. A destroyer captain's duty was to build as well as to destroy.

But although it was necessary to leave Carling in complete control this was not the time to quit the bridge. He had to appear to be taking no notice while remaining instantly available to deal with any emergency. He went over to the T.B.S. and listened on the hand-set with one ear, his back to Carling, and the other ear cocked listening to what Carling was doing. Carling acted quite normally, called down to the chartroom to give him a course for the proposed movement, gave the necessary helm order, and called for twenty knots.

'George to Harry. George to Dicky. George to Eagle,' said Krause on the T.B.S. He waited for the replies. 'I'm coming up round the left flank. Look out for me, Harry.'

'Aye aye, sir.'

'I don't think I got the sub. I chased through the convoy,' he went on. 'Maybe I gave him a fright, though.'

The British officer who had lectured on anti-submarine

warfare at Casco Bay had been fond of quoting an army story of the previous war, in which two infantry privates put their clothes through a newly-invented machine for delousing them.

'Why,' said one, bitterly, after inspecting results. 'They're all alive still.'

'Yes,' said the other. 'But I expect they've had the hell of a fright.'

Usually—too often—an encounter between a U-boat and a destroyer ended merely in the U-boat having had more or less of a fright and receiving no hurt. To cleanse the sea of the U-boat vermin called for killing; no amount of narrow escapes would deter the U-boat captains with their fanatical *esprit de corps*—and with the iron hand of Doenitz to force them into action.

'It's us that's having frights up here, sir,' squawked the T.B.S.

Was there reproach in that remark? Krause felt a pang as he heard it. No one was more sharply aware than himself that the destroyer captains under his command had fought through two and a half years of war and had probably resented bitterly the accident that had put them, two-and-a-half stripers, under the command of a three-stripe American who had never fired a shot even though he was nearly twenty years older. The convoy had had to sail; the Allies had had to scrape together an escort for it; and he had happened to be the ranking officer. Luckily they could not be aware of the other circumstances which rankled as badly in Krause's heart, that he had been marked with the words—utterly damning although innocent enough in appearance—'fitted and retained,' and that he had been twice passed over for promotion and had only made commander with the expansion of the navy in 1941.

What they *were* aware of was that twice today at wild moments their commanding officer had vanished into the rear of the convoy. The fact that he had engaged in desperate action each time, that *Keeling* had been doing work that had to be done and for doing which she was best situated at the moment, would not be so apparent to them. There might be heads wagging about the inexperience— or even worse—of their commanding officer. It was painful, horribly painful, to think about that; it was infuriating as well. Krause could have burst into a roaring rage, but it was very much his duty not to do so. He that is slow to anger is better than the mighty, and he that ruleth his spirit than he that taketh a city. It was his duty to stay unangered, to speak in a flat tone, with every word distinct, and with no trace of emotion.

'I am six miles behind you,' he said. 'I'll be up to you in half an hour. Coming up on the left flank. Over.'

He turned away from the T.B.S. with a horrid mixture of emotions. That remark may have been merely a light-hearted one, but it rankled.

'I think, Mr Carling,' he said; it was for another reason now that he had to appear unconcerned and unexcited. 'She'll take another couple of knots at least. Better try her.'

'Aye aye, sir.'

He was hungry and thirsty, and this would be an ideal moment in which to eat and drink; he had no idea what had happened to the last pot of coffee for which he had sent the messenger—all he knew was that he had not tasted it; the last coffee he had drunk had been the icy cold contents of the pot before that one. But now he was hungry and thirsty and yet had no appetite; with the strain he was undergoing and had undergone the thought of food was actually distasteful to him. Yet it was essential that he should eat and drink if he were to remain equal to the demands upon him.

'Messenger!'

'Yes, sir.'

'Go down to the wardroom. I want a pot of coffee and a sandwich. But no onion. Remember to tell the mess-boy that or he'll put some in for sure. Wait for it and bring it up yourself.'

'Aye aye, sir.'

No onion; if ever there was another chance of smelling oil he wanted to be sure of whether he smelt it or not. This might even be a good moment to get down to the head, although it was by no means necessary yet. No; as it was not necessary it would be better not to leave Carling in sole charge. The quartermaster, crouching over the table with the red flashlight, was endeavouring to write up the deck log. It would be a poor job he would make of it, with *Keeling*'s recent evolutions, and in the absence of the hourly readings from the engine-room, but he was scribbling away industriously and fast. Now there was bustle through the ship, voices, clatter on the ladders, and Krause realized that the quartermaster was working in that fashion in anticipation of being relieved at the change of watch. Shadowy figures were crowding up into the pilot-house. Another watch was over. The convoy was another thirty miles or more nearer safety.

Thursday. Middle Watch—2400–0400

'You did a good job, McAlister,' said Krause as the helm was relieved. 'Well done.'

'Thank you, sir.'

With McAlister at the wheel *Keeling* had pointed herself straight up the U-boat's wake, straight for the U-boat itself.

Carling saluted in the darkness and reported his relief. He went through the ceremonial sentences—ceremonial and yet every word important—with an apparent calm.

'Mr Nystrom has the deck, sir,' concluded Carling.

'Thank you, Mr Carling. Very well.'

The flat tone; essential that there should be no suggestion of anything unusual.

'Cap'n, please, sir, I got your coffee.'

It was rather a plaintive voice. The messenger had carried that tray up four ladders, with *Keeling* leaping on the waves and the ladders crowded with the changing watch, and now there was a crowded pilot-house and as always only the jealously-guarded chart-table on which to put the tray.

'On the table,' said Krause. 'Quartermaster, make room for it. Thank you, messenger.'

Because he had chosen that particular moment to send for coffee the messenger had lost ten full minutes of his watch below. The fortune of war for the messenger, but Krause would have waited until the watch was changed if he had noticed the time. Krause pulled off his right-hand fur glove and wedged it in his left armpit; his hand was cold but he still had full use of it. He poured himself a cup of coffee, fumbling in the darkness, and sipped at it. Scalding hot, too hot to drink despite its long journey up from the wardroom. But the taste and the smell of it were sufficient to start his digestive processes working again. He longed for that coffee; he was accustomed to drinking eight big cups every day of his life and had always guiltily put aside the self-accusation that he was a coffee-hound dependent on a drug.

154

While the coffee cooled he bit into the sandwich. No onion, just bread and cold corned beef and mayonnaise, but he found himself in the darkness snapping at it like a wolf, biting and chewing frantically. During the last sixteen hours or so of ceaseless activity he had eaten half a sandwich. The present one vanished in a few bites, and Krause lingeringly licked the traces of mayonnaise from his fingers before addressing himself to the coffee. It was now exactly cool enough—just hotter than most people would care to drink it—and he emptied the cup without taking it from his lips and poured himself another in passionate anticipation. He sipped at it; *Keeling* was pitching very considerably and heeling a good deal, but he held the cup level in the darkness even when an unexpected lurch caused him to shift his footing. A towering pitch on *Keeling*'s part sent the coffee, when next he sipped, surging up his upper lip as far as his nose, and it ran down to drip from his chin, but he drank all the rest and felt in the darkness for the pot hoping there would be a third cupful in it. Of course there was not—there never was; only, as far as he could guess, a thimbleful at the bottom of the pot which he tossed off.

It crossed his mind that he could send for another pot, but he virtuously put the temptation aside. He would not be led astray into self-indulgence; he could be firm in the matter of coffee when he had had nearly enough. He had cast the napkin aside from the tray in his initial eagerness, and now it was hopeless to try to find it in the darkness; his handkerchief was out of reach in his bundled clothes, but he wiped his mouth on the back of his hand, secure in the knowledge no one could see him, and then pulled on his glove again. He had eaten and drunk without a moment's interruption, and the food and drink brightened his outlook; his momentary depression had vanished. Yet as he moved away from the table he was very conscious of fatigue in his legs—the first time he had noticed it. He determined at that same moment not to notice it; he had often enough before stood balancing on a heaving deck for sixteen hours at a stretch. There was duty still to be done, and endless vistas of days and nights of duty.

'What do you have on the screen?' he asked down the voice-pipe.

Someone down there gave him distances and bearings; the convoy half a mile abaft his starboard beam although out of sight. A pip three miles ahead.

'That's the British corvette, sir.'

'Very well.'

'Screen's very fuzzy, sir. And it's jumping, too.'

'Very well.'

Over the T.B.S.

'George to Harry. Do you hear me?'

'Harry to George. I hear you. Strength three.'

'You bear from me zero-eight-zero. Do you have me on your screen?'

'Yes, we have you, bearing two-six-two, distance three and a half miles.'

'Very well. I'll cross astern of you. I'll reduce speed and start sonar search now.'

'Aye aye, sir.'

He put down the hand-set.

'Mr Nystrom, we'll come down to standard speed. Start sonar search.'

'Aye aye, sir.'

'Set a course to pass astern of *James* and *Viktor*. Keep well clear of the convoy.'

'Aye aye, sir.'

156

Krause's leg weariness asserted itself again, to his considerable annoyance. He had no business to feel tired yet. And he was gloomily conscious that despite his recent meal depression was only just over the horizon of his mind. He knew it because suddenly, agonizingly, the thought of Evelyn came up into his mind. Evelyn and her handsome black-haired young San Diego lawyer. That was a dreadful thought here in this dark Atlantic night, heaving over a black invisible ocean. Evelyn was quite justified in growing tired of him, he supposed. He was dull. And he had quarrelled with her—he should not have done so, but it was hard to avoid it when she resented the amount of time he spent in his ship; she could not understand—that was his fault for not being able to explain. A cleverer man would have made his feelings, his compulsions, clear to her. Three years ago now, and the memories as bitter as ever.

Thinking about it was every bit as bad as the actual experience had been. 'Fitted and retained'—those hideous words which meant so much to him and so little to Evelyn. The quarrels, and then the piercing frightful pain of the news about Evelyn and the lawyer. The pain was as bad as ever, far worse than anything physical Krause had ever experienced. Two years the marriage had lasted; a month of happiness—shamefaced happiness. Evelyn's amused astonishment at finding she had married a man who knelt down and said his prayers in all sincerity night and morning; her slightly more irritated surprise that her husband would not leave some dull duty in his ship to his executive officer in order to attend a party; these spoilt it a little.

Krause tried to shake off the memories; he was not self-analytical enough to be aware that this was typical mid-watch depression, that it was in these hours when vitality was at a low ebb between midnight and four in the morning that he was assailed by these regrets and yearnings, but he struggled against them. For that matter, it was because of that black-haired lawyer that he was here now, on the tossing Atlantic. He had asked for service on the Atlantic seaboard; he could not face the possibility of seeing Evelyn in San Diego or Coronado, or of hearing fragments of gossip about her. If it had not been for that lawyer he might have died along with so many of his friends at Pearl Harbour.

That could have been a cheering thought, but Krause did not find it so. In part this black mood was due to the reaction from the tension of war-like operations. Krause, like many good fighting men, felt a sharp keying-up, something akin to exhilaration, in battle, and now, in this comparatively quiet moment, he was paying for it with interest, the more painfully because this was the first time he had had the experience. His infinite sadness encompassed him as closely and as impenetrably as the darkness of the night, while he stood on the bridge suffering useless agonies thinking about Evelyn and her lawyer, and wishing for the moon, wishing that in some impossible fashion he had been able to bring both experience and purity to his marriage. The ping-ping of the sonar was a dirge of his dead happiness.

'Eagle on the T.B.S., sir,' said Nystrom, and Krause went to it.

'Eagle to George! Eagle to George!'

Urgency in that English voice.

'George to Eagle. Go ahead.'

'Contact bearing oh-five-oh from us. We're running it down.'

'I'll turn towards it. What range?'

158

'Very distant.'

'Very well.'

The sadness was gone, not only gone but forgotten, as if it had never been. Krause called down to the chartroom for a course.

'I'll take her now, Mr Nystrom.'

'Aye aye, sir.'

'Dicky to George. Dicky to George!'

The T.B.S. summoned him at the moment when he had given the new course.

'We've got a contact too. Distant, bearing nine-seven. And we've got a pip as well. Bearing one-oh-one, range twelve miles.'

'Very well. I'll come over to you after I've helped Eagle.'

'George! George!' Another voice breaking into the circuit. 'Harry here. Do you hear me?'

'George to Harry. I hear you.'

'We've got a pip. Range twelve miles, bearing two-four.'

'Very well.' Something must be said besides 'very well.' 'I'll send Eagle to you as soon as I can.'

This was a fresh attack, perhaps the decisive one, timed for this moment, with the middle watch half-through and vitality and alertness at their lowest in the blackest part of the night.

'Eagle to George. Contact's turning. Looks as if she's heading your way.'

'Very well.'

'Sonar reports contact, sir. Distant, bearing zero-nine-zero.'

'Very well.'

So nearly dead ahead that there was no purpose in altering course yet.

'Eagle to George. Contact bearing two-seven-one from me. Range one mile.'

'It bears zero-nine-zero from me, distant contact.'

'Oh-nine-oh, distant. Aye aye, sir. We're turning after it.'

'I'll alter course to zero-eight-five.'

'Oh-eight-five. Aye aye, sir.'

Otherwise the two ships, not much more than two miles apart, would be heading straight for each other in the darkness.

'Left smartly to course zero-eight-five.'

'Left smartly to course zero-eight-five, sir. Steady on course zero-eight-five.'

'Sonar reports contact ahead, bearing indefinite. Strong up Doppler.'

Strong up Doppler; as he had expected, U-boat and *Keeling* were heading almost straight for each other at the moment the report was transmitted.

'Eagle to George. Contact's still turning. Bearing two-seven-six. Range one-five-double oh. We're still turning after it.'

'I'll hold my course at present.'

Two ships setting to partners in the dark. The sub. might complete its circle; she might double back in an 'S' turn. The problem was either to intercept her or drive her back upon *Viktor*, and to do one or other of these things, or both, without collision and without interference with each other's instruments.

'Dicky to George! I am attacking.'

The Canadian voice had broken in.

'Very well.'

This was like a juggler keeping three balls in the air at once.

'Sonar reports contact bearing zero-eight-seven. Range one mile. No Doppler.'

'Who's on the sonar?'

'Ellis, sir,' replied the talker.

That was good; there was less chance of being deceived by a *pillenwerfer*.

'Eagle to George. It looks as if she's turning back again.'

'Very well. I'll go on holding my course.'

'Sonar reports distant explosions, sir.'

'Very well.'

That would be Dicky's depth-charges going off.

'Sonar reports contact dead ahead. Strong up Doppler. Range fifteen hundred yards.'

'Very well. George to Eagle. He's coming right at me again. Keep clear.'

'Eagle to George. Aye aye, sir.'

That English voice was cold and steady, bearing no hint of the excitement of the hunt.

'Eagle to George. We are on course oh-one-oh.'

Viktor was squarely astern of the U-boat, and heading to intercept her if she turned to starboard.

'Sonar reports contact dead ahead. Strong up Doppler. Range twelve hundred yards.'

Apparently the U-boat had not detected *Keeling*'s presence as yet. All her attention had been directed to evading *Viktor*, possibly; or her listening devices had been confused by *Viktor*'s nearness; or the fact that U-boat and *Keeling* were exactly bow to bow might be rendering them ineffective.

'Sonar reports contact confused, sir. Approximately dead ahead. No Doppler. Range approximately eleven hundred.'

'Very well.'

The U-boat must by now have become aware of *Keeling*'s presence, and was doing something about it.

'Sonar reports contact dead ahead. It's a *pill*, sir. Range one thousand.'

She had let loose a *pillenwerfer*; Ellis had detected that, but the bubbling thing had prevented him from ascertaining what new course the U-boat had taken.

'Sonar reports possible contact bearing zero-nine-two, range eleven hundred yards. *Pill* still dead ahead.'

So the U-boat had altered course to port most likely; that was its best chance. And thanks to the *pillenwerfer* she had increased her distance—she had stolen a march on *Keeling*.

'Right standard rudder. Steer course one-zero-zero. George to Eagle. Contact seems to have altered course to port and dropped a *pill*. I am altering course to starboard. One-zero-zero.'

'One-double oh. Aye aye, sir.'

'Sonar reports confused contact, sir, on port bow.'

With *Keeling* turning, the contact would likely to be indefinite.

'Eagle to George. We've only got the *pill*, sir. No other contact.'

'Very well.'

Keeling and *Viktor* had the sub. between them, and although on their present courses they would be rapidly separating it was the best arrangement until the situation cleared up.

'Sonar reports confused contact bearing zero-eight-five. Range twelve hundred yards. Sounds like the *pill*.'

Undoubtedly it *was* the *pill*; but it was hard to imagine what the sub. was doing. A sudden sharp alteration of depth might have added to the confusion. Better to hold on as he was doing even though both he and *Viktor* were diverging from the last-known position of the sub.

'Sonar reports contact bearing zero-eight-zero. Range thirteen hundred yards. Contact weak.'

Getting too far away altogether.

'Left smartly to zero-nine-zero. George to Eagle. I am turning to port. Course zero-nine-zero.'

'Course oh-nine-oh. Aye aye, sir.'

'Steady on course zero-nine-zero.'

'Very well.'

'Sonar reports faint additional contact, range indefinite, bearing three-five-zero.'

Three-five-zero? Right abaft his beam despite his turn?

'George to Eagle. Do you get anything bearing three-five-zero from me? Range indefinite.'

'We'll try, sir. Three-five-oh.'

There was something strange about this. But there was always likely to be something strange about a blindfold hunt for an enemy below water.

'Eagle to George! Eagle to George! We've got something. Very faint. Bearing two-two-oh from us.'

'Get after it, then, quick.'

Abaft *Viktor*'s beam, too. Much nearer the safety of the convoy with its propeller noises. Almost out of the danger circles drawn by the wheeling destroyer. The sub. had fooled them both completely. Hard to imagine what she had done. Perhaps she had dropped two *pillen-werfers* and circled sharply between them and had got away at a very different depth. *Viktor* had less of a turn to make than he had. Better to send her after the contact while he turned away out of her wake and came down on the outside.

'Right standard rudder. Steer course two-six-zero.'

Keeling came round, wallowing in the trough, corkscrewing on the quartering sea, and the hunt went on again. Round and round went the destroyers, chasing the faint contacts, dodging each other as they passed in the darkness. *Viktor* just headed off the U-boat from the convoy; *Keeling* missed her as she circled, and *Viktor* missed her as she doubled back. Then closer contacts. Depth-charges from *Viktor*. Depth-charges from *Keeling*, rumbling in the windy night, momentarily illuminating the fathomless depths below, and deafening the sonar so that there were long anxious waits before the search could be resumed. Bearings and courses called back and forth between the ships. Circle and turn. This U-boat captain was a foxy fellow. Seas coming in over the low freeboard as *Keeling* turned her defenceless quarter into them; seas crashing against the forecastle as she wheeled towards them. Hunting and hunting, with every small indication of vital importance; straining to keep the mind alert to draw rapid deductions from vague data. Sudden reports coming in from *James* and *Dodge*, out on the flanks, fighting their own battles, but with their situation having to be borne in mind as well. 'Left rudder.' 'Right rudder.' Orders repeated. Orders countermanded as *Viktor* turned unexpectedly. A tiring game with death, but never tedious with every moment tense.

'Right standard rudder. Steer course zero-four-zero.'

'Right standard rudder to——'

'Sonar reports torpedoes fired, sir.'

The talker broke in on the quartermaster's repetition of Krause's order, and tension acutely rose in the pilot-house where it had seemed as if tension could not possibly be screwed up any tighter.

'George to Eagle. Torpedoes fired.'

'We heard 'em, sir.'

'Steady on course zero-four-zero,' said the quarter-master. There was discipline in the pilot-house.

Torpedoes; the quarry had poison fangs and was slashing back with them at its tormentors.

'Sonar reports torpedoes' sound fading out,' said the talker.

They were not aimed at *Keeling*, therefore. That had seemed likely to Krause already, bearing in mind her changing course and distance from the contact.

'Eagle to George. We are turning away.' The English liaison officer's voice was positively more languid than usual. 'Course oh-seven-oh. Oh-eight-oh.'

Krause stared out into the darkness where the torpedoes were speeding at fifty knots towards *Viktor*. There might be a sheet of flame and a detonating explosion out there in five more seconds. Subs did not fire torpedoes at escorting vessels as often as one might have expected. They were too small and too elusive a target and of too shallow a draft. And probably Doenitz's orders were strict that each U-boat should do her best to expend all her twenty-two torpedoes on bulging cargo vessels.

'Sonar reports——'

'Eagle to George. Those torpedoes have missed, sir.'

'Very well.' He could be as nonchalant as any Englishman. No; better not to pose; better to try to establish a warm relationship. 'Thank God for that. I was worried about you.'

'Oh, we can look after ourselves, sir. Thank you all the same.'

But those were precious seconds to waste on amenities. No time to spare, not with a U-boat trying to break out of the circle. Krause snapped an order over his shoulder at the helmsman before speaking into the T.B.S. again.

'We're coming in on course zero-eight-zero.'

'Oh-eight-oh. Aye aye, sir. We'll keep away to starboard.'

Viktor's compulsory turn away had stretched the circle almost to breaking point—it was to gain herself that relief that the sub. had fired the torpedoes, perhaps; only with a faint hope of making a hit. It was necessary to narrow the circle again, to press the pursuit, to continue the contest, as always with one destroyer trying to close in, one steering to intercept, each ready to exchange roles in the intricate figures of the movements in the stormy dark—desperate manœuvres like nothing ever contemplated by admirals a few years ago planning peace-time exercises under 'simulated wartime conditions.' Left rudder. Right rudder. Deep pattern. Thunder and storm and strain. And *James* firing star-shells out on the left flank, while look-outs reported gunfire in that direction, and sonar reported distant explosions as *Dodge* fought off attackers on the right, and the convoy lumbered along in the darkness, heading eastward, steadily eastward, towards infinitely distant safety.

Thursday. Morning Watch—0400-0800

Then Nystrom addressing himself to him while *Keeling* steadied herself on yet one more new course.

'Report having been relieved, sir——'

The mid-watch was over; thirty more miles gained. Four hours had passed half in misery and half in desperate concentration.

'Very well, Mr Nystrom. Get some rest while you can.'

'Aye aye, sir.'

166

Rest? That called his attention to the fact that his legs were aching frantically. His muscles, unconsciously taut with the mental tension, protested as violently as did his joints the moment he thought about it. He moved stiffly to the captain's stool in the starboard corner of the pilot-house. He never sat on that stool while at sea; he had a theory that captains should never sit down—it was allied to the theory that all self-indulgence was suspect—but theories were liable to be discarded under practical test. He could have groaned both with pain and relief as he sat down, but instead it was 'Right standard rudder. Steer course zero-eight-seven.'

And now that he had sat down he knew it was pressingly necessary to get down to the head again; and with the self-indulgence of sitting also came the overwhelmingly tempting thought of pots and pots of fiery hot coffee to pour down his throat. But they were closing fast on a contact. Count the seconds. Force the weary brain to think clearly, to try to guess the U-boat captain's next move, as the closing range broke off the contact.

'Mr Pond!'

'Fire one. Fire two. "K" guns fire.'

Once more the underwater thunder and lightning, once more the rapid thinking, the sharp helm orders.

'Sonar reports indications confused, sir.'

'Very well. Mr Harbutt, take the conn.'

'Aye aye, sir.'

His barely rested legs would hardly carry him down the tossing ladder as he went down to the head with the red spectacles over his eyes; on his way back he had to pull with his hands to take some of his body weight as his hesitant feet felt their way from rung to rung.

The brief interval away from the bridge gave him time

to think about other problems besides the present and instant one of catching the submarine with which he was in contact. He gave the orders as he was at the top of the ladder, and he heard the result over the ship's loudspeaker as he came back into the pilot-house.

'Now hear this. Hear this. There won't be any routine general quarters this watch. If general quarters goes it'll be the real thing. The watch below can have a full four hours in unless there's an emergency.'

Krause was glad he had thought of that and decided upon it. He had been in touch with the enemy all day long, and most of the time he had got along without calling all hands to battle stations. The routine of general quarters an hour before dawn would cut into his men's rest and was not necessary with the whole ship keyed up and ready for action as she was. The strain of Condition Two was bad enough. *Keeling* had been supplied with new weapons and new instruments. The presence of the additional men to man them had strained her living accommodation to the utmost, and yet she did not have enough trained ratings available to supply three watches in Condition Two—and even if she did have them Krause had no idea where they would sleep or how they would be fed. The shortage of trained ratings had led him to divide his ship's company into four sections and to institute a routine of watch-and-watch while in Condition Two. He wanted to impose no additional burden on his men, and he wanted to give them all the rest he could. He was more fortunate regarding his officers. Most of them were doing four on and eight off, but even so they might as well be spared an unnecessary call to general quarters.

It had taken Krause all the time he had spent going up and down the ladder to come to this decision; when he re-entered the pilot-house he was ready to take over the handling of the immediate problem. The removal of the red spectacles was a kind of symbolic act, transferring his attention from within the ship to outside it.

'Sonar reports uncertain contact, range indefinite, approximately bearing two-three-one.'

'Is that the first contact since I went below, Mr Harbutt?'

'Yes, sir.'

'Where's *Viktor*?'

Harbutt told him. In the three minutes the situation had moved slowly along usual lines.

'I'll take the conn, Mr Harbutt.'

'Aye aye, sir.'

'Right full rudder. Steer course one-six-two.'

'Right full rudder. Steer course one-six-two, sir.'

He was back in the hunt again.

'Steady on course one-six-two, sir.'

'Eagle to George. I am closing in on course nine-seven.'

'Very well.'

This particular chase had already lasted three long hours. Although they had not damaged the sub. they had at least contrived to keep her from attacking the convoy; they had forced her away to the flank out of the convoy's path. Three hours was not a long time for a U-boat hunt; the British Navy had a record of one that had lasted more than twenty-four hours. But at the same time the sub. he had been chasing had been using her batteries extensively, going a full six knots much of the time instead of creeping along at three or hanging motionless. The U-boat captain, although he still must have plenty of air, must by now be experiencing a certain anxiety about his batteries, even assuming (as was most likely the case) that when the contact was first made he had only recently submerged and had begun the battle with full air banks and a full charge.

But the U-boat captain's worries, while dodging two destroyers, while being depth-charged, while exhausting his batteries, were not to be compared with Krause's. He had herded his enemy away to the flank, but that had left the front of the convoy open to attack. *Dodge* and *James* had their hands full, judging by the reports they were making when they had time to spare. It could only be a question of time before the prowling enemy should find the weak spots for which he was probing. To guard the whole circuit round a large convoy with two destroyers and two escort vessels was not just difficult; it was impossible, against a determined enemy under good leadership. In his next moment of leisure, while the next pattern was being fired (so far had *Keeling* and Krause progressed towards being war-hardened during these twenty hours of battle, that the firing of depth-charges brought a moment of leisure) Krause conjured up a picture of the ideal escorting force—three more escort vessels to guard the front while he and *Viktor* acted as a pursuit force; two more to reinforce *Dodge* and *James*; one to cover the rear; yes, and another pursuit force as well. With eight escort vessels and four destroyers a good job could be done; and air cover; the thought of air cover shot up in Krause's weary mind like a rocket. He had heard of the small carriers that were being built; with radar-equipped planes they would give a wolf-pack a whole lot more to think about. Escort vessels and destroyers and baby flat-tops were coming off the ways as fast as America and England and Canada could build them—newspapers and classified pamphlets assured him of that; somehow they would be manned, he presumed, and in a year or so convoys would be well guarded. But meanwhile it was his duty to fight his way through as best he could with the means at his disposal. Every man's work shall be made manifest.

'Right full rudder. Steer course zero-seven-two,' said Krause. 'George to Eagle. I am heading to cross your wake after your next attack.'

He had forgotten about sitting down, but his legs had not forgotten. They reminded him about it with vicious aches as he stepped back from the T.B.S. He sank on to the stool and spread his legs. After all, this was in the darkness, and the people in the pilot-house were hardly able to see their captain lounging in such a slack fashion. He had compounded with his sense of what he could permit himself regarding sitting down, admitting that it was necessary, but he still had qualms about what would be the effect upon discipline and *esprit de corps* if the men upon whom he kept such a taut hand should see him slacking off with so little excuse.

'After look-out reports fire in the convoy, sir,' said a talker.

He was on his feet again, with hardly time to think of this as retribution for his self-indulgence. There it was; now the rockets were soaring into the night above the flames which he could see; now there was another sharp red glow lighting the upper works of one ship, silhouetting the upper works of another—a torpedo explosion as he watched; the length of the interval told him that this was not a 'spread' bursting as it reached various targets. A U-boat had been deliberately marking down victims one after another.

'Sonar reports contact bearing zero-seven-seven,' said the talker.

He and *Viktor* were in touch with one U-boat; at any

minute a false move by her captain might mean her destruction. Behind him men were dying in the night, the victims of cold-blooded sharpshooting. He had to choose; it was the most painful moment he had ever known, more painful than when he had heard about Evelyn. He had to leave those men to die.

'Depth-charges away,' said the T.B.S.

If he abandoned the present hunt he could not be sure of making contact with the other U-boat; in fact it was most doubtful that he would. And she had done her damage for the present.

'Sonar reports contact confused,' said the talker—that was *Viktor*'s depth-charges exploding.

He might save some lives; he *might*. But in the darkness and confusion of the disordered convoy even that was unlikely, and he would be seriously endangering his ship.

'I am turning away to port,' said *Viktor*.

'Very well.'

The U-boat which had done the damage would now be harmless for a short space at least while reloading her tubes. It was humiliating, it was infuriating, that he should find comfort even for one moment in such a thought. Fighting anger and baffled rage surged up inside him, a yearning to run amok, to hit out wildly. He could feel the tension rising within him. He could lose all patience and see red, but twenty-four years of discipline saved him. He imposed self-control upon himself; Annapolis may have taught him that, or perhaps his much-loved father in his boyhood. He forced himself to think as coldly and as scientifically as ever.

'Sonar reports contact bearing zero-six-eight.'

'Left smartly to course zero-six-four. George to Eagle. I am turning to port to intercept.'

Men were dying behind him, men he was supposed to protect. What he had to do was to solve little trigono-metrical problems in his head quickly and accurately, and give his orders calmly, and issue his information intelligibly, and anticipate the submerged U-boat's movements as freshly and as rapidly as he had done ever since yesterday. He had to be a machine that did not know emotion; he had to be a machine that did not know fatigue. He had to be a machine uninfluenced by the possibility that Washington and London might think him a failure.

'Sonar reports contact bearing zero-six-six, range one thousand,' said the talker. 'But it sounds like a *pill.*, sir.'

If it were a *pill.* which way was the U-boat turning? What depth would she take up? He applied himself to those problems while the men in the convoy died. He gave his two hundredth successive helm order.

The darkness was not as impenetrable now. The white wave-tops could be seen overside, and even as far ahead as the bow from the wing of the bridge. Day was creeping towards them from the east, an unutterably slow transition from black to grey; grey sky and grey horizon and a slate-grey heaving sea. Weeping may endure for a night, but joy cometh in the morning. It was not true. The heavens declare the glory of God. These heavens? As Krause noted the coming of the light the well-remembered verses came up into his mind—they had come up in his mind in the old days of Pacific and Caribbean sunrises. Now he thought of them with a bitter, sardonic revulsion of mind. The shattered convoy on the flank; the frozen corpses on the life-rafts; the pitiless grey sky; the certainty that this agony was going to endure until he could bear it no longer—it was more than he could bear already. He wanted to throw in his hand, to cast aside all thought of his duty, his duty to God. Then he drew himself back from the temptation.

'George to Eagle. I am holding my course. Keep clear.' His voice was as flat and as precise as ever.

The fool hath said in his heart, There is no God. He had nearly said that too, while he could still square his shoulders and while his aching legs could still carry him to the T.B.S.

'Contact bearing zero-six-seven, range eleven hundred yards.'

'Very well.'

One more attempt to destroy the hidden enemy. And not one more only; dozens, hundreds if necessary. While *Keeling* moved in to the attack, while the talker repeated the ranges, there was time to bow his head. Cleanse Thou me from secret faults.

'Stand by for deep pattern, Mr Pond.'

'Aye aye, sir.'

Balked by the U-boat's turn; helm orders to get into position again; orders to *Viktor* to head her off. Let us not be weary in well doing.

The wind was still blowing, the sea was still rough, *Keeling* was still corkscrewing and rolling and pitching. It was as if he had been in that gale and balancing upon that heaving deck for a hundred years. His darkness-accustomed eyes were gradually aware of the interior of the pilot-house —for hours he had seen nothing of it except for one or two glimmering dials and the quartermaster's red flashlight. Now he could see it; the shattered windows—one pane with a clean bullet hole but the rest in splinters; fragments of glass over the deck; and his discarded trays—a cup here, a napkin, trampled and dirty, there.

'Get this mess cleaned up, Mr Harbutt.'

'Aye aye, sir.'

And there was something strange about *Keeling*'s appearance in the growing light. Her upper works were coated with ice, frosted white. Stanchions and stays, torpedoes and life-lines, ice was over them all. The commission pennant at the masthead instead of streaming in the wind was frozen in an untidy loop against the halliard. He could see *Viktor* now, after this long night of talking with her over the T.B.S. I have heard of Thee by the hearing of the ear, but now mine eye seeth Thee. She stood out white against the grey with the ice upon her also. Now he could actually see her making the turn she had just announced to him over the T.B.S. He had to make the corresponding move; now he could judge it by eye in confirmation of his mental trigonometry.

'Left standard rudder. Steer course zero-six-zero.'

It might certainly be called daylight now. At this time yesterday he had secured from general quarters. Today he had saved his men that fatigue. Was that only yesterday? Was it only last evening that those bullets had ripped through the pilot-house? It might well have been last year. And at this time yesterday he had been able to get below; he had eaten bacon and eggs and filled himself with coffee. He had said his prayers and he had had a shower. Unbelievable happiness. It reminded him that during the twenty-four hours since that time he had taken nothing except a sandwich and a half and a few cups of coffee. And he had been on his feet nearly all that time too; he was on them at this moment. He shuffled—he could not walk—to the stool and sat down again, the muscles of his legs throbbing painfully as they relaxed. Palate and throat were dry; he felt nauseated and hungry at the same time. He watched *Viktor* moving in; he listened to the reports from the talker.

'Permission to light the smoking lamp, sir?' asked Harbutt.

Krause's mind struggled out of his concentration like a man with his feet embedded in a bog.

'Permission granted. Meet her, Quartermaster! Steady as you go.'

'Now hear this, hear this,' began the loudspeaker, broadcasting the permission he had just granted. Harbutt had a cigarette in his mouth and was filling his lungs with smoke, breathing deeply as if he were inhaling the air of Paradise. And all over the ship, Krause knew, the men whose duty kept them on deck were happily lighting cigarettes and breathing them in; through the night no one had been able to smoke whose post of duty was such that match or glowing cigarette could be seen by an enemy. Whiffs of cigarette smoke drifted past his nostrils, wafting with them a momentary memory again of Evelyn. She had smoked—she had been a little puzzled, almost amused, by the fact that her husband did not do so. Coming back from duty to the little house at Coronado he had always been conscious, on first entering the door, of the faint aroma of cigarette smoke combined with the tiniest hint of the perfume Evelyn used.

'Sonar reports contact bearing zero-six-four, range eleven hundred yards.'

The U-boat captain had outwitted him again, turning to starboard when he planned to head him off on a turn to port. It would call for a long circle to get at him again. He gave a careful order to the quartermaster and conveyed the information to *Viktor*.

'Messenger! Ask the signal-bridge if they have Com-convoy in sight yet.'

Innumerable things to do even while he was wheeling

about trying to kill a U-boat which would kill him at the first opportunity. Another turn; *Viktor* had been unable to come round sharply enough to depth-charge the U-boat; it might be possible for *Keeling* unless the U-boat captain did the right thing at the right time—as he had done repeatedly before.

'You timing that, Mr Pond?'

'Yes, sir.'

'Contact bearing zero-five-four, range eight hundred yards.'

Missed again; the U-boat's smaller turning circle had saved her. Ten degrees on *Keeling*'s bow meant the U-boat was magically safe from her with both vessels turning as hard as they could.

'Eagle! This is George. Ten degrees on my port bow, range eight hundred yards, turning fast.'

'Our asdic's got her on an indefinite range. We'll come in on her, sir.'

'Very well. I'll come round to starboard. Over. Quartermaster! Right standard rudder. Steer course zero-nine-five.'

'Right standard rudder. Steer course zero-nine-five, sir.'

The messenger was hovering beside him.

'Signal-bridge reports Comconvoy in sight, sir. Message just coming in. Long message, sir.'

'Very well.'

And here was pink-faced Dawson, the communications officer, freshly shaved and spruce, with his clip-board of messages.

'Anything important, Mr Dawson?'

'Nothing special, sir.' Thank God for that. 'Except the two weather forecasts, sir.'

More freezing weather? Snowstorms? Gales?

'What do they say?'

'It's going to moderate, sir. By twenty hundred wind south to south-west, force three.'

'Thank you, Mr Dawson.'

As Krause turned to the T.B.S. the fleeting thought passed through his mind that Dawson now would be going down to the wardroom and would have breakfast. Ham and eggs, probably, and buck-wheat cakes, a stack swimming in syrup. And coffee, gallons of coffee.

'She's doubled round the other way, sir,' said the T.B.S. 'We're turning to port, course oh-six-oh, sir.'

'Very well. Keep after her. I'll come round on to your starboard quarter. Over. Right standard rudder. Steer course one-two-five.'

'Right standard rudder. Steer course one-two-five, sir. Steady on course one-two-five.'

'Very well.'

The ranges and bearings reported by the talker were being noted by his mind as they came in. For the moment *Keeling* was not the active pursuer; *Viktor* had taken over that role and he was jockeying *Keeling* into position to charge in again if *Viktor* were balked. In this comparatively passive role—although they were likely to exchange at any moment—he had more leisure than when hot on the U-boat's heels. More leisure, even though that was not a great deal, but time at least to take the signal-pad from the waiting messenger from the signal-bridge. Even time to feel, before his eyes focused on it, a feeling of sick apprehension in his stomach while he prepared to read.

COMCONVOY TO COMESCORT. KNOWN LOSSES DURING NIGHT . . .

Four names staring at him in the signalman's ill-formed print; he went on to read that the convoy was straggling badly and that the list might not be complete. *Cadena* had saved some lives. Comconvoy went on to submit that it was necessary to cover the rear of the convoy in consequence of straggling.

CHANCE OF PICKING UP SURVIVORS.

'Eagle to George! Eagle to George! She's still going on round. You'll be crossing her bows, sir.'

'Very well. I'll attack.'

Krause waited for a range and bearing. He did trigonometry in his head and thought about the U-boat skipper.

'I'll come in on course one-two-zero. Over. Left smartly to course one-two-zero.'

But the next bearing told him that the submarine was turning back in the opposite direction.

'Right rudder—handsomely.'

He had been going to give a course when inspiration came to him, and then inspiration was confirmed by the next bearing that came in.

'Meet her! Left rudder! Steady as you go!'

'Sonar reports contact dead ahead close range.'

Inspiration and prompt action had brought its reward; he had this elusive fellow right under his bows. It had been not a feint but a double feint and he was lunging past the disengaged foil.

'Mr Pond!'

'Standing by, sir.'

'Sonar reports no contact, sir.'

'Fire one!' said Pond. 'Fire two!'

Down went the depth-charges, and the first deep rumble and lofty pillar of water marked the descent of the first. Sonar, accurate and sensitive though it was, had many serious defects. It could make not even a rough estimate of the depth of the pursued submarine, it gave no results at a closer range than three hundred yards, it could only be used at speeds of twelve knots or less, and it was deafened for several minutes by depth-charge explosions. A destroyer captain was under the same handicap as a duck hunter with a beautiful hard-hitting gun would be with weights on his wrists to slow down his swing, with no power of estimating the height of the flying duck, and if he had to shut his eyes two seconds before he pulled the trigger and keep them shut for half a minute afterwards.

'Right standard rudder. Steer course two-one-zero.'

The deficiencies of sonar should be made good one way or another; improvements in design might make it more robust; it should not be difficult to devise a gun or a sling that would throw a depth-charge a quarter of a mile ahead—but then the depth-charge would go off just as the destroyer was over it and it would blow the bottom out of her.

'Steady on course two-one-zero.'

'Very well.'

These thunderous explosions, those volcanoes of water, had brought no results. Not one of the four depth-charges in that pattern had burst within the necessary thirty yards of the hidden target. *Viktor* was coming round to take up the attack, and the messenger from the signal-bridge was still at his elbow. Krause had a brief interval available in which to divert his weary mind from the problem of fighting an individual U-boat to a consideration of the welfare of the convoy as a whole; he could re-read that horrible message. A chance of picking up survivors; a chance—the torpedoings had been some hours ago and they would be many miles behind. If they were on life-rafts they would be dead by now in this tossing icy sea. If they were in boats

—no, it would take even a destroyer all day to go back, search for them, and rejoin the convoy.

'Eagle to George. We've got her ten degrees on our starboard bow, sir.'

'Very well. Come on round after her.'

Cover the rear of the convoy? He wished he had a ship to spare to do that. Four names on that list of the lost; that made six ships out of the convoy which had been sunk during this twenty-four-hour battle. Dead men by the hundred. And of the enemy one probable sinking and one faintly possible. Would Washington think that was a profitable exchange in this bloody game of beggar-your-neighbour? Would London? Would Doenitz, in his case-mated advance headquarters at L'Orient? No matter what anyone thought, was it basically profitable? And no matter even then; he had his duty to do, whether it was a losing phase of the war or a winning one. He could only go on, fight on to the end of his strength.

'Eagle to George. Attacking now.'

Range and bearing from the talker, noted automatically by the weary mind. Lieutenant Fippler the gunner officer, awaiting his attention—what could he want? *Viktor*'s first depth-charge was exploding.

'Come right handsomely. Meet her! Steady!'

Keeling's bows were pointed at the fringe of the area of tortured water, to lose no time in making the next attack if one were possible. And still he held the message-pad in his hand, and still the wind blew—no sign of moderating as yet—and still *Keeling* rose and plunged and corkscrewed over the heaving sea. He handed back the message-pad.

'Very well,' he said. There was nothing else to say in that repect. He was doing all he could. This is the day which the Lord hath made.

'Stand by, Mr Pond!'

'Aye aye, sir.'

The next bearing showed that the U-boat had turned aside, as was to be expected.

'Right standard rudder. Steer course—three-two-zero.'

Krause was just conscious of that hesitation in his order, and was indignant with himself as far as there was time to be. He had had to glance at the repeater before giving that course; with these distractions he had not been able to carry the tactical situation in his head.

'Sonar reports no contact, sir.'

'Very well.'

'Fire one!' said Pond.

Krause turned to Fippler now. Those seconds while the pattern was being fired, while the depth-charges tumbled down through the dark water, were for Krause moments of freedom, when he could turn his mind to other matters. He need not grow expectant or hopeful about the result of the attack until the depth-charges had had time to burst and the sub. had had time to give evidence of damage—if she were damaged.

'Well, Mr Fippler?'

He raised his hand in reply to Fippler's salute. Fippler was being very formal; not a good sign.

'If you please, cap'n, I have to report about the consumption of depth-charges.'

Depth-charges were exploding behind them at this moment.

'Well?'

'Thirty-four expended, sir. This pattern makes thirty-eight.'

In the last twenty-four hours *Keeling* had flung more than seven tons of high explosive over the side.

'Well?'

'We've only six left, sir. That's all. I got the extra ones up that we had up our sleeve from the crew's living quarters last watch.'

'I see.'

One more burden on his shoulders. A destroyer without depth-charges might be as wise as a serpent, but would be as harmless as a dove. But the present pattern was completed. He had to handle his ship.

'Right standard rudder. Steer course zero-five-zero.'

A minute more—one only—to decide upon his orders. Yesterday, before he became an experienced fighting man, these seconds would be spent in eager watching, at a time when nothing could really be expected for quite an interval, a whole minute, perhaps.

'Thank you, Mr Fippler. We must leave off firing patterns, then.'

'That's what I was going to suggest, sir.'

Six depth-charges left? One day's fighting had consumed nearly all the supply. Not much more fighting would exhaust it altogether. Yet the mathematicians had calculated the odds; the size of the area searched by a pattern varied with the square of the number of depth-charges. Halve the pattern and the chances of a hit were only a quarter of the previous chance. Divide it by three and the chances were only one-ninth. Only one-ninth. Yet on the other hand a single depth-charge bursting within the hearing of a U-boat had an important moral effect, would deter it, would induce it to take evasive action, at least for a time.

There had been time enough now for the last pattern to have taken effect, if it had. Krause looked back over the starboard quarter, at the area where the foam of explosions was dying away. There was nothing but foam to be seen there. *Viktor* was hovering, waiting to pick up the contact.

Regarding the question of future patterns. Tomorrow morning he would just be within the radius of air cover. All the classified pamphlets he had read, all the lectures he had heard at Casco Bay, had emphasized the reluctance of U-boats to engage under the menace of air attack. With the weather moderating he might expect some air cover. Moreover, it was notorious that recently U-boats had refrained from attacking convoys in the eastern quarter of the Atlantic. Those secret charts of sinkings, month by month, that he had seen, all demonstrated this fact.

'Eagle to George! He's turning inside us again. On our starboard bow. Range about one-one-double oh.'

Krause gauged the distances and bearings with his eye.

'Very well. Keep after him now. We'll come in on him next time round.'

'Aye aye, sir.'

'Quartermaster, right standard rudder. Steer course zero-nine-five.'

Krause visualized the pattern of three depth-charges, in line, and the pattern of four, diamond shaped, and the other pattern of three, 'V' shaped. He remembered the blackboard at Casco Bay, and the diagrams there with the small circles showing the 'limits of lethal effect' dotted over the three-hundred-yard circle marking 'limits of possible position of sub.' Mathematically the pattern of four was far superior to the pattern of three.

He listened to Eagle again on the T.B.S., gauged her course, waited for the next sonar report, and turned *Keeling* again further to starboard.

During the past twenty-four hours he had been prodigal

with his depth-charges, as he had when a little boy been prodigal with his pennies on his first entrance into the County Fair. But in those days when, with empty pockets, he had ruefully contemplated all the other things for which he needed money a kindly father and a smiling mother had each of them smuggled a dime, a whole dime each, into his hot hands; when dimes were important to buy food in that household. But now there was no one to refill *Keeling*'s magazines with the depth-charges he had squandered. Krause shook off the memories which had crowded, in one single second, into his tired brain. For that one second in that bleak and cheerless pilot-house he had felt the hot Californian sunshine, and heard the barkers and the calliope, and smelt the cattle, and tasted the spun sugar— and known the utter confidence of the child with a loving parent on either side of him. Now he was alone, with decisions to make.

'We'll fire single charges, Mr Fippler,' he said. 'The timing will have to be exact. Allow for the last estimated course of the target and for the time of the drop according to the depth setting.'

'Aye aye, sir.'

'See that the torpedo officers at the release stations are instructed to that effect before they come on duty. I won't have time.'

'Aye aye, sir.'

'Tell Mr Pond now. Very well, Mr Fippler.'

'Thank you, sir.'

'Right standard rudder. Steer course two-eight-seven.'

That was the best course to intercept.

'George to Eagle! I'm coming in now.'

The single depth-charge could make no attempt to allow for the U-boat's evasive action. It could only be dropped where she would be if she took none. That was not a likely spot; but the odds against any other spot were far higher. The single charge made it more urgent than ever that he should take *Keeling* in to the attack with the utmost exactitude. But he always had tried to do that; he could not be more exact than he had been. He had to think clearly, methodically, and unemotionally, even if he had to goad his exhausted mind to perform its functions, even though it was becoming agonizingly urgent that he should get down to the head, even though he was thirsty and hungry and his joints ached vilely.

It was time to vary his methods; the U-boat captain might have grown accustomed to the routine *Keeling* had been employing lately.

'George to Eagle. I shall come straight through after attacking this time. Keep on my port bow and move in down my wake as soon as I am clear.'

'Aye aye, sir.'

Thursday. Forenoon Watch—0800–1200

He listened to the ranges and bearings; there was no chance of the sub. turning inside him. He realized now that some time back, when Fippler was addressing him, the watch had been changing. A different voice had repeated his helm orders; there had been a coming and going in the pilot-house. Carling was back again awaiting an opportunity to report; but Nourse was at the depth-charge release, the telephone instrument at his lips. He was glad to see him there.

'Very well, Mr Carling.'

Carling had had some hours of sleep, and his belly was

full of ham and eggs, and he was in no pressing hurry to get to the head.

'Contact bearing two-eight-two. Range close.'

A good interception, tangential to the circle in which the U-boat was presumably turning, as far as he could calculate.

'Mr Nourse!'

Nourse was timing the moment carefully.

'Fire one!' said Nourse.

The single depth-charge seemed strange and out of place after all those patterns of four. *Keeling* kept steadily on her course. Here came *Viktor*, steering to pass port side to port side, very close indeed, changing rapidly from a full face silhouette to a detailed picture of a ship in profile in frosted ice, the Polish ensign blowing briskly in the breeze, her commission pennant streaming; the muffled-up figures of her look-outs were clearly visible, the people on her bridge—Krause did not know if the British liaison officer to whom he was talking was there or lower down—and then the depth-charge crews at their exposed station astern.

'Eagle to George. Do we look as cold as you do, sir?'

So he had to joke as well as fight U-boats. He had to goad his weary mind into a prompt reaction, and think of some lighthearted wisecrack, and he was a man who joked with difficulty. He thought academically along the lines of what he believed would be considered funny, and produced an academic pun.

'George to Eagle. You look North Polish.'

Keeling's port bow smacked into *Viktor's* wake as soon as she passed. Back to business.

'George to Eagle. I am turning to port. Quartermaster, left standard rudder. Steer course zero-zero-zero.'

He had reversed the circle, turning anti-clockwise now

after several clockwise circles. But perhaps the U-boat captain was paralleling his thoughts.

He went out on to the port wing of the bridge, treading warily on the treacherous surface, and watched *Viktor*'s going down to attack. With the bearing changing so rapidly it was not easy to tell by eye if she was altering course at all while running down her contact. The pilot-house even with its shattered windows was warmer, when he returned to it, than the wing of the bridge.

'Eagle to George. We've got her right ahead.'

He hoped it would be an unpleasant surprise for the U-boat captain to emerge from one attack and find himself steering straight into another. He hoped more passionately that the attack would be successful, that *Viktor*'s next pattern would shatter the sub. into an uncontrollable derelict. He saw the depth-charge explosions; three only, one in the wake and one on each side. *Viktor* was using a 'V' shaped pattern, then, one charge for the place where the U-boat ought to be and one on each side allowing for a turn to starboard or to port.

'George to Eagle. I am turning to port. Keep away.'

'Aye aye, sir.'

'Left full rudder. Steer course zero-six-nine.'

Keeling headed for the centre of the magic circle that she and *Viktor* marked out with their wakes.

'Contact bearing zero-seven-nine. Range distant.'

That looked as if the U-boat had doubled back after *Viktor*'s attack. He would know better with the next reading; meanwhile he must keep his bows on the target.

'Right smartly to course zero-seven-nine.'

'Sonar reports contact dead ahead. Range distant.'

Was the U-boat on a reciprocal course, then? Towards? Or away?

'Captain to sonar. "Is there any Doppler effect?"'
'Sonar answers "No," sir.'
'Very well.'
'Sonar reports contact dead ahead. Range fifteen hundred yards.'

Suspicions grew in Krause's mind—unless the U-boat, crippled, was lying stationary. That was too good to hope for, and the next report strengthened Krause's suspicions.

'Sonar reports contact dead ahead. Range thirteen hundred yards. Sonar reports it sounds like a *pill.*, sir.'

That was it, then. It was some time since this U-boat had used that device. But which way had she turned after dropping the thing? Had she dropped it before *Viktor* made her attack or after? It seemed to be a matter of pure chance, but he made himself analyse the situation, looking over at *Viktor*'s position, judging the distance ahead, trying to think of what the U-boat captain would do when he heard *Viktor* moving straight in on him, and quite ignorant of whether *Keeling* had turned to starboard or port. It was the first time in a long while that *Keeling* had turned to port. The U-boat captain would guess she would turn to starboard, and would himself turn to port. Then he must make a further turn to starboard.

'Right smartly to course zero-eight-nine.'

While the helmsman was repeating the order the next report came in.

'Contact dead ahead. Range eleven hundred yards. Still sounds like a *pill.*, sir.'

'George to Eagle. He's dropped a *pill*. I am moving out to starboard. Move in on my port beam and search.'

'Aye aye, sir.'

The sub. had won itself a respite of two or three, or four or five minutes.

'Sonar reports contact with *pill.* bearing zero-nine-nine, range nine hundred yards.'

If he knew what the endurance of those things was it would help him with his estimates, but—he searched back through his memory of all he had heard and read—no data on that point had been supplied to him.

'Sonar reports no contact, sir.'

The bubbles had ended, then; the *pillenwerfer* had ceased to bob precariously in the limbo of the deep, hauled up by its bubbles and drawn down by gravity. Gravity had won and the mysterious thing was now sinking down and down in the darkness to the sea bed.

'Sonar reports no contact, sir.'

The ripples were widening in the pond; with the passage of every second the circle marking 'possible position of U-boat' was growing larger and larger.

'George to Eagle. I've had no contact.'

'Neither have we, sir.'

Maybe that last attack of *Viktor's* had hit home, maybe the moment after dropping the *pillenwerfer* the U-boat had been crushed in by a depth-charge close alongside; maybe she had gone down without trace. No; that was unlikely enough to be quite disregarded. The U-boat was still some-where near, malignant, dangerous. But at twelve knots *Keeling* was very near the circumference of the circle out-side which the U-boat could not possibly be as yet. *Viktor* was well advanced beyond the centre of that circle.

'Left standard rudder. Quartermaster, call out your heading. George to Eagle. I am circling to port. Turn to port, too.'

'Aye aye, sir. Asdic's getting echoes from cold layers, sir.'

Very likely. Perhaps the U-boat captain, with a sharp eye on the thermometer readings recording the outside water temperature, had noted a steep rise in the temperature gradient, had sought the cold layer which that indicated, and was now lying deep, deep down, trimmed to a milligram, deathly silent, balanced miraculously upon the invisible and fragile support of a stratum of denser water. The Lord is in His holy temple; let all the earth keep silence before Him—that was a blasphemous thought.

'Passing zero-four-zero. Passing zero-three-zero. Passing zero-two-zero.'

Keeling was coming round; seconds were passing rapidly, and every second precious. Over the port quarter *Viktor* was turning less sharply, searching in a quarter so far unexplored.

'Passing three-four-zero. Passing three-three-zero. Passing three-two-zero.'

Now *Viktor* was on her port bow; now she was right ahead.

'Sonar reports no contact, sir.'

'Very well.'

'Passing two-eight-zero. Passing two-seven-zero. Passing two-six-zero.'

'Sonar reports echoes, sir. No contact.'

'Very well.'

The same kind of echoes as *Viktor* had reported from a little farther away. Many cold streaks of water here, deflecting away the sonar beam if the U-boat was indeed lying stationary here. But she might have slipped away unobserved; she might be two miles, three miles distant by now, her crew laughing derisively at the spectacle of two destroyers circling round and round and round, seeking where they could not possibly find.

'Passing two-zero-zero. Passing one-nine-zero. Passing one-eight-zero.'

They were completing the circle. Was it any use going on with the search? Krause considered the question with the rigid and unrelenting analysis he applied to his nightly review of his actions during the day before his evening prayers. Would it be feeble, faint-hearted, irresolute, light-minded, to abandon the search? He was aware of his fatigue; was he allowing his fatigue to influence his judgment? He wanted to get down to the head; he wanted food and drink. Was he allowing these human weaknesses to deflect him from a determination which he ought to maintain? This was the only kind of self-analysis that Krause ever knew. With his mind's eye he looked coldly at the wriggling worm, the weak and sinful creature which was Commander Krause, spineless in the presence of temptation and untrustworthy in the presence of an opportunity to err. Yet he came, reluctantly, to admit that perhaps in this case the feeble creature was right.

'Passing one-two-zero. Passing one-one-zero.'

'Steady on course zero-eight-zero,' he ordered, and then, into the T.B.S. 'I am going east to the head of the convoy. My course zero-eight-zero.'

'Oh-eight-oh. Aye aye, sir.'

'Make one more sweep and then patrol round the stragglers.'

'Patrol round the stragglers. Aye aye, sir.'

'Steady on course zero-eight-zero, sir.'

'Very well.'

He could not quite remember when he had begun this hunt, but it must be seven hours ago or so. Now he was giving it up. He felt a moment of regret, a moment of self-doubt. Submarine hunts had been called off before this, often enough; but that did not mitigate the feeling of failure even so. Over on *Keeling*'s port side, from just forward of the beam to the quarter, the convoy was just in sight over the horizon. It had certainly straggled during the night as a result of the torpedo attack; it was spread out like smoke trailing from a stack. *Viktor* would have her hands full covering all that vulnerable flank and herding the stragglers back into formation. He went wearily over to the stool and sank down on it. Thigh muscles and calf muscles, knee joints and hip joints, were all aching horribly, and in those first few seconds after he had sat down they ached even more sharply with the returning circulation. The physical exhaustion and discomfort were sufficient at the moment to distract his mind from his disappointment and feeling of mental lassitude. Hours and hours ago he had told *James* he would send *Viktor* over to help her; and he had told *Dodge* he would bring *Keeling* to her assistance. Light-heartedly he had made the promises, conditional ones—'as soon as I can'; 'after I've helped Eagle'—without a suspicion of how long and how fruitless his chase would be. He called up *Dodge* and *James* on the T.B.S. and listened to their reports, bracing himself to pay close attention. *Dodge* was seven miles away on his starboard bow— that was how far her operations during the night had drawn her—making her way back to her station having lost contact with the enemy. Looking in that direction through his binoculars, he could just see her, a more solid nucleus in the hazy horizon. *James* was over on the left flank beyond the convoy, out of sight but close up to station.

'One moment, please, sir,' said the T.B.S., the wording, so oddly like that of a long-distance operator, in quaint contrast with the precise English accent. A new voice made itself heard in Krause's listening ear.

'This is Lieutenant-Commander Rode, commanding, sir.'

'Good morning, Captain,' said Krause. Formality always boded ill.

'As soon as we are in visual touch I shall make a report to you, sir. I am taking this opportunity of calling your particular attention to it.'

'You can't tell me now?' asked Krause.

'No, sir. Jerry's been in on this circuit more than once during the night. He has an English-speaking rating who chips in with rude remarks, and I wouldn't like him to hear this.'

'Very well, Captain. I shall await your report.'

It could only be bad news, of course. Fuel problems almost for certain; depth-charge shortages very likely. But at this moment he had his own personal problem, the extreme necessity of getting down to the head. That was something that, having been postponed for hours, could not be postponed one minute more after thinking about it. Charlie Cole was entering the pilot-house.

'Wait for me a minute, Charlie,' said Krause. 'Take the conn, Mr Carling.'

'Aye aye, sir.'

As he lowered himself heavily down the ladders there was some comfort in the thought that Cole was on the bridge, even though the conn was officially handed over to Carling. He climbed heavily back again. This ship of his, with which he was so utterly familiar, seemed foreign to him in his present condition. The sights and sounds and smells which he knew so well seemed to threaten him, like jagged reefs surrounding a ship creeping into narrow, uncharted waters. He had been so long on the bridge, and in a state of such intense concentration, that the real world seemed unreal; furthermore, he had to keep that real world out of his mind, so as not to break the chain of his thinking.

It was a major physical effort to climb the last ladder to the bridge where Cole was awaiting him, and when he had achieved it he sank unashamedly on the stool.

'I've ordered something for you to eat, sir,' said Cole. 'I suppose there's no chance of your taking it in the wardroom.'

'No,' said Krause.

His mind was still at work assembling the details of keeping his command as efficient as possible. He fixed his eyes on Cole; the tanned, fleshy face was somewhat drawn with fatigue. Over the cheeks sprouted a thick growth of beard, something most unusual, for Lieutenant-Commander Cole was careful about his appearance.

'You spent the night in the plot,' said Krause, accusingly.

'Most of it, sir.'

'Have you eaten anything yourself?'

'Not much, sir. I'm just going to.'

'You'd better. I want you to have a good breakfast, Charlie.'

'Aye aye, sir. I'll just go aft first and see——'

'No. I don't want you to, Commander. A good breakfast, and then I want you to turn in for at least two hours. That's an order, Commander.'

'Aye aye, sir.'

'At least two hours. Very well, Charlie.'

'Aye aye, sir.'

There was no more than half a second's hesitation about Charlie Cole's salute. He did not want to leave his captain there on the bridge, with his white face and his hollow cheeks and his staring eyes. But there was no chance of argument when an order had been given. That was naval discipline, which had them all in a rigid grip, which the exigencies of war did no more than tighten slightly. *Keeling* was in the presence of the enemy and Krause on the bridge was at his post of duty and it was inconceivable that he should leave it. Navy Regs and the Articles for the Government of the Navy were quite definite about that. Consideration of any other course led into flights of fancy wilder than the thoughts of a lunatic. Krause could have summoned the medical officer to the bridge, he could have had himself certified as unfit for duty, and then he could have left his post and taken a rest. Only a lunatic could think of an officer going voluntarily through such a humiliation, and it would be beyond any lunatic's imagination to conceive of a man with Krause's rigid pride and overwhelming sense of duty submitting to it. Certainly the possibility never developed even in embryo in Krause's thoughts. It was as far from his mind as a dereliction from duty would be, which meant that it never came into existence at all.

Here was a messenger with a tray.

'Exec. told me to bring this first without waiting for the rest, sir,' he said.

It was coffee; the inevitable set-up with the cream and sugar that he never used, but he viewed it as Galahad would have viewed the Holy Grail. Krause tugged off his gloves and snatched at it. His hands were numb and trembled a little as he poured. He swigged off the cup and refilled and drank again. The warmth as the coffee went down called his attention to the fact that he was cold; not acutely, perishingly, cold but chilled through and through as if nothing would ever quite warm him again.

'Get me another pot,' he said, replacing the cup on the tray.

'Aye aye, sir.'

But as the messenger turned away the Filipino mess-boy took his place, also with a tray in his hands; a white cloth covered it, and the humps and valleys of the cloth hinted at much beneath. When he lifted the cloth he saw marvels. Bacon and eggs—no, ham and eggs with hashed brown potatoes! Toast, jelly, and more coffee! Charlie Cole was a wonderful man. Yet it was a proof of the weariness of Krause's legs that he sat on the stool contemplating these wonders for a short space wondering what to do next. The stool was just too high for him to hold the tray on his knees; the alternative was to put the tray on the chart-table and eat standing up, and Krause experienced a brief hesitation before he decided upon it.

'On the table,' he said, and hobbled after the mess-boy. And when he addressed himself to the tray then he experienced another momentary hesitation. It was almost as if he were not hungry; he might almost have told the boy to take the tray away again. But with the first mouthfuls that feeling disappeared. He ate rapidly, with the cold wind from the broken windows of the pilot-house blowing round him. Fried eggs may not have been the most convenient things to eat while standing up on a heaving deck, but he did not care, not even when yellow drips fell on his sheepskin coat. He shovelled the potatoes into his mouth with the spoon. He spread jelly on the toast with an egg-smeared knife. He wiped his plate with the last fragment of toast and ate that too. Then a third cup of coffee, not swigged down madly like the first two, but drunk more at leisure, savouring it like a true coffee-hound, with the added pleasure of knowing that there was a fourth cup yet to be drunk. The pleasure was not even spoiled when a sudden recollection came to him of a duty yet unfulfilled. He bowed his head for a moment.

'I thank Thee Oh Lord for all Thy mercies——'
There had once been a kind and understanding father.

Krause was fortunate in that memory; that father had been able to smile at the excusable naughtiness of a little boy even though he led the life of a saint himself. Krause was not harassed by the thought of sin at having forgotten to say his thanks until his meal was nearly completed. That would be understood and forgiven him. The letter killeth but the spirit giveth life. Krause's severest and most unrelenting judge, of whom he went in fear, was Krause himself, but that judge had luckily never taken ritual sin under his jurisdiction.

He finished the third cup and poured the fourth, and turned to find the messenger beside him with yet another pot on a tray. He had given the order before he knew about the breakfast tray, and now he contemplated the results a little aback.

'Can't drink that now,' he said, and looked round for help. 'Mr Carling, would you have a cup of coffee?'

'I could use it, sir.'

Carling had been on the chilly bridge for two whole hours. He poured himself a cup and added cream and sugar to reveal himself as the sort of man he was.

'Thank you, sir,' said Carling, sipping.

In his present state of well being Krause could exchange a grin with him. Wink-wink-wink; out of the tail of his eye he could see a signal flashing far down on the northern horizon. That would be *James* sending the message about whose coming he had been warned, yet he could finish his fourth cup without any diminution of pleasure. He pulled on his gloves again over his chilly hands, told the mess-boy to remove the tray, and limped back to the stool again. The meal had eased some of his weariness; he was deliberately seating himself so as not to incur more fatigue than necessary. A whole day of battle had made a veteran of him.

The message reached him from the signal-bridge as soon as he sat down.

'JAMES' TO COMESCORT. OWING TO PROLONGED ACTION DURING NIGHT . . .

It was exactly what he had expected. *James* was down to the danger point as regards oil fuel. She had no more than nine depth-charges left. One day's hard steaming or half an hour's action with the enemy would equally leave her helpless. The message only contained these bare facts; it made no submissions, and the only excuse it made was in its opening words. If he were to detach *James* now she would at economical speed fetch Londonderry safely. If he retained her it could be highly questionable. He could imagine that tiny little ship lying helpless off the northern coast of Ireland, a prey to any enemy—and there might be many—in the air or below the surface or even on it. Yet she still had value as part of the escort. With her guns she could out-fight—only just—a submarine on the surface. Her nine remaining depth-charges, dropped singly but at the right moments, might keep a submarine away from the convoy for a vital few hours. Her sonar might guide *Keeling* or *Viktor* in to a decisive attack; even its steady pinging, heard by a listening submarine, might have a deterrent effect.

If they lived through today and tonight he might expect some air cover tomorrow, and then it would not be wildly difficult to take her in tow—one of the merchant vessels could do it. He balanced possible loss against possible gain. The captain of the *James* had been perfectly correct in calling his commanding officer's attention to the condition of his ship; it would have been negligence on his part not to do so. Now the responsibility was Krause's. He took the pad and pencil and began to print out the reply. Despite the hot coffee he had drunk he was only just warm enough to control the pencil sufficiently to be legible.

COMESCORT TO 'JAMES.' CARRY ON USING UTMOST ECONOMY IN FUEL AND AMMUNITION.

That much was easy, once the decision had been reached. But it might be well to add a heartening word, and it was strange how his mind, still capable of grasping and analysing facts, balked like a stubborn mule at the demand for something further. He wrote 'WE CANNOT SPARE YOU' and then, with the utmost deliberation, crossed those words out with three thick lines to make sure they would not be transmitted. They were perfectly true, but a sensitive or touchy recipient might read them as an answer to an unexpressed appeal to be released from escort duty, and there was no such unexpressed appeal in the message he had received. Krause would not willingly hurt any man's feelings except for the good of the cause in which he was fighting, and it would emphatically not be for the good of the cause to hurt the feelings of the captain of the *James*. He sat with pencil poised trying to think of the right thing to say. No inspiration came to him. There was only the hackneyed expression which he must use since his mind refused to think of anything better.

GOOD LUCK.

He was in the act of handing the pad back to the messenger when the next idea came.

WE ALL NEED IT.

That would soften the cold official wording. Krause knew academically that a human touch was desirable in these relationships even though he himself had never felt the need of it. He would be perfectly content to do and die in reply to a baldly worded order from a superior and would feel no resentment at the absence of a polite phrase.

What he did feel was a dull envy of the captain of the *James* who had no more to do now than to obey orders and no more responsibility than to execute them to the best of his professional ability. He gave the pad to the messenger. Be thou faithful unto death—he nearly said those words aloud, and the messenger, on the point of saluting, seeing him open his mouth and shut it again, waited to hear what he had to say.

'Signal-bridge,' said Krause harshly.

'Aye aye, sir.'

With the departure of the messenger Krause was aware of a new and strange sensation. For the moment he was not being compelled to do something. It was the first time in more than twenty-four hours that instant and important decisions were not being forced on him. There were a hundred minor tasks he could profitably undertake, but he could actually choose between them at leisure. In his fatigued state of mind he contemplated this strange fact as someone in a dream—not in a nightmare—contemplates a new and odd development in what he is dreaming. Even when Carling came and saluted, this new condition was not disturbed.

'Next change of course due in ten minutes, sir,' said Carling.

'Very well.'

It was a routine change of course on the part of the whole convoy, and Carling's warning was merely in accordance with Krause's standing orders. The convoy could wheel without Krause's intervention being called for. And yet—perhaps he should intervene. The convoy was in disorder, and the wheel would accentuate that and prolong it. It might be better if the wheel did not take place. Krause mentally drafted the order he would flash to

Comconvoy. 'Negative change of course, maintain present course.' No. Better to let matters continue. The convoy would be expecting the change of course, and might be confused if it did not materialize. And when the next routine change of course became due there would be certain confusion as to which change was expected of them this time. 'Order, counter order, disorder'; at more than one lecture at Annapolis he had heard that quotation, and during twenty years of service he had seen its truth demonstrated scores of times. He would let the routine continue.

'Commodore signalling for change of course, sir,' said Carling.

'Very well.'

What was this? Something else new and strange. An unreal brightness in the bleak pilot-house. The greyness of the morning was lifting; it was unbelievable. Up in the sky, forward of the starboard beam, Krause actually saw it, a pale, watery sun, more like the moon than the sun but the sun all the same, just visible through the high, thin cloud blowing before its face. The sun; for five seconds it was definitely bright enough for the stanchions to cast the faintest shadows, moving on the deck as the ship rolled. The faint shadows endured for one roll of the ship, moving to port and then to starboard before fading out again while the pale disc vanished for good behind the high cloud. Truly the light is sweet and a pleasant thing it is for the eyes to behold the sun.

'Execute, sir,' said Carling.

'Very well.'

Krause heard the helm order given and repeated. Next moment, it seemed to him, he found himself falling off his stool, swaying right over to one side, falling endlessly as he did sometimes in nightmares. He caught himself up before he had swayed actually more than an inch or two. It was no nightmare. He had really been asleep and had nearly fallen from the stool. He straightened himself up and stiffened his back profoundly shocked at his behaviour. Drowsiness shall clothe a man with rags. It was quite disgraceful that he had allowed sleep to creep up on him unawares. He had never had the experience before in his life. It was only thirty hours since he had been awakened in readiness for yesterday's general quarters after two hours of perfectly sound sleep. There was absolutely no excuse for him to nod off. But now he had had his warning. He had discovered the insidiousness of the enemy he had to fight against. He would never let it happen again. He got down from the stool and stood erect. The protests of his leg muscles would keep him awake; and his feet were painful now that he stood on them. It really seemed as if his shoes were far too tight for him, as if his feet had grown a size larger during the night. He thought for a moment of taking off his shoes—old and tried companions though they were—and sending down for the slippers in his cabin. But the idea only grew up in his mind to be cut down again instantly. A captain had an example to set and should never appear at his post of duty in slippers; and self-indulgence whether physical or moral was something treacherous and rightly suspect—he had had a clear example of that just now when he fell asleep on his stool. And—and—perhaps if he stood long enough his feet would go numb and cease to hurt him so.

'Mr Carling, we had better come to course one-two-zero and patrol back again across the front of the convoy.'

'One-two-zero. Aye aye, sir.'

A few minutes ago the pinging of the sonar had been a monotonous lullaby lulling him into unconsciousness. Now it was a hard persistent reminder to him to do his duty. I will not give sleep to mine eyes nor slumber to mine eyelids. His eyes did not feel dry or swollen; it was no effort at all to keep his eyelids lifted. That meal that he had eaten had helped to betray him, enmeshing him in the torpor that comes with a full belly—one more example of the dangers of self-indulgence.

He forgot all this when the warning bell rang beside the voice-tube. His feet did not feel painful as he strode to answer it.

'Captain.'

'Cap'n, sir, there's a pip just showing up. At least I think it's a pip, sir. Screen's very bad. Pip bearing zero-nine-two, range nine miles, sir. Now it's gone. Not sure, sir.'

Was it better to turn in that direction or maintain the present course? At the moment they were heading to interpose between the possible pip and the convoy; it would be better to maintain course.

'I think it's there again, sir. Wish I could be sure.'

The radar had behaved as well as a radar could be expected to behave for several days now; it was due to start acting up at any time. And at that range—Krause knew the figures, but automatically he did a square root in his head and multiplied by a coefficient—a sub. trimmed right down would hardly appear on any radar screen. In any case his present course was a satisfactory one for the next few minutes.

'How would that pip bear from *Dodge*?' he asked down the tube. He could have arrived at a fair approximation mentally, and would have trusted it in the heat of action, but now there was time to spare, for a wonder.

'Zero-seven-zero, range thirteen and a half miles, sir,' replied the plot.

The little ship's radar antenna was not as lofty as *Keeling*'s; she could offer no confirmation, then, and certainly there was no chance at present of getting a cross-bearing.

'Very well,' he said.

'If this is a pip, sir,' said the tube, 'the range and bearing's staying constant. It may be the screen.'

'Very well.'

It might be a defect of the radar; on the other hand—he went out on to the starboard wing of the bridge and looked over the quarter. There was a disgraceful amount of smoke rising from the convoy. Captains were calling for an extra knot or two to jockey their ships back into station, and this was the result. With the wind moderating and backing the smoke was rising higher than yesterday; it would mark the position of the convoy for fifty miles. It might easily be in sight of a sub. out there, and if that sub. was doing an 'end around' in consequence it could easily be maintaining a constant range and bearing from *Keeling*. What was the use of radar at all if the ships he was supposed to protect announced their presence to enemies far beyond radar range?

There was no bitterness in Krause's soul as he asked himself that question. He was beyond that stage, just as he was beyond the stage of buck-fever. He had matured very considerably during the last day. An excellent upbringing as a child; a sound Annapolis training; long experience at sea; even these were not as important as twenty-four hours at grips with the enemy. He noticed that the gloved hand that he laid on the rail detached a thin sliver of ice; there was a row of water-drops along the rail's lowest curve. A rapid thaw was in progress. The ice was melting from stays and guys. The commission pennant had unfrozen itself and now flapped as it should. He was quite calm even though he had a possible submarine not far outside the range of his guns, and the marked contrast between his condition now and his excitement when yesterday's first contact was made was not due to the apathy of fatigue.

In the pilot-house the voice-tube had an announcement to make to him.

'I can't see that pip any longer, sir.'

'Very well.'

They continued to churn along diagonally across the front of the convoy. *Dodge* was plainly in sight on her station beyond the starboard flank.

'Permission granted,' said Carling into a telephone. He caught Krause's eye and explained. 'I've given permission to shift steering cables, sir.'

'Very well.'

Krause's standing orders left that decision to the officer of the deck, and Carling had given permission without consulting his captain, as he was entitled to do. If there were a sub. just outside radar range it might not be the best moment to choose. But the change should be made daily, and at the present moment there were no contacts. And it was to Carling's credit that he had accepted that responsibility; it was possible he had learned something in the last twenty-four hours.

In *Keeling*'s present position it was easy to get a good view of the starboard half of the convoy; visibility was certainly nine miles now. Through his binoculars Krause could see the ships, various in their paint and design, still trailing astern; close beyond them he could see *Viktor*'s unmistakable foremast as she rode hard on them. They were gradually closing up. Satisfied, Krause gave the order.

'Time to head back, Mr Carling,' he said.

'Aye aye, sir.'

206

Krause pretended unconcern; it was his duty to know how Carling reacted.

'Left standard rudder. Steer course zero-six-zero,' said Carling.

It had not been a very exacting test, to lay *Keeling* on a course patrolling back again across the front of the convoy, but Carling had passed it quickly and correctly. If the Navy was going to expand as prodigiously as apparently it was going to, Carling might easily be commanding a destroyer in battle in six months' time—if he lived.

'Steady on course zero-six-zero,' said the helmsman.

It occurred to Krause that it might be provident to get down to the head again; it was over an hour since he had drunk four cups of coffee.

'Periscope! Periscope!' shouted the starboard-side look-out. 'Starboard beam!'

Krause sprang out, binoculars to his eyes, sweeping the sea on the starboard beam.

'Still there, sir!'

The look-out pointed madly with his hand while staring through his binoculars.

'Zero-nine-nine! Three miles—four miles!'

Krause trained his glasses slowly outwards; the 8-shaped area of vivid magnification which he saw advanced farther from the ship with the movement of the glasses. He saw it —it was gone—he caught it again, as he balanced with the roll of the ship. The slender grey cylinder sliding along over the surface, with a ripple of white at its base, a thing of immeasurable, serpent-like menace.

'Right full rudder,' he roared, and in the same breath as a fresh thought came up into his mind, 'Belay that order! Steady as you go!'

Carling was beside him.

'Make sure of that bearing!' he snapped over his shoulder.

Then, slowly, as if with sneering self-confidence, the periscope very gradually dipped below the surface. The wind passeth over it and it is gone; and the place thereof shall know it no more.

'One-six-zero, sir,' said Carling; and then added, honestly. 'Couldn't be sure, sir.'

'Very well.'

Krause stared on through his glasses. He wanted to make certain that the periscope did not immediately reappear for a further look round. He made himself count to twenty slowly.

'You have the conn, Mr Carling,' he said. 'Come to course one-seven-zero.'

'One-seven-zero. Aye aye, sir.'

During the time the periscope had been visible *Keeling* and submarine had been on practically opposite courses. Krause had belayed his order for an immediate turn to encourage the sub. in the idea that the periscope had not been sighted. The last information the sub. had was that *Keeling* was still peacefully heading away from the point of danger; the sub. might continue in a fool's paradise, believing that she had slipped unobserved through the gap between *Keeling* and *Dodge*, and thinking that she was heading without opposition for that very important tactical point close in to the convoy and broad on its bow from which she could launch a series of torpedoes at its vulnerable beam.

'George to Dicky! George to Dicky!' said Krause into the T.B.S. 'Do you hear me?'

'Dicky to George. I hear you. Strength four.'

'I sighted a periscope a minute ago, distance three to

208

four miles and bearing approximately one-six-zero from me.'

'Three to four miles. One-six-oh. Yes, sir,' said a calm Canadian voice.

'It seemed to be heading on course two-seven-zero, for the flank of the convoy.'

'Two-seven-oh. Yes, sir.'

'I am now on course one-seven-zero to intercept.'

'One-seven-oh. Yes, sir. Here's the captain, sir.'

An incisive voice made itself heard in Krause's ear.

'Compton-Clowes speaking.' The Canadian captain was one of the rare examples of a Canadian with a hyphenated name. 'My officer of the watch took your data, sir. I am turning to course oh-two-oh to intercept.'

'Very well.'

From where he stood Krause could see the silhouette of the upper works of the little ship foreshortening as she made the turn. Krause wondered if perhaps a course more directly towards the last-known position of the sub. might not be more forceful. Compton-Clowes apparently thought it would be safer to make sure of an intercepting position, and likely enough he was right. The most important objective was to drive the sub. away from the convoy. To destroy the sub. was an important objective but not the only one. Expecially—Krause knew just what Compton-Clowes was going to say before he started speaking again.

'If we get into a position to attack, sir,' said Compton-Clowes. 'I shall be forced to use single depth-charges. My supply is low.'

'So is mine,' said Krause.

The analogy of the handicapped duck hunter who had to shut his eyes before shooting could be carried a little further. Seeing that only single depth-charges could be used it was as if the duck hunter, with all his previous handicaps, now had to abandon his shot-gun for a rifle—for a smooth-bore musket.

'We have to turn him away,' said Krause. 'Keep him down until the convoy gets by.'

'Yes, sir. My noon report about my fuel will be coming in to you soon.'

'Is it very bad?' asked Krause.

'It is serious, sir, but I wouldn't say it is very bad.'

It was some sort of comfort to hear that something was only serious.

'Very well, Captain,' said Krause.

Even Krause was aware of a certain unreal quality about the situation, to be carrying on a quiet conversation in this manner while both ships were heading towards a hidden submarine. They might be two bankers discussing the state of the money market rather than two fighting men moving into battle. But hard reality pushed far enough became unreal; nothing more could excite surprise or dismay, just as a lunatic feels no surprise at his imaginings. Physical fatigue played its part in keeping Krause cold and calm—and very likely was doing the same with Compton-Clowes—but mental satiety was more important. Krause was making these opening moves in the battle much as he might go through a ritual game to oblige some children; something that might as well be well done, but in which he felt no passionate personal interest.

'Good luck to us both, sir,' said Compton-Clowes.

'Thank you,' said Krause. 'Over.'

He spoke down the voice-tube to the plot.

'How long before we cross the sub.'s predicted course?'

'Twelve minutes, sir.'

That was Charlie Cole's voice again. Had two hours

elapsed since he had given Cole that order to take two hours' rest? Perhaps it would be as well not to inquire. If Cole were dead asleep in the deepest bowels of the ship he would hear about the sighting of a periscope, and it would take a great deal to keep him out of the chartroom then.

Thursday. Afternoon Watch—1200–1600

Yet it was likely to be two hours; here was the watch changing. Carling saluting and going through the ritual of reporting being relieved. One thing must be promptly done.

'You have the conn, Mr Nystrom.'

'Aye aye, sir.'

His weary legs carried him to the loudspeaker.

'This is the captain. You men just coming on watch had better know that we sighted a periscope ten minutes ago. We're after him now. Keep on your toes.'

He was glad he had secured from battle stations yesterday. Otherwise the ship might have been at general quarters ever since yesterday morning; every member of the ship's company might be as tired as he was, and that would not be so good. Krause knew that there were men who did not go on even trying to produce their best when they were tired.

On the wing of the bridge he took stock of the situation. *Dodge* over there would not be very far ahead of the leading ship of the right-hand column of the convoy when the chase came. Nor would *Keeling* be too far for that matter. It was the same speeding up of time. Leisure at first, and then events moving more and more rapidly, space contracting and time hurrying.

'Sonar reports distant contact bearing one-six-zero, sir,' said the talker suddenly.

Already? The sub. had not followed, submerged, the best course she could have chosen, then.

'Contact ten degrees on my port bow,' said Krause into the T.B.S.

'Aye aye, sir.'

'I'll take the conn, Mr Nystrom.'

'Aye aye, sir.'

He was practically on a collision course with the sub., it seemed. It was the first meeting of the blades in a bout with a new opponent. In the old days with his opponent's foil button in front of the wire of his mask, and the feeling of the first contact running quivering up his wrist and arm, it had been necessary to size up an opponent as rapidly as possible, to gauge the strength of the other man's wrist, the rapidity of his movements and reactions. Krause was doing the same now, remembering that over-long exposure of the periscope and taking into account this not very suitable underwater course of the sub. The captain of this new sub. was not like the man who had shaken off *Keeling*'s pursuit, and *Viktor*'s, earlier in the day. He had less finesse and less caution. He might be inexperienced, he might be over-bold, he might even be fatigued.

'Sonar reports distant contact bearing one-six-one,' said the talker.

No need for a helm order as yet, with the bearing so little altered. Better to wait. Nourse was at his side.

'I'd better fire single charges, sir?' said Nourse.

It was a statement with a question mark at the end. Nourse could give his opinion but the responsibility was Krause's. The handicapped duck hunter had a choice; one shot with a shot-gun or six with a rifle. Krause thought of all the patterns *Keeling* had fired without result. The objective was to keep the U-boat down, slow, blind, and comparatively harmless until the convoy had passed on. But one well placed pattern might destroy her, and this seemed as good an opportunity as ever might present itself. The temptation was enormous. And then Krause thought of what his situation would be like if he fired all his depth-charges now and missed. He would be practically helpless, useless. The objective had not changed.

'Yes. Single charges,' said Krause.

He had forgotten the weariness of his legs and his aching feet; tension had not mounted as rapidly this time but he was tense again, with the need for rapidity of decision.

'Sonar reports——'

'Periscope!' said the other talker breaking in; in the pilot-house they heard the yell from forward at the same moment. 'Forward look-out reports periscope dead ahead.'

Krause put his glasses to his eyes; the port side 40 mm., just forward of the bridge, suddenly began to fire tonk-tonk-tonk. Then nothing for a moment. Krause had just seen the splashes thrown up by the 40 mm. shells. Then the two talkers both began to speak at once.

'Sonar first,' said Krause.

'Sonar reports contact bearing one-six-four, range two thousand yards.'

'Forward look-out reports periscope disappeared.'

'Gun forty-two opened fire at periscope dead ahead. No hits.'

This U-boat captain certainly had a different technique. He had not trusted his listening instruments. He had not been able to resist taking a peep through his periscope. What would be his reaction at the sight of *Keeling*'s bows pointing right at him? Helm over, most probably. But which way? On across *Keeling*'s bows or an instinctive flinching away? The next report might show. And dive deep or stay at periscope depth? Dive deep, most likely.

'Deep setting, Mr Nourse.'

'Aye aye, sir.'

'Sonar reports contact dead ahead, range fifteen hundred yards.'

She was crossing *Keeling*'s bows, then. She had probably used left rudder.

'Right smartly to course one-eight-zero.'

'Right smartly to course one-eight-zero. Steady on course one-eight-zero.'

'Sonar reports contact dead ahead, range thirteen hundred yards.'

He had anticipated the U-boat's movement, then. She had come sharply round. Better lead her another ten degrees more.

'Right smartly to course one-nine-zero.' Then into the T.B.S. 'Contact crossing my bows, range thirteen hundred yards. I am turning to starboard.'

'Aye aye, sir.'

'Steady on course one-nine-zero.'

'Very well.'

'Sonar reports contact bearing one-eight-zero, range eleven hundred yards.'

Ten degrees to port? Suspicious. If sonar had reported a Doppler effect at the same time it would be more suspicious, though. Wait. Wait.

'Sonar reports contact bearing one-seven-five, range twelve hundred yards.'

That was it. The sub. was circling right away. *Keeling*'s last turn had been worse than unnecessary; it had increased distance and wasted time. Krause felt a momentary annoyance with himself. But how far round would the sub. turn? Lead her or follow her?

'Left standard rudder. Steer course one-seven-five.' Into the T.B.S. 'Contact's circling. I am turning back to port.'

'Aye aye, sir.'

Dodge was drawing up to her station on the edge of the ring, ready to enter into the combat. The convoy was closing on them steadily. There were many factors to be borne in mind at the same time.

'Contact bearing one-seven-two, range twelve hundred yards.'

Wait for it. Wait. Wait.

'Contact bearing one-six-six, range steady at twelve hundred yards.'

She was coming right round, then, and at a very slow speed.

'Left full rudder. Steer course one-five-five.' Into the T.B.S. 'I am still turning to port.'

'Aye aye, sir.'

'Sonar reports contact dead ahead, range one thousand.'

This time he had scored a point. He had closed on his victim by two hundred yards and still had her dead ahead. He must rub the advantage in and anticipate again.

'Left full rudder. Steer course one-four-zero.'

Round they went in the circle, closing in to the point of equilibrium.

'Dicky to George! Dicky to George! Contact, sir. Bearing oh-six-four, range one thousand.'

'Come in, then.'

The rat had doubled away from one terrier to head for the jaws of the other. A pity that both terriers were so nearly toothless. Krause watched *Dodge* steady herself on her new course; saw her swing a trifle and then a trifle more as the desperate U-boat came out of her circle.

215

Quick thinking was necessary. In one hundred and eighty seconds the two ships would be meeting—long seconds when chasing a sub.; horribly short when closing on another ship at right angles. He must give way and give way so as to be in the most suitable station for taking up the chase if *Dodge*'s attack failed.

'Right full rudder. Steer course zero-eight-five. Come on in, Dicky. I am turning to starboard.'

'Aye aye, sir.'

Long seconds again now, watching whether the rat would run into the other terrier's jaws or would just evade them, listening to the sonar bearings, deciding on whether the present course was the most suitable. *Dodge* was still turning to starboard. Time to turn to port again yet?

'Steady on course zero-eight-five.'

'Torpedoes fired!' said the talker.

One second for thought. The U-boat's stern was pointing straight at *Keeling*'s port beam; the U-boat's bows were pointing, as far as he could tell, somewhat away from *Dodge*'s bows. *Dodge* was distant, *Keeling* was near. The U-boat must be aware of *Keeling*'s proximity; it was probable she did not know of *Dodge*'s approach. Foil-blade pressed against foil-blade; one second—one-tenth of a second—for thought. *Keeling* must be the target.

'Right full rudder. Steer course one-seven-zero.'

Not quite a right angle turn. The torpedoes would be aimed to cross nearly ahead of *Keeling*'s present position; allow for the advance and *Keeling* would be as nearly parallel to the tracks as he could judge.

'All engines ahead flank speed!'

'Torpedoes approaching!' said the talker.

'Make your report the way you've been taught,' snapped Krause at the talker. 'Repeat.'

216

'Sonar reports torpedoes approaching,' stammered the talker.

It was absolutely essential for the talkers to report in due form. Otherwise confusion was certain.

'Steady on course one-seven-zero,' said the helmsman.

'Very well.'

'Engine-room answers "All engines ahead flank speed," sir.'

'Very well.'

Time to spare for the T.B.S. now, which was demanding his attention.

'Torpedoes fired at you, sir!' said the Canadian voice, urgent, distressed. 'I see you've turned.'

'Yes.'

'Good luck, sir.'

Good luck to the man who might be dead in ten seconds' time. Good luck to the ship which might be a sinking wreck or a pillar of fire. He had taken the best action, laying his ship parallel to the torpedo tracks. With the call for flank speed the churning of *Keeling*'s propellers, working furiously against the inertia of the ship, might perhaps have some effect on deflecting a torpedo coming right at them, especially as it would be set for a shallow run against a destroyer. In any case the propellers' quickening beat would kick *Keeling* a few yards farther away from the firing-point than she would otherwise have been, and every yard, every foot, counted. Inches might make the difference between life and death; not that life or death mattered, but success or failure did.

'Sonar reports echoes confused, sir,' said the talker.

'Very well.'

'Torpedo to starboard!'

'After look-out reports———'

'Torpedo to port!'

Look-outs were shouting and talkers talking. One leap to the starboard wing of the bridge. There was the indescribably menacing track along *Keeling*'s side, not ten yards away, straight along it. Luckily it was a torpedo of the old-fashioned type with none of the rumoured homing devices that the Germans were supposed to be putting into production.

'T'other one went over there, sir,' said the port-side look-out, pointing vaguely.

'How far?'

'Good two hundred feet, sir.'

'Very well.'

Back to the pilot-house.

'All engines ahead standard speed. Left full rudder. Steer course zero-eight-five.'

It was forty seconds since the alarm was given. Forty of those long seconds, and during this time he had been neglectful. He had not watched *Dodge* to see the effect of her run-in. She had come farther round still. Her turning circle was remarkably small. She was handier than *Viktor*, and considerably handier than *Keeling*. Those tiny ships, fantastically uncomfortable to live in, were good anti-submarine craft all the same, even though a single torpedo would blow them to pieces. She was coming round again— it must be remarkably pleasant to handle a ship that could turn inside a U-boat's turning circle.

It was time to head round towards the most likely point of interception.

'Left standard rudder. Steer course zero-two-zero.'

His turn away and even his momentary increase in speed had considerably enlarged his distance.

'Dicky to George. We've got him right ahead of us. We'll be firing any minute now.'

'Very well.'

'Glad he missed you, sir. Very glad.'

'Thank you.'

'We're turning to starboard again.'

'Very well.'

Krause turned to the helmsman.

'Left standard rudder. Steer course three-three-zero.'

The convoy was unpleasantly near. It would not be long before sonar would start complaining about interference. This new enemy was a dangerous man, free with his torpedoes. He would have to be watched very closely indeed if he were like that, giving him as little opportunity as possible for a beam shot, and that meant considerable precaution in manœuvring round him. At the same time he now had two torpedoes the fewer—he was ten per cent less deadly to the convoy than he had been. Doenitz might take him to task—if he lived to return to L'Orient—for those two wasted fish. He might ask why he had not fired a full spread; he might ask why he had fired at all at a shallow-draft fighting vessel with full power of manœuvre and on the alert. The question as to whether or not it was profitable to use torpedoes against escort craft was a difficult one for the Germans to answer. It was foolish, a foolish waste of time, and yet attractive, to think of luring the U-boat into wasting all its torpedoes in that fashion. The sub. would not fire eighteen more torpedoes and miss every time. He must be delirious to give it a thought. Over-tired, perhaps.

'Dicky to George. Firing now.'

'Very well. I'll come in. Right standard rudder. Steer course one-one-zero.'

A single pillar of water in *Dodge*'s wake. Just the one shot, yet sufficient to deafen *Dodge*'s sonar.

'Sonar reports underwater explosion, sir.'

'Very well.'

'Sonar reports indications confused.'

'Very well.'

What had this U-boat captain been doing during his three minutes' grace between *Dodge*'s arriving close to him and dropping the charge? Starboard? Port? His own sonar indications had not been very conclusive. And what was the U-boat doing now, with *Keeling*'s sonar deafened?

'Sonar reports contact bearing zero-seven-five, range fourteen hundred yards.'

So he had guessed wrong. Round after him.

'Left full rudder. Steer course zero-six-five. George to Dicky. Contact bearing zero-seven-five from me, range fourteen hundred yards.'

'Zero-seven-five. Aye aye, sir. I am turning to starboard.'

Round after him. Round again. Coach *Dodge* in against him. Jockey into position and drop a single depth-charge, resisting the temptation to make it a full pattern. Remember that this fellow might fire a spread at any moment. Keep the flagging mind alert. Think quickly. Forget the weary legs and the aching feet which had not, after all, gone numb. Keep from thinking about the ridiculous and yet penetrating need to get down to the head again. Round and round, ever on the alert for something to happen at any moment.

Something did. *Keeling* on one run, *Dodge* on another, had each dropped a charge. Hopeless to expect any results from such a feeble attack.

'After look-out reports sub. astern.'

Krause leaped to the wing of the bridge. A grey shape showing there, a quarter of a mile away, bridge and hull in

full view. The guns in the after gun-mounts began to fire.
Wang-o, wang-o.

'Right full rudder!'

Next moment it was gone, plunging violently below the
surface.

'Meet her! Steady as you go!'

'Sonar reports close contact dead ahead.'

'Mr Nourse!'

'Sub. alongside! Sub. alongside!'

That was a scream from the port-side look-out. Almost
scraping alongside, not ten feet between them. Krause
could have hit her with a rock if he had had a rock to
throw. As it was there was nothing to throw. Not a depth-
charge at the port-side 'K'-gun; the five-inch could not
depress so far. Tonk-tonk-tonk went the port-side 40 mm.;
Krause saw the splashes in the water beyond—it would not
depress sufficiently either. Painted on the side of the
U-boat's bridge was a golden-haired angel in flowing
white robes riding a white horse and brandishing a sword.
The U-boat's bow submerged again at a sharp angle and
the bridge plunged forward into the water again. Bang-
bang-bang-bang. Someone had got a fifty-calibre machine-
gun into action too late.

'Left full rudder!'

Right in *Keeling*'s wake the U-boat broke surface again
in a flurry of spray and vanished instantly, to reappear
again and disappear again. The assumption was obvious
that one of her bow-planes was jammed on rise. It might
be an ordinary mechanical failure; it might be that one of
those depth-charges had by a miracle exploded near
enough to damage it.

'Right full rudder!' bellowed Krause, his voice loud
enough to be heard from end to end of the ship.

Here was *Dodge* coming right towards them; in the excitement of finding a sub. close alongside he had forgotten all about *Dodge*, who was coming in to the attack as she had every right to do. The two ships, no more than a cable's length apart, were wheeling towards each other, heading for a common meeting point where the crash would be tremendous, fatal to both ships probably. Instinctive action, instinctive application of the ordinary rules of the road, saved them. Slowly each ship ceased to swing inwards; for a hair-raising moment inertia carried them on towards each other, and then the kick of the propellers against the turning rudders, the solid, wedge-like thrusts of the rudders against the water, swung the ships slowly outwards again. *Dodge* went past *Keeling*'s port side hardly farther than the sub. had been a minute ago. Someone waved airily to Krause from *Dodge*'s bridge and then passed rapidly by at the combined speed of both ships. Krause found himself shaking a little, but as always there was no time to worry; not if he wanted to get *Keeling* into position to follow up the attack that *Dodge* was going to deliver.

'Meet her!' he roared. 'Left full rudder!'

He went back into the pilot-house forcing himself to be calm; it was helpful to be greeted by the talker's monotonous voice.

'Sonar reports contacts confused.'

Sonar down below was doing its job in an orderly fashion, whether ignorant or not of all the things that were going on top-side.

'Meet her! Steady as you go!'

He was judging *Dodge*'s course by eye, and trying to anticipate the sub.'s next move.

'Dicky to George! Dicky to George!'

'George to Dicky. Go ahead.'

'We've no contact, sir. Must be too close.'

Yesterday that situation would have called instantly for a full pattern of depth-charges; today there was no question of wasting all *Dodge*'s remaining offensive power on the ten-to-one chance that the sub. was near enough within the possible three-hundred-yard circle to receive damage.

'Hold your present course. I'll cross your stern.'

'Aye aye, sir.'

'Left standard rudder! Meet her! Steady as you go!'

'Steady on course——' said the helmsman; Krause had no ears for the figures; he was planning to pass across *Dodge*'s wake sufficiently far from her to give his sonar a chance to pick up an echo from the sub.; *Dodge* would be going twice as fast as the sub., so that was the area to search. With a jammed plane the sub. could with care manage to keep submerged by trimming her ballast tanks; even below the surface she might manage to clear . . .

'George! George! Here he is!'

Krause looked forward over the starboard bow at *Dodge*. There was nothing to see except the little ship steaming along apparently peacefully.

'Too close!' said the T.B.S., and at the same time through the ear-phones came the sound of gunfire, echoed a second later over the air. *Dodge* was turning rapidly to port. Guns were firing; over the water came the sound of small-calibre machine-guns. Round came *Dodge*. Grey against her grey side was something else, the surfaced U-boat, bow to stern with her, circling as she circled, each ship chasing the other's tail. As *Dodge* came broadside on to Krause's view a great red eye opened in *Dodge*'s side and winked once at Krause. A pillar of water rose in the sea half-way between them; something black shot out of the base of the pillar, turning end-over-end with incredible rapidity, rising out of Krause's sight and roaring overhead with a sound like the fastest underground train ever heard. *Dodge* had banged off her four-inch at extreme depression and the shell had ricochetted from the surface, luckily bouncing high enough to pass over *Keeling*. Hard to blame the gunners; with *Dodge* turning so rapidly and *Keeling* crossing her stern the situation was changing so rapidly they could not have guessed that *Keeling* would come into the line of fire.

Other bangs, other rattles, as the ships wheeled. The U-boat captain must have despaired of effecting a repair and come to the surface to fight it out. Close alongside *Dodge*, his men must have run to their guns over the streaming decks as she emerged. And, closer to the surface than *Dodge*'s gun, her gun would bear on *Dodge*'s loftier side while *Dodge*'s gun would not depress sufficiently. And what would that four-inch do to that fragile little ship?

In a moment, it seemed, they had turned the half-circle and *Dodge*'s bow and the U-boat's stern were presented to Krause's view; already the U-boat was disappearing behind *Dodge* on the other side.

'Right full rudder!' said Krause. He had been so fascinated by the sight that he was allowing *Keeling* to steam straight on away from the fight. 'Meet her! Steady as you go!'

'Steady on course——'

'Very well. Captain to gunnery control. "Stand by until you have a chance at a clear shot." '

A sudden flare-up forward in *Dodge*; smoke pouring from her below her bridge. The U-boat had scored one hit at least. The embattled ships were coming round again, and he was going in the opposite direction, hovering on the outskirts like a distracted old lady whose pet dog had engaged in a fight with another dog.

224

'Gunnery control answers "Aye aye, sir." '

He must get clear, turn, and come in again. With cool judgment and accurate timing he could break into the battle. He would have to ram, picking the U-boat off *Dodge*'s side as he might pick off a tick. It would be a tricky thing to do. And he might easily tear the bottom out of *Keeling*, but it was worth trying, even in the face of that probability. They were turning counter-clockwise; best if he came in counter-clockwise too. That would give him more chance.

'Left standard rudder! Meet her! Steady as you go!'

Endless seconds as *Keeling* drew away from the fight. He had to allow himself sufficient distance to time his run-in. Krause watched the increasing distance. He had his glasses to his eyes; as they came round again he could see the figures on the U-boat's deck; he saw two of them drop suddenly, inert, as bullets hit them.

'Left full rudder!' Long, long seconds as *Keeling* turned with exasperating slowness.

'Meet her!'

As Krause braced himself to make the run-in the situation changed in a flash. Keyed up and eager, watching through his glasses to time his movement exactly, he saw *Dodge*'s bow seemingly waver in the smoke that surrounded it. It was ceasing to turn to port. Compton-Clowes was putting his wheel over. The deduction exploded a further series of reactions on Krause's part.

'Right standard rudder! Captain to gunnery control. "Stand by for target on port beam." Meet her! Steady as you go! Steady!'

Keeling's turn to starboard presented her whole port side to *Dodge* and the sub. All five five-inch guns came training round as she turned, and at the same instant the sub. with her wheel hard over and taken momentarily by surprise by

Dodge's abrupt alteration of rudder diverged from her. Ten yards—twenty yards—fifty yards of clear water divided the two ships, and before the U-boat could turn back into the sheltering embrace of her enemy the five-inch opened, like a peal of thunder in the next room, shaking *Keeling*'s hull as a fit of coughing will shake a man's body. The sea seemed suddenly to pile up around the grey U-boat, the splashes were so close and so continuous around her; it was as if there was a hillock of water there, with the square grey bridge only dimly to be seen in the heart of it like an object in a glass paper-weight—and, in the heart of it, too, over and over again, a momentary orange glare as a shell burst. Also in the heart of it showed momentarily a vivid red disc, just once. Through the noise of the gunfire and the vibration of the recoil Krause heard a rending crash and felt *Keeling* undergo a violent shock which made everyone on the bridge stagger; a shock wave like a sudden breath passed into and out of the pilot-house. And before they had steadied themselves the guns fell silent, ending their fire abruptly, so that Krause was conscious of a moment's unnatural silence, just long enough for him to feel fear lest the main armament had somehow been put out of action. But a glance reassured him. The U-boat was gone. There was nothing in the foaming water over there. The eye-pieces of the binoculars which he raised again to his eyes beat against his eyelashes until he forced his hands to quiet themselves. Nothing? Surely there were some things floating there. And something came and went, came and went again; not strange-shaped wave-tops but two huge bubbles bursting in succession on the surface.

In that moment the unnatural silence was ended and Krause became conscious of sounds close beside him, snappings and bangings, and voices. From the wing of the bridge he looked down aft, and what he saw first was a bird's nest of twisted iron seen dimly through smoke. It was an effort to recall what he should have seen there. The port-side 20 mm. gun tub just abaft the stack was gone, gone. Below it the deck was riven and twisted, with smoke eddying from it, and at the root of the smoke a glimmer of flame visible in the pale daylight, and, just beyond, the torpedoes in their quadruple mount with their brassy warheads. There shot up in Krause's mind the recollection of the Dahlgren experiment just before the war when it was proved—to the satisfaction of all except those who died— that T.N.T. detonated after a few minutes' steady cooking.

Petty, the damage-control officer, hatless and excited, was running to the spot with a team following him. He should not have left his central post. They were dragging hoses. Krause remembered suddenly what there was stored there.

'Belay those hoses!' he bellowed. 'That's gasoline! Use foam!'

One hundred gallons of gasoline in two fifty-gallon drums, for the motor whale-boat which *Keeling* carried. Krause swore a bitter vow that in future he would have a Diesel boat, or else no boat at all; at any rate no gasoline.

Those drums must have burst and the fiery stuff was spreading. The flames were reaching eagerly for the torpedoes.

'Jettison those fish!' hailed Krause.

'Aye aye, sir,' answered Petty, looking up at him, but Krause doubted if he had understood what had been said. The flames were roaring up. Flint, the ageing Chief recalled from Fleet Reserve was there, and looked more sensible.

The convoy was perilously near. He did not dare launch live torpedoes. Krause had been a destroyer officer most of his professional life; for years he had lived with torpedoes in consequence, visualizing their use in every possible situation—save perhaps this one. The old dreams of charging in upon a column of battleships for a torpedo attack had no place here. But at least he was familiar with every detail of the handling of torpedoes.

'Flint!' he yelled, and Flint looked up at him. 'Jettison those fish! Get rid of 'em! Launch 'em dead! Lift the tripping latches first!'

Flint understood him. He had not been able to think for himself, but he could act when someone thought for him. He sprang through the edge of the flames on to the mount, and went steadily from tube to tube carrying out his instructions. The lifted tripping latches would not engage the torpedo starting lever when the tubes were fired. Tonk! A dull noise, a puff of smoke, and the first torpedo plunged over the side like a swimmer starting a race, but only to dive straight down to the bottom. Tonk! That was the second. Then the third. Then the fourth. They were all gone now. Fifty thousand dollars' worth of torpedoes tossed deliberately to the bottom of the Atlantic.

'Well done!' said Krause.

The flames were bursting up through the holes in the deck, but one young seaman—in his cold-weather clothes Krause could not determine his rate, but he could recognize him and would remember him—had a foam-nozzle in each hand and was playing on the flames from the very edge of the blaze. Other nozzles were appearing now and he could be sure the fire would be smothered. He weighed in his mind the proximity of number three gun-mount's handling-room. No. That was safe. He had many other things to think about. It was only three and a half minutes since the gunfire had ceased, but he had been improperly employed during that time doing his damage-control officer's work. He looked round at *Dodge* and at the convoy and plunged into the pilot-house.

'Dicky on the T.B.S., sir,' said Nystrom.

There was long enough to note that Nystrom was steady, pop-eyes and all. His manner still had the faintly apologetic flavour that characterized it at other times and might excite prejudice against him.

'George to Dicky. Go ahead.'

'Submit we turn in to look for survivors, sir,' said the T.B.S.

'Very well. Permission granted. What is your damage?'

'We've lost our gun, sir. Our four-inch. Seven dead and some wounded. He hit us right on the mount.'

'What other damage?'

'Nothing serious, sir. Most of his shells went right through without exploding.'

At twenty yards' range those German four-inch would be travelling at practically muzzle velocity. They would be liable to go right through unless they hit something solid like a gun-mount.

'We have our fires under control, sir,' went on the T.B.S. 'I think I can report definitely that they are extinguished.'

'Are you seaworthy?'

'Oh, yes, sir. Seaworthy enough with the weather moderating. And we'll have the holes patched in a brace of shakes.'

'Seaworthy but not battleworthy,' said Krause.

Those words would have had a dramatic, heroic ring if it had not been Krause who said them in his flat voice.

'Oh, we've still got our Bofors, sir, and we've two depth-charges left.'

'Very well.'

'We're going into the oil, sir. Enormous pool of it—it'll reach you soon I should think, sir.'

'Yes, I can see it.' So he could, a circular sleek area where no wave-top was white.

'Any wreckage?'

'There's a swimmer, sir. We'll get him in a minute. Yes, sir, and there are some fragments. Can't see what they are from here, sir, but we'll pick them up. It'll all be evidence, sir. We got him all right.'

'We sure did.'

'Any orders, sir?'

Orders. With one battle finished he had to make arrangements for the next. He might be plunged into another action during the next ten seconds.

'I'd like to send you home,' said Krause.

'Sir!' said the T.B.S. reproachfully.

Compton-Clowes knew as much about escorting convoys as he did, probably more even despite his recent intensive experiences. Nothing could be spared, not even a battered little ship armed with Bofors and two depth-charges.

'Well, take up your screening station as soon as you've picked up the evidence.'

'Aye aye, sir. We're getting a line to the swimmer now, sir.'

'Very well. You know your orders about him.'

'Yes, sir.'

Instructions regarding the treatment of survivors from U-boats were quite detailed; Naval Intelligence needed every scrap of information that could be gleaned from them. Possession had to be taken immediately of every scrap of paper in any survivor's pocket before it could be destroyed. Any information volunteered was to be carefully noted.

'Over,' said Krause.

The spreading oil had reached *Keeling* now. The raw smell of it was apparent to everyone's nostrils. There could be no doubt about the destruction of the U-boat. She was gone, and forty or fifty Germans with her. The Nazi captain had died like a man, even if—as was likely—it was a mere mechanical failure for which as captain he was responsible, which had prevented him from diving. He had fought it out to the end, doing all the damage he could. Through Krause's mind drifted the unsummoned hope that if he had to die he would die in a like fashion although in a better cause, but he would not allow his mind to dwell on such time-wasting aspirations. On the surface the U-boat had fought a good fight, handled superbly, far better than she had been handled under water. That might be a trifle of evidence for Naval Intelligence—the U-boat captain might be a surface ship officer given command of a submarine after insufficient underwater training and experience. Discipline in the U-boat had endured to the end. That last shot she fired, the one that had hit *Keeling*, had been fired by someone with a cool head and iron nerve. Amid that hell of bursting shells, probably with the training mechanism jammed, he had caught *Keeling* in his sights while the U-boat turned and had pressed the firing pedal as his last act before his death. The dead which he slew at his death were more than they which he slew in his life.

Those dead were in *Keeling* and he had stood here idle for several seconds when there was so much to be done. Out on to the wing of the bridge to look down on the scene of the damage. The fire was out; patches of foam were still to be seen drifting about the deck with the movement of the ship. Petty was still there.

'Go back to your post, Mr Petty, and let's have your report.'

'Aye aye, sir.'

The ship's damage–control system had not stood the test of war; he would have to take some action about that. Two seamen were making their way past the shattered part of the deck carrying a stretcher between them; fastened into it was an inert shape. Storekeeper Third Class Meyer. Down to the loudspeaker.

'This is the Captain. We got that U-boat. The oil from her is all round us now. *Dodge* has picked up a survivor. We hit her a dozen times with the five-inch. And he hit us. We've lost some shipmates. Some have been hard hit.' The sentences were dragging. It was hard to make his mind think of suitable things to say. 'It was in the line of their duty. And we'll make the next U-boat pay for them. We've still a long way to go. Keep on your toes.'

It was not a good speech. Krause was no orator, and now once more he was, without realizing it, in the throes of reaction after the extreme tension of the battle, and his fatigue accentuated the reaction. Inside his clothes he was cold and yet sweating. He knew that if he relaxed for a second he would be shivering—trembling. On the bulkhead beside the loudspeaker hung a small mirror, a relic of peacetime days. He did not recognize the face in it—he gave it a second glance for that very reason.

The eyes were big and staring and rimmed with red. The unbuttoned hood hung down beside cheeks that were sprouting with bristles. He still did not think of it as his face until he observed at the base of one nostril a dab of filth—relics of the mayonnaise that had been smeared there so long ago. And there was yellow egg on his chin. He wiped at it with his gloved hand. All round his bristly lips he was filthy. He needed to wash, he needed a bath and a shave, he needed—there was no end to the list of what he needed, and it was no use thinking about it. He dragged himself back into the pilot-house and sank down on to his stool, once more commanding his tired body not to tremble. Next? He still had to go on. The sonar was still pinging; the Atlantic was still full of enemies.

'Mr Nystrom, take the conn.'

'Aye aye, sir.'

'Take station to patrol ahead of the convoy.'

'Aye aye, sir.'

Petty giving his damage report. Watching Petty's face as he spoke, concentrating his attention. This was the first time Petty had been tested in action, and it was not fair to judge him finally; and he must put in a word of admonition, but carefully phrased as it would be in the hearing of all in the pilot-house.

'Thank you, Mr Petty. Now that you've had the opportunity of seeing your arrangements in action you will know what steps to take to improve them.'

'Yes, sir.'

'Very well, Mr Petty.'

Fippler made his gunnery report on the battle circuit. He had counted seven distinct hits in the fifty-odd rounds fired.

'I should have thought it was more,' said Krause.

'It may have been, sir. May have been plenty we didn't see.'

'But it was good shooting, Mr Fippler. Well done.'

'Thank you, sir. And number four gun still has a round in the breech. Request permission to unload through the muzzle.'

That was one way of asking permission to fire the gun

off. A round left in the heated gun was too dangerous to unload in the ordinary way, and as a result of the chemical changes caused by the heat it would be unreliable in action. Krause looked round him. A sudden unexpected gun going off might puzzle the convoy but could hardly alarm them further than they had been alarmed already.

'Permission granted, Mr Fippler.' Think of everything; keep the mind concentrated so as to miss no detail. 'Send someone first to warn the ship over the loudspeaker about what you're going to do.'

'Aye aye, sir. Thank you, sir.'

It might alarm the convoy, but the sudden unexpected crash of a gun might well disturb the ship; false alarms were to be avoided if possible for fear of blunting the edge of the men's attention.

Now he could get down to the head. He did not know how many hours it was since he had thought he should do that as a precautionary measure; now it was something of the most urgent and pressing importance. He heard Fippler's warning being given over the loudspeaker as he went down the ladder, but it did not register because he was now having to grapple with the problem of whether or not to break radio silence and inform London of the growing helplessness of his command. That was a problem calling for so much thought that he had no attention to spare for anything else, with the result that he forgot all about his recent conversation with Fippler and while still in the head he was taken completely by surprise by the crash of number four gun going off. The sudden galvanization into tension, the reaction from it when he remembered the actual state of affairs, and his annoyance with himself—his shock that he could have forgotten so quickly —left him shaken again. But he deliberately took two more minutes away from the bridge, and washed his face and hands, soaping and rubbing vigorously. That made him feel considerably better. He actually remembered to pick up his hood and gloves before setting himself to make the weary climb back up the ladders to the bridge.

Thursday. Dog Watches—1600–2000

The watch was changing as he began the ascent with painful feet and aching legs; the ladders were crowded with men climbing up and men coming down. They were chattering and talking animatedly to each other, like schoolboys between classes; perhaps the recent exciting events had keyed them up, but they showed no sign of weariness.

'Did you hear the Kraut?' asked one young seaman loudly, 'He said——'

Someone else caught sight of Krause on the ladder and nudged the speaker into silence as they made way for their captain.

'Thank you,' said Krause, pushing past them.

He had been nearly sure before this that on the lower deck he was known as the Kraut. Now he knew. It was inevitable that he should have that nickname. It was only among the officers that he was known by his Annapolis nickname as Squarehead Krause.

In the pilot-house two men turned to salute him; Charlie Cole of course and Temme the doctor.

'You got him all right, sir,' said Cole.

'Yes, we did, didn't we?' said Krause.

'Reporting casualties, sir,' said Temme, and then, glancing down at the scrap of paper he held. 'Three killed.

Gunner's Mate Third Class Pisani, Seaman Second Class Marx, Mess Attendant Second Class White. All of them badly mutilated. Two wounded. Seaman Second Class Bonnor, Storekeeper Third Class Meyer. Both of them hospital cases. Meyer has it badly in both thighs.'

'Very well, Doctor.' Krause turned to receive Nystrom's salute and statement that Harbutt now had the deck. 'Very well, Mr Nystrom.'

'I've prescribed something for you, Cap'n,' said Cole, 'in consultation with Doc.'

Krause looked at him a little stupidly.

'Something on a tray, sir,' said Cole.

'Thank you,' said Krause in all gratitude, the thought of coffee rising in his mind like sunrise. But Cole obviously had more to say and the doctor was obviously waiting to support him in what he had to say.

'About the funerals, sir,' said Cole.

Certainly the thought of burying the dead had not crossed Krause's mind.

'Doc. here thinks——' said Cole, with a gesture he brought Temme into the conversation.

'The sooner they're buried the better, sir,' said Temme. 'I've no room for corpses down below. I've four other bed cases, you know, sir, the survivors from the burning ship.'

'We may be in action again any time, sir,' said Cole.

Both statements were perfectly true. A destroyer, as full of men as an egg is of meat, had no space to spare for mutilated bodies. Temme had to consider the likely possibility of having dozens more casualties on his hands.

'Commander tells me it may be three days or more before we reach port, sir,' said Temme.

'Quite right,' said Krause.

'On the table, there, messenger,' said Cole.

The 'something on a tray' that they had prescribed had arrived. The three of them moved over to the table. A quick gesture by Cole sent the quartermaster and the messenger away out of earshot. Krause lifted the napkin; there was a full meal there. Besides the pot of coffee was a plate of cold cuts painstakingly arranged, bread already buttered, potato salad, a dish of ice-cream. Krause looked at it all not entirely comprehendingly—at everything except the coffee.

'Please, sir,' said Cole, 'eat it while you've time. Please, sir.'

Krause poured himself coffee and drank, and then mechanically picked up the knife and fork and began to eat.

'May I arrange about the burials, sir?' asked Cole.

The burials. Krause had heard about the deaths of Pisani and Marx and White without emotion, too involved at that time with other problems and too encompassed by distractions for those deaths to affect him. Now he found himself eating with this discussion going on. Pisani had been young and dark and handsome and vital; he remembered him perfectly well. But the convoy had to go through.

'We've nearly two hours more of daylight, sir,' said Cole. 'And I can get it all set in ten minutes while you're eating your dinner. We might not have another chance.'

Krause rolled an eye on him while chewing a mouthful of cold meat. Before he became captain of his own ship, while still head of a department, he had done his share of prodding or luring a dilatory captain into giving necessary orders. That was what was happening to him at this moment. The discovery, in his present condition, affected him more than the thought of the dead men. It stiffened him.

'I shall have to take the service,' he said, coldly.

'Yes, of course, sir,' agreed Cole.

It would never do for the captain to be lounging on his stool in the pilot-house while someone else buried the ship's dead. The profoundest respect must be paid to the poor relics of the men who had given their lives for their country.

'Very well, then, Commander,' said Krause. Those were official words, and with them he took a fresh grip on the reins which Cole may have thought were lying loosely in his hands. 'You may give the necessary orders. Thank you, Doctor.'

'Aye aye, sir.'

Knife and fork in hand he could not return the salutes; he gave a sideways nod of his head. The food was very important to him at this moment. He was desperately hungry. He finished the cold meat, the bread, the salad, and he had begun on the ice-cream as Cole's voice made itself heard over the loudspeaker, announcing that the dead would be committed to the deep from the main-deck aft, detailing who should be present from each man's division, and adding a few really well-chosen words about the rest of the ship's company marking the solemnity of the occasion by remaining at their posts of duty. Krause thought about another pot of coffee. The men were dead; the first men who had died under his command. In war men died and ships sank.

Actually Krause was both too weary and too harassed with other problems to feel any emotion about men meeting the fate that he was ready to meet himself. But in a moment of horrible clarity he thought of himself as cold and indifferent, and there was a lightning stab of pain when he thought of how his coldness and indifference must have hurt warm-hearted Evelyn.

'All set, sir,' said Cole, saluting.

'Thank you, Charlie. Stay here while I'm down on the main-deck.'

Down the ladders again, forcing himself to forget Evelyn, forcing himself to forget how his feet hurt him, forcing his mind to abandon for the moment the problem of breaking radio silence and to apply itself to arranging the necessary sentences in his mind. The three stretchers at the ship's side; the flags over them; and, with the waning day, a thin gleam of pale sunshine breaking through from the western horizon. The sonar pinging on monotonously as he spoke. The realization that Cole had done an excellent job of organization as the men bent to lift the inboard ends of the stretchers and as the beat of the propellers ceased for a few seconds when the stretchers were tilted and the bundled-up shapes slid out from under the flags—Cole must have been watching from the bridge to give the signal at the right time. The wind blowing through his cropped hair as he stood bare-headed and three men stepped forward with rifles at Silvestrini's command to fire three small volleys over the boundless sea. Then back again, up the heart-breaking ladders with feet that had to feel for the rungs, dragging himself up to the pilot-house.

'Thank you, Charlie. Well done.'

Lifting his binoculars immediately to his eyes to look round him and take note of the condition of his command. What he had been doing was undoubtedly in the line of duty, but he felt uneasily that he might have been better employed although he could not say how. He swept the horizon aft of the ship with his glasses; visibility was improving steadily. The convoy appeared to him in fair order, although the commodore had the eternal signal flying 'Make less smoke.' *Dodge* and *James* were up to station, leading on either flank. Somewhere astern of the convoy, *Viktor*; with the convoy interposed he could not be sure he saw her, but he fancied he could at times see that odd foremast against the pale sunset. The weather forecasts had been really accurate; here was the wind down to force three, south-westerly. That would be of considerable importance with regard to the corvettes' urgent need of fuel. Tomorrow with luck he could expect air cover, and with the ceiling as high as this the cover would be really effective. He hoped London would appreciate his need.

Night was taking much longer to fall than it had done yesterday, thanks to the thinness of the cloud cover, and daylight would come appreciably earlier tomorrow morning, he hoped. At even thou shalt say Would God it were morning. Those two faint lights against the western sky were not stars. They were . . .

'Rockets in the convoy!' shouted the after look-out. 'Two white rockets right astern!'

Krause stiffened out of the easy mood into which he was nearly falling. Rockets meant trouble; two white rockets meant a torpedoing, unless it was a false alarm, set off by some panicky captain. There was a long moment during which Krause hoped it was a false alarm. *Viktor* was somewhere close to where the trouble was. He had to decide whether he should turn about and go to her help; there was no question of sending either corvette with their limited fuel supply.

'Commodore signals general alarm, sir,' said the signal-bridge down to him.

'Very well.'

There were powerful arguments against turning back. Night would be falling before he reached there. He would be astern of the convoy again, with all the prolonged delay before he could rejoin it, especially if the convoy were to get into serious disorder. Whatever mischief a U-boat might do had by now been already done; he could not remedy that. Nor could he hope to avenge it with his small remainder of depth-charges. He might pick up survivors—but *Cadena* and *Viktor* were on the spot and he would not be there for half an hour. But what would the men on board the convoy think of him if they saw him placidly steaming along ahead of them while their comrades died astern? He went to the T.B.S. *Dodge* and *James* answered promptly enough; they were aware of trouble in the convoy and asked for orders; he could only tell them to stay on station. But he could not raise *Viktor* on the circuit at all. He said, 'George to Eagle. George to Eagle. Do you hear me?' and received no reply. *Viktor* was ten miles away —possibly more by now—and it was quite possible that she could not hear. It was faintly possible that her hands were so full she had no time to reply, but it was hardly likely. Krause stood holding the hand-set, yearning inexpressibly to hear one single word even from that nonchalant English voice. The Commodore was blinking away, his light directed straight at *Keeling*; it must be a message for him. And it must be urgent, for it was almost too dark for Morse messages to be safe. The Commodore was taking a chance transmitting in these conditions, and the Commodore was not the sort of man to take chances.

Someone came dashing down from the signal-bridge with the pad.

COMCONVOY TO COMESCORT. 'CADENA' REPORTS 'VIKTOR' HIT.

'Very well.'

No more indecision.

'I'll take the conn, Mr Harbutt.'

'Aye aye, sir.'

'What's your heading?'

'Zero-nine-three, sir.'

'Right full rudder. Steer course two-seven-three. Mr Harbutt, the commodore tells me *Viktor* has been hit; she's somewhere astern of the convoy. I'm going back to her.'

'Steady on course two-seven-three, sir.'

'Very well. All engines ahead flank speed.'

'All engines ahead flank speed. Engine-room answers "All engines ahead flank speed," sir.'

'Very well.'

Just time to get to the T.B.S. and tell *Dodge* and *James* what he was doing.

'You'll have to cover the front as well as the flanks,' he added. 'Go easy with the fuel.'

'Aye aye, sir.'

Convoy and *Keeling* were rushing at each other. There was still light enough in the western sky to silhouette the ships against it; but aft the sky was already dark and it was quite possible they would not see *Keeling* approaching. And they were in disorder. Ships were out of station; there were no safe lanes through the convoy. And the ships would be moving unpredictably avoiding danger or trying to regain station. But he must go on. *Viktor* was hit. He felt overwhelming sorrow at the thought, even while he stood, poised and ready and keyed up. The sorrow would only endure for a few seconds before it was thrust aside by the urgencies of the moment. Napoleon long ago in the heat of battle had heard of the death of a favourite soldier and had said, 'Why have I not time to weep for him?' Krause had fifteen seconds in which to feel sorrow. Then . . .

'Right rudder. Meet her. Left rudder. Meet her.'

Keeling was plunging for the gap beside the Commodore. She had to snake past her. The gap was widening.

'Right full rudder!'

The ship behind was sheering across. A rapid calculation of the distance of the dark shape beyond. *Keeling* leaned over as she turned.

'Meet her! Steady as you go! Left rudder, handsomely. Meet her. Left rudder. Meet her.'

Keeling sped across the bows of one ship and across the stern of another, and then down alongside a dark shape. They were through.

'All engines ahead standard speed.'

'All engines ahead standard speed. Engine-room answers "All engines ahead standard speed," sir.'

'Very well.'

Minutes were precious, but he must have *Keeling* going slow enough now for the sonar to be effective.

'Resume sonar search.'

'Object on the starboard bow! Close!'

Object? Periscope? Krause sprang out with his glasses to his eyes. There was still the faintest twilight. The object was a fragment of a ship's lifeboat, just three or four feet of the shattered bows, almost awash. A man was lying there, face upturned, arms outspread, but alive; Krause could see him trying to lift his head to see what was approaching. Next second *Keeling*'s bow wave struck it, washing high over the face. Krause saw it again as it passed down the side of the ship. Waves washed over it again. That dim shape out there must be *Cadena*. Forget that just visible face with the waves flowing over it.

'Eagle on the T.B.S., sir,' said Harbutt.

Eagle? *Viktor* on T.B.S.? A thrill of hope; Krause picked up the hand-set.

'George to Eagle. Go ahead.'

'We've got it in the engine-room, sir,' said the lacka-daisical English voice. '*Cadena*'s standing by. She's taking us in tow.'

'I have *Cadena* in sight,' said Krause.

'Well, we're just beside her, sir. Engine-room's flooded and all power lost. We've just rigged this jury battery circuit for the radio-telephone.'

'One moment. Mr Harbutt! That's *Cadena* there taking *Viktor* in tow. Circle them at half a mile.'

'Aye aye, sir.'

Back to the T.B.S.

'I am patrolling round you at half a mile.'

'Thank you, sir. We're doing our best to save her.'

'I am sure you are.'

'The bulkheads are standing up to it pretty well, sir, and we're shoring them up. Trouble is there are plenty of leaks in the other compartments too. We're dealing with them as well.'

'Yes.'

'*Cadena*'s got our surplus men. We've put a hundred ratings on board her. We lost thirty in the engine-room.'

'Yes.'

'We've a five degree list to starboard and we're down by the stern, sir, but we'll tow all right.'

'Yes. Is *Cadena* passing that tow line satisfactorily?'

'Yes, sir. Another fifteen minutes, I should say, and we'll be under way.'

'Good.'

'We can use the hand steering, sir, and we'll be under control to a certain extent.'

'Good.'

'Captain asks me to report to you, sir, that *Kong Gustav* took it just before we did. He thinks she was hit by three

244

fish at short intervals. It must have been a spread fired at close range.'

'It sounds like it.'

'She sank in less than five minutes. *Cadena* picked up her captain and some of the crew, sir.'

'Yes.'

'We got ours while she was sinking, sir. Asdic didn't hear the shots. There was a lot of interference.'

'Yes.'

'We had only one depth-charge left, sir. We set it on safety and dropped it.'

'Good.'

The explosion of depth-charges in sinking ships had killed many swimmers who might otherwise have been saved.

'The captain asks me to thank you, sir, for all you've done. He says those were fine hunts we had.'

'I wish I could have done more,' said Krause.

This was like a conversation with a voice from the grave.

'And the captain asks me to say good-bye, sir, in case he doesn't see you again.'

'Very well.' Never had that Navy phrase been of more use than at this moment. But even so it was insufficient— it was only a stop gap. 'Tell him I'm looking forward to seeing him in Londonderry.'

'Aye aye, sir. The towing hawser's going out now. They'll be taking the strain soon.'

'Very well. Report results. Over.'

All the light had faded from the sky now. It was dark, but not solidly dark. It was possible to see, on the starboard beam, the two dark shapes that were *Cadena* and *Viktor*. *Keeling* was circling about them, her sonar searching the depths, her radar scanning the surface. Krause's brain took up mathematics again. A circle a mile in diameter was over three miles in circumference; it would take *Keeling* twenty minutes to complete the circle. A U-boat two miles distant from her, well out of range of her sonar, would need twenty minutes at six knots to creep in those two miles to launch a killing spread at half a mile's range before *Keeling* came round again. He was covering those two ships as effectively as was possible. And it was most necessary that he should. Destroyers were precious. If he could possibly bring *Viktor* into port he meant to do so. She would be ready for sea again in one-tenth of the time it took to build a new one, and with all her valuable, irreplaceable equipment. And *Cadena* was full of men. She had saved many lives on this voyage; and big ocean-going tugs of her type were scarce and almost as valuable as destroyers. There could be no doubt that his duty lay in covering *Viktor* and *Cadena*, and in leaving the rest of the convoy to the two corvettes. There was some cold comfort to be found in the thought that in this matter he was not confronted by a dilemma calling for painstaking weighing of chances. The T.B.S. demanded his attention again.

'We're making way now, sir. We're making three knots and we're going to work up to five, but the captain's worried about the bulkheads if we do. She's steering—she's steering after a fashion, sir.'

'Very well. Course zero-eight-five.'

'Oh-eight-five. Aye aye, sir.'

Thursday. First Watch—2000–2400

Harbutt saluting in the darkness.

'Report having been relieved, sir.' The rest of the formula. 'Mr Carling has the deck, sir.'

'Very well, Mr Harbutt. Good night.'

The T.B.S.

'Four knots is the best we can do, sir. The list gets worse if we make any speed. I fancy there's a flap of plating sticking out from the hole, and it scoops the sea in and it's bad for the after bulkhead.'

'I understand.'

'We're learning how to steer her, sir.'

'I understand.'

Here in *Keeling* all was as still as the grave. Over there in that patch of blackness men were working with desperate haste. They were shoring up bulkheads, working in pitch darkness relieved only by the faint light of flashlights. They were trying to patch up leaks, with the deadly gurgle—gurgle—gurgle of water bubbling in around them. They were trying to steer, passing helm orders back from the bridge through a chain of men, struggling with a hand-steering gear while the ship surged unpredictably to port and to starboard, threatening at any moment to part the towing hawser.

'Mr Carling!'

'Sir!'

A careful explanation of the situation, of *Cadena*'s course and speed, of the necessity to maintain a constant sonar guard around her. *Keeling* must describe a series of ellipses round her as she struggled on at four knots, each ellipse a trifle—an almost inconsiderable trifle—nearer safety. It would be a neat but easy problem to work out how to handle *Keeling* at twelve knots circling round *Cadena* at four.

There were other problems not so easy. With every hour that passed the convoy would be four or five miles farther ahead. It would be long days before *Viktor* could be brought into port. The question of *Keeling*'s fuel supply would become urgent before long. He would have to appeal to London for help; he would have to break radio silence. He could take that bitter decision. He would have to do it. But . . . There were the German direction-finding stations; there were German submarines at sea. Doenitz would by this time be fully aware of the position, course, and even the composition of the convoy; that information would be relayed to him by the subs. At that rate there would seem to be no serious objection to breaking radio silence. But there was. The moment the German monitoring system informed Doenitz that the convoy had sent out a message he would ask himself the reason, and there could only be one reason—that the convoy was in such bad straits that it needed help urgently. It would be enough to prompt Doenitz to turn every available sub. against the convoy. It would tell the captain who had fired on *Viktor* that his torpedo had hit home and that *Viktor* need no longer be reckoned with. If the convoy went ploughing along in silence Doenitz and the sub. captains could not be sure that it was not still in a condition to hit back. It was a very important point.

Yet with the convoy practically unguarded and *Viktor* so far from home, help was essential. It was very doubtful whether *Dodge* and *James* had sufficient oil to enable them to reach Londonderry. *Keeling* herself could do practically nothing to beat off a determined attack on *Viktor* and *Cadena*. He had to call for help; he had to swallow his pride; he had to take the risk. His pride did not matter, but it was possible to reduce the risk to a minimum. If he were to send the message now Doenitz could employ the whole night in directing his subs. to the attack. There were seven or eight hours of darkness still ahead, and during those hours there would be little that London could do to help him. It would be better to get the message off later, at one or two in the morning. That would still allow plenty of time for the Admiralty to get air cover over him at dawn, and it would cut down the interval as far as possible during which Doenitz could concentrate against him. Two in the morning would be early enough; his message would go straight through to the highest authority, he knew. Half an hour for that; half an hour for the Admiralty orders to go out; an hour for preparation. Two hours' flight; he would have air cover at dawn. He would send the message at two in the morning—perhaps at one-thirty.

Krause had reached that decision, standing in the pilot-house with Carling directing the ship as she patrolled round *Cadena* and *Viktor*. He was standing because he knew that if he sat down he would go to sleep. He had already caught himself once actually swaying on his feet. Krause had heard of the Mexican bandit who during the 1917 troubles had kept his district terrorized by his method of executing his enemies. He had hoisted them up nearly to the top of roadside telephone poles, one to each. There with their hands bound behind them they were stood with their feet on the climbing supports and ropes round their necks attached to the tops of the poles. Each man stood there, and as long as he stood he lived. When he tired, when his foot slipped, the noose strangled him. Some of them would stand for days, an example to the whole neighbour-hood. Krause was in like case. If he sat down he went to sleep, and if he stood—if he stood, as he was doing now, it was unbearable. Feet and muscles and joints all cried out with agony. Unbearable? He had to bear it. There was nothing else to be said about the matter. They that wait upon the Lord shall renew their strength.

He must not go to sleep, and so he went on standing, and

while he stood he forced his mind to think about the wording of the message he was going to send. A signal should
convey all necessary information; then he should tell about
Viktor's helpless state, the unguarded condition of the
convoy, the fact that he was dropping far astern, the need
for fuel—nonsense; it would take all night to tell all his
troubles. All he need say was something like 'Help urgently
needed.' They would know in London that he would not
send any message otherwise; with all their experience they
could guess his troubles. Then there was no need for the
'urgently.' If it was not urgent he would not be asking.
Then why say 'needed?' The one word 'help,' the mere
fact that it was sent, would tell the whole story. And there
was the faintest possible chance that a single word sent
like that might slip unnoticed past Doenitz's monitoring
system. No. That was too wild a hope to be reckoned with,
but the brevity of the message would be a serious handicap
to the German experts trying to break the code. No, he had
forgotten—he must be growing stupid. By cryptographic
regulations all short messages must be 'padded' with
indifferent material up to a minimum length, which
Dawson would know about. That was the decision of the
cryptographic experts, and he could not contravene it. Yet
the main conclusion he was reaching was sound enough.
He must appeal for help; at zero-one-forty-five tomorrow
he would send out the message with the one word 'help'
and leave the padding to Dawson.

Having reached that decision, and ceasing to concentrate his mind on the matter, Krause found himself swaying on his feet again. This was quite absurd; he had been
awake for less than forty-eight hours, and he had had two
or even three hours of good sleep the night before last. He
was a weak and beggarly element. He must not merely

keep standing but he must keep thinking, or he was lost. Strange that he found himself longing for more action, for more need for quick thinking and rapid decision, to key himself up again. But any further action could only be disaster. His command could face nothing further. He made himself stump up and down on his weary legs in the cramped pilot-house. It occurred to him to send for more coffee, and he told himself he would not be indulging in a slavish habit but taking necessary action to keep himself awake. But first he must go to the head; he put on the red spectacles and went down the ladders. He stumbled over the coamings like a farmer at sea, and it seemed to him as if he would never be able to drag his dead-weight body up those ladders again, and yet he did. He simply must not allow this lassitude to overcome him. When he reached the pilot-house he walked again; head up, chin in, chest out, shoulders back as he had done on parade at Annapolis. Until he had braced himself up he would not allow himself more coffee.

It was really something of a relief to be summoned to the T.B.S. again.

'Eagle to George. Do you hear me?'

'George to Eagle. I hear you. Go ahead.'

'Submit that we abandon ship, sir.' The cynical English voice was not cynical. It was grave; there was a little break in it before it went on. 'Very sorry, sir.'

'You have no choice?' asked Krause.

'The collision mats weren't large enough, sir. Nor was the hand-billy pump. The water's been gaining on us steadily—we couldn't keep it under and it came in faster all the time.'

So it would; the lower the helpless hull sank the greater would be the number of holes below the surface and the greater would be the pressure forcing in the water.

251

'We've fifteen degrees of list now and the main-deck's under water abaft the bridge, sir.'

'I'm sure you've done all you can. Permission granted to abandon ship,' said Krause. 'Tell your captain I have no doubt he has done all in his power to save his ship. And tell him I am sorry about his bad luck.'

The tired brain was being driven to work normally, to choose carefully the right words to employ towards an ally.

'Aye aye, sir,' said the English voice, and then the old nonchalance came back into it. 'Well, good-bye for now, sir, and thank you for a nice party.'

Krause turned away from the T.B.S. unhappily. When he had first heard that voice he had never dreamed for a moment that he would come to feel something of affection for its owner.

Friday. Middle Watch—2400–0400

It was just light enough in the pilot-house to be aware of the change of watch, talkers handing over head-phones, the wheel being relieved, Carling saluting.

'Mr Nystrom has the deck, sir.'

'Very well, Mr Carling.'

'Good night, sir.'

'Good night, Mr Carling. I'll take the conn, Mr Nystrom.'

'Aye aye, sir.'

With a couple of helm orders he edged *Keeling* up closer towards the dark patch that was *Cadena* coming alongside *Viktor*. At one moment they distinctly heard a few words coming down wind and over the sea—someone was using a speaking-trumpet and it had traversed in their direction.

'Sonar reports loud breaking up noises, sir,' said a talker.

'Very well.'

That was the requiem of a brave ship. It was two and a half years since *Viktor* had got away from Gdynia in defiance of all the power of the Luftwaffe, and had escaped from the Baltic in the teeth of the Nazi Navy. For two and a half years she had fought a desperate fight; she had been the only home left to her exiled crew, and now she was gone.

Four blasts from *Cadena*'s siren, startlingly loud in the night. 'F' for Fox—rescue completed.

'Come right handsomely. Still right. Meet her. Steady.'

He took *Keeling* carefully up to within hailing distance of *Cadena*—watching like a hawk as she turned—and then stepped out to the bull-horn.

'*Cadena*! Comescort.'

The speaking trumpet hailed back.

'Have you saved everyone?' asked Krause.

'Yes. We've got 'em all.'

That was a great relief. Krause had had a momentary mental picture of the British liaison officer with all his insouciance falling between the two grinding hulls with his bones snapping as the water leaped at him.

'Course zero-eight-seven,' hailed Krause.

'Eighty-seven,' said the speaking trumpet.

'Make your best speed to rejoin the convoy.'

'Twelve knots if I can,' said the speaking trumpet.

'I'll screen you ahead,' said Krause. 'Use the modified zig plan. Number Seven.'

'Modified zig? But——'

'That's an order,' said Krause. 'Modified zig. Number Seven. This is zero minute.'

'O.K. then,' said the speaking trumpet grudgingly.

It was remarkable how nearly every merchant captain resented zig-zagging. The almost universal feeling was that it was safer to get through the dangerous zone as quickly as possible; yet five minutes spent with a manœuvring board and a pair of parallel rulers working out an approach problem would convince anyone that zig-zagging made the attacking submarine's task considerably harder and postponed the moment when a shot might be got in. And an unpredicted change of course at the moment of firing usually meant a clean miss. Zig-zagging lessened very appreciably the chances of a hit; it did not even need Krause's experience at anti-submarine school of a few minutes in a sub.'s conning tower planning an approach to convince a thinking man of that.

'You heard that conversation, Mr Nystrom?'

'Yes, sir.'

'Take the conn, then. Screening position ahead of *Cadena* at five hundred yards' distance.'

'Aye aye, sir.'

'Messenger! Bring me a pot of coffee.'

Now that *Viktor* had sunk it was necessary to think again regarding his decision to appeal for help. At dawn he and *Cadena* would be close up to the convoy, so that the situation was greatly modified. And yet there was still the question of *James*'s oil fuel and the general helplessness of the escort. Despite the fact that *Viktor* would cause no further delay tomorrow would be a long day; air cover might make a great deal of difference—all the difference. But London would be endeavouring to provide it in any case. Was it worth while now to break radio silence, to incur the incidental risks which he had already debated, for the sake of the difference between certainty and likelihood? Was it? Krause tried to plod about the pilot-house. He had almost to repress a mutiny in his aching legs and feet as he did so. His mind was not mutinous; it was merely unwilling. He drove himself into weighing the pros and cons. The coffee would undoubtedly help.

'On the table, messenger.'

There was not enough light for him to see what he was doing, but he was practised in pouring coffee into a cup in the dark. As always, that first cup tasted like nectar, and the last of the first cup tasted possibly even better than the first sip because of the delightful knowledge that there was a second cup to follow. He drank the last of the second cup lingeringly, like a lover reluctant to part from his mistress. Let us eat and drink, for tomorrow—for within the next hour he had to reach a decision.

'Take that tray back to the wardroom, messenger,' he said.

The personal factor must be entirely disregarded. How Washington and London would be affected in their opinion of him must not influence him at all. It was his duty to think only about the convoy, about fighting the war. He must not spend a moment worrying lest he be thought of as an officer who went crying for help without sufficient justification. A good name is rather to be chosen than great riches; his good name, like his life, was at the service of his country. Promotion cometh neither from the east nor the west—what did he care about promotion? There is no discharge in that war. The Bible texts bobbed up in his mind as he tried to think. He could not ignore them.

Again, was it merely his personal weakness that was inclining him to call for help? Was he subconsciously trying to relieve himself of responsibility? Head up, shoulders back. Krause grudgingly gave himself a passing grade after a short but merciless self-examination. At the same time and equally grudgingly he acquitted himself of the other charge, that he was unwilling to break radio silence because of the possible effect on his own career. 'Fitted and retained.' Those words were as painful as the memory of Evelyn, but, for all their damning negation, he would not allow them to influence his decision.

The bell rang at the voice-tube, and Krause forgot feet and legs and the problem of breaking radio silence as he sprang to answer it.

'Captain.'

'Cap'n, sir, there are pips ahead of us.'

'Pips?'

'Pips or a pip, sir. This screen's getting fuzzier all the time. And the range unit's acting up.'

'But what is it you see?'

'Just something, sir. Thought it was two pips, but now I'm not sure. But it's right ahead of us, bearing around zero-eight-four—zero-eight-eight sometimes.'

'It's not the convoy?'

'No, sir. That's out of range. This pip's about at the limit.'

'Very well.'

Not so well, of course. A pip. Something on the surface right ahead. A U-boat, going full out to overtake the convoy? Very possibly. A straggler from the convoy? Likely enough. It was something that must be dealt with. 'I'll take the conn, Mr Nystrom.'

'Aye aye, sir. *Cadena*'s making all of twelve knots, sir.'

'Thank you. Right standard rudder. Steer course two-four-zero.'

'Right standard rudder. Steer course two-four-zero, sir,' said the helmsman in the quiet of the pilot-house. A pause while *Keeling* turned; long enough for Krause to work out on which leg of the zig *Cadena* would be in three minutes' time. 'Steady on course two-four-zero, sir.'

'Very well.' He had to go out on the starboard wing of the bridge to see the dark form of *Cadena*. 'Right rudder, handsomely.'

Cadena's next zig was due now. As *Keeling* drew up to her his straining eyes detected her change of silhouette as she put her rudder over. 'Meet her. Left rudder. Meet her. Steady as you go.'

To come alongside a zig-zagging ship within hailing distance in the darkness called for the most careful handling. The two ships came closer and closer together. Over there a light flashed momentarily. They were growing nervous, unable to guess what *Keeling* was trying to do. Someone had switched on a flashlight and pointed it at her.

'Port look-out reports a light from *Cadena*, sir,' said a talker.

'Very well. Right rudder. Meet her.'

He reached the bull-horn just as the speaking-trumpet voiced an anxious appeal.

'*Keeling*!'

'Comescort. I'm going on ahead of you. There's something suspicious several miles ahead bearing about zero-eight-six true.'

'What is it?'

'I don't know and I'm going to find out. Maintain your present base course and keep a good look-out ahead.' A few more seconds for thought. 'I'll warn you if there's danger. If you see me fire a gun make a radical change of base course, to zero-four-two true.'

'O.K.'

'Maintain that course for half an hour and then return to zero-eight-seven if you've heard nothing from me.'

'O.K.'

He hoped *Cadena* had understood, and then he remembered that on board her, probably on her bridge at that moment, were the Polish captain and the British liaison officer. They had heard him and would keep *Cadena*'s captain in line.

'Good-bye. Right full rudder. Steer course zero-eight-six. All engines ahead flank speed.'

Krause's orders were quietly repeated. Up here in the pilot-house everyone was aware of what was going on. Down below in the engine-room they would be ignorant. They would be conscious of *Keeling* having circled; they would not be able to guess what new crisis demanded the increase in speed. Their troubles were minor ones. All they had to do was to obey orders. Krause allowed the engine-room staff to disappear from his mind—a passing twinge of envy was left there like the passing swirl left by a sinking ship. These next few free minutes, while heading towards the unknown danger, he must think once more about breaking radio silence.

'Permission to change the clocks, sir?' said Nystrom, looming up beside him.

Change the clocks? Krause held himself back from a stupid repetition of the words. It was something he had forgotten all about, and yet something he should have remembered. They had just passed from one time zone to the next; they were an hour further forward into the day.

'Mr Watson's orders?' he asked.

'Yes, sir.'

Watson, as navigating officer, had been charged by Krause to alter the ship's time at the most convenient moment.

'Permission granted,' said Krause.

258

Nystrom could not know that he had broken into an important chain of thought in his captain's mind. Yet Nystrom's request had a powerful bearing on the subject of Krause's thoughts. Now the deadline he had once set himself for appealing for help was long past. He had been a fool not to think of that; even though it was only a nominal change and not an actual change—dawn was no nearer to them in actual minutes than it would have been if the time had not changed—the moral effect was profound. Besides, Krause was now reminded that the night was considerably shorter on an easterly course, heading for the sunrise. In any case, they were heading not only for the sunrise but towards a suspicious object, and at flank speed. He addressed himself to the voice-tube again.

'What do you make of that pip now?' he asked.

'It's still there, sir.'

'Is it big, or little? Can't you guess?'

'I'd say it was big, sir. Perhaps it's two pips like I said, sir. And I think it's moving, sir. Keeping on the same course as us.'

'But we're overtaking it?'

'Near as I can tell, yes, sir.'

He would have to identify the thing before he took any further action; not so easy in the darkness. Ten to one it was only a straggler from the convoy. He tried to raise *Dodge* and *James* on the voice circuit, but had to abandon the attempt in exasperated disappointment. They were out of T.B.S. range, unless—unless—that was a horrible thought. He could put it aside in any case. They could not both have been sunk without the look-outs observing some kind of explosion reflected from the high cloud in the darkness of the night.

'Can you estimate the range of that pip now?' he asked.

'Well, no, sir. Can't say that I can.'

Another voice came up the tube immediately after that unsatisfactory reply. It was Charlie Cole. Krause could not believe he had been asleep; probably he had been prowling round the ship inspecting.

'The bearing's constant, sir,' said Cole. 'And I'd say there are two pips for certain.'

'Thank you, Charlie.'

'And I'd say we're overtaking them fast.'

'Very well.'

Two pips being rapidly overtaken could only mean stragglers. There was no urgent anxiety, then. Krause reached that comforting conclusion and a second afterwards caught himself from swaying forward unconscious. Sleep was waiting like some half-tamed beast of prey ready to spring the moment he relaxed his vigilance. He was nearing the end of his second day without any sleep at all; two days of almost constant tension and strain. Two days spent almost entirely on his feet, too; there was no possible chance of forgetting that. Krause was glad when the bell pinged again.

'I got it tuned for a second just then, sir. Two pips for certain. And range four miles—that might be pretty accurate. Bearing zero-eight-six.'

'Very well.'

Better not to close too fast. Better to have the sonar working. Wait five minutes.

'All engines ahead standard speed. Resume sonar search.

'Engine-room answers "All engines ahead standard speed," sir.'

The abrupt diminution of vibration, the reduction in the sound of *Keeling*'s passage through the water, told their own story, as did the resumption in the steady pinging of the sonar.

'Sonar reports indications confused, sir.'

That would right itself as soon as *Keeling*'s speed fell to twelve knots.

'Forward look-out reports objects dead ahead, sir.'

'Very well.'

That would be three miles ahead, if Cole's estimate of range had been accurate. The look-out was doing his work well to sight the objects at that distance on a night like this.

'Captain to forward look-out. "Continue to report what you see." '

Friday. Morning Watch—0400-0800

He himself was standing, staring forward. At present he could see nothing there in the darkness. Nystrom was beside him, also gazing forward, and Krause became aware out of the tail of his eye that another figure was standing beside Nystrom—young Harbutt. The watch was changing.

'Forward look-out reports objects appear to be two ships, sir.'

'Very well.'

'Ships for sure, sir,' said Harbutt.

Now Krause could see them, something more than solid nuclei in the darkness. They were just ships, stragglers from the convoy. He felt considerable exasperation at having been subjected to his recent tension merely on their account.

'Forward look-out reports two merchant ships dead ahead, about two miles, close together, sir.'

'Very well. Captain to forward look-out. "We have those ships in sight from the bridge." '

'Reporting having been relieved, sir,' said Nystrom, and went on through the time-honoured formula.

'Very well, Mr Nystrom.'

'Sir,' said Harbutt. 'Have you any orders about general quarters this morning?'

Something else he had forgotten all about. In a hour, unless he countermanded his standing orders as he had done yesterday, general quarters would be sounded and the whole ship would be roused. The reasons that motivated his cancellation yesterday still held good. His men were doing four on and four off; they might as well have all the rest they could. He ought to have remembered it.

'No general quarters this morning unless it's the real thing,' he said. 'Put it on the loudspeaker.'

'Aye aye, sir.'

As they approached the dark ships he heard the announcement made.

'Now hear this. There'll be no——'

One of Uncle Sam's ships had acquired the nickname a few years ago of 'the beno ship,' because of the numerous announcements over her loudspeaker beginning that way; but those announcements had given warning that there would be no liberty that afternoon, and similar unpleasant news. This was different.

They were close up to the nearer ship now; he could see her churning wake.

'Left rudder. Meet her. Steady as you go.'

Now he could recognize her; a tanker with bridge and engines aft. That was *Hendrikson*. They were hailing already from her bridge by megaphone. Krause stepped out to the bull-horn; on his way he collided violently with a figure who had suddenly appeared at his elbow.

'Admiralty message, sir,' said the figure. It was Dawson's voice.

'One minute,' said Krause, although the words brought

a surge of life and excitement back into his numb body. He bellowed into the bull-horn. 'Comescort. What are you doing back here?'

'Ve touched that bastard over dere,' said a voice in reply. 'Buckled our bow plates. Yust saved ourselves. He will hear from my owners.'

'You don't seem to be much hurt. What did you do to him?'

'Hope I did plenty.'

'Can you maintain course and speed?'

'Yes.'

Keeling was fast drawing past *Hendrikson*; they were almost out of hailing distance.

'Maintain your course with modified zig. Plan Number Seven. Look out for *Cadena* coming up astern.'

'O.K.'

'Mr Harbutt, take the conn. Hail that fellow over there and find out what his damage is. If he's all right get him into column astern of the tanker and screen them both.'

'Aye aye, sir.'

'Now, Mr Dawson.'

Dawson had his clip-board; he had taken the dim red flashlight from the chart-table and shone it on the message. Krause took both clip-board and flashlight from him.

'Some of it's badly scrambled, sir,' apologized Dawson. 'I've done the best I can with it.'

Some of the words were only jumbles of letters. The others stood out with startling effect as Krause read them in the faint red light.

REINFORCEMENT DESPATCHED. A muddle of letters. ESCORT GROUP CAPTAIN EARL OF BANFF SNO. More muddles. EXPECT AIRCRAFT OP ORD 278-42 APPENDIX HYPO. More muddles.

'I'm sure of *that*, sir,' said Dawson, stabbing a finger at OP ORD. 'Here it is.'

Attached to the clip-board in addition to the message was the reference—HIS CHALLENGE UW YOUR ANSWER BD.

'Just as well,' said Krause. 'Messenger!'

'Yes, sir.'

'Ask the exec. to come to the bridge.' He had hesitated before speaking. The sentence he had framed in his mind—'My compliments to the executive officer and I would be glad if he were to come to the bridge'—had been ridiculously pompous, an echo of old battleship days in peacetime, and he had had to reframe it to suit wartime conditions in a destroyer.

He studied the message again. It was nearly twelve hours old, having taken much longer to come through than the previous Admiralty message, which had been given priority. The channels were congested but the Admiralty must have worked out that this would reach him in time for him to take the necessary action. But it was wonderful news that reinforcements were on their way. SNO meant senior naval officer in accordance with British usage, not one of those odd collections of letters like DSO or MBE which merely meant a decoration. And the SNO was a captain. That meant that he would be superseded in the command. His responsibility for the convoy would be ended. Krause found himself madly regretting that—regret without any alloy of relief. He would have liked to finish the job himself. His woolly fatigue was stirred into a resentment.

'I didn't dare guess at those scrambles, sir,' said Dawson. 'There were some numerals——'

'Very well, Mr Dawson.'

It was a little odd—strangely British—that the Admiralty should go to the trouble of informing him that Captain

Earl, who was going to take over command, came from Banff. Krause thought of the Canadian Rockies and Lake Louise; but there might be a Banff in Britain, the same as there was a Boston and a Newport. But in that case why mention it? It could only be of importance if Earl was a Canadian. The explanation suddenly shot up in Krause's mind, adding a trifle of amusement to temper his irritation and resentment. This must be one of those English lords— Captain the Earl of Banff. And with the British 'aircraft' was the usual and not the unusual way of saying 'plane.'

'Yes, Cap'n?' said Cole, arriving.

'Read this,' said Krause, handing over clip-board and flashlight.

Cole bent to read, the flashlight held within two inches of the paper. It was Krause's bounden duty to inform his second in command of news as important as this.

'That's fine, sir,' said Cole. 'You'll be able to take a rest.'

He could not in the darkness see the expression on Krause's face, or he might have used other words.

'Yes,' said Krause, harshly.

'Sent at eighteen hundred G.C.T.,' commented Cole. 'And it says the relief has already been despatched. Won't be long before we meet them. They'll do a high-speed run without zigging. Well, they can't arrive too early.'

'No,' said Krause.

'Do you know this Captain Earl, sir?' asked Cole.

'That's not his name,' said Krause, and for the life of him he could not help feeling superior. 'He's a lord. The Earl of Banff.'

'An earl? But you haven't ever spoken to him, sir?'

'No,' said Krause. 'Not to remember. I mean I am sure I haven't.'

The last sentence was jerked out of him by conscience to

make up for the one before it. Krause had met many British naval officers, but he would certainly have remembered meeting the Earl of Banff, and it was dishonest to imply that he was capable of forgetting it.

'You can't risk a guess about these cipher groups, Dawson?' asked Cole.

'No, sir. I was saying so to the captain. There are numerals in them, which makes it hard.'

'No doubt about the numerals,' commented Cole. 'Time of meeting not stated. Position not stated. But that plane will be here within an hour of sunrise, sir. You can be sure of that.'

'I think so,' said Krause.

'I never heard better news in my life, sir,' said Cole. 'Thank you for letting me in on it.'

It was quite obvious that Cole had not the least notion that Krause could feel any bitterness regarding his supersession.

'Cap'n, sir,' said Harbutt.

During this last conversation they had been aware of Harbutt carrying on a bellowed conversation through the loud-hailer, giving orders to the wheel, and occasionally swearing to himself.

'Yes, Mr Harbutt?'

'The other freighter's *Southland*, sir. She's pretty well caved in on the starboard quarter, they tell me. But most of the damage is above water-line and they can cope with the leaks. *Hendrikson*'s damage is all above water-line. I've got 'em into column, *Southland* leading. She says she can make ten and a half knots, and *Hendrikson*'s good for eleven. And here's *Cadena* coming up astern, sir.'

'How far ahead's the convoy?'

'Four miles is what radar guesses, sir. Can't see 'em yet.'

'Very well, Mr Harbutt. Get *Cadena* into column as well and patrol ahead of them.'

'Aye aye, sir.'

Cole addressed himself to Dawson as Harbutt withdrew.

'You're sure of this challenge and reply?' he asked.

'As sure as I am of anything, sir,' said Dawson.

It was necessary to size up Dawson's capabilities and mentality. He had not spoken overboldly or pathetically.

'Just as well,' said Cole, repeating Krause's very words. 'We might have him here in two hours.'

'How do you make that out, Charlie?' asked Krause. In the nick of time he had repressed an exclamation of surprise.

'We're on G.C.T. now, sir,' replied Cole. 'Sunrise this morning here will be zero-six-thirty-five. It's zero-five-twenty now. You can see it's getting light already, sir.'

So it was. Undoubtedly it was. Cole's and Dawson's figures were not black shadows; a hint of their white faces was perceptible. Two hours! It was fantastically unbelievable.

'We're well on schedule,' said Krause.

'Ahead of where they'll expect us to be, sir,' supplemented Cole.

The Admiralty could have no certainty about the position of the convoy. In view of their recommendation of two days ago—two days? It seemed more like two weeks—of a radical change of course, and in view of the numerous D.F. bearings on U-boats that they must have had, they might guess that the convoy was far behind schedule. But it had ploughed steadily on with almost no delay.

'*Dodge* and *James* have to know about this,' said Krause, tapping the clip-board with his gloved hand. 'I'll tell 'em. I couldn't raise them last night. They were too far.'

'I'd better stand by, sir,' volunteered Dawson, with a queer hint of apology in his voice. 'Perhaps——'

What Dawson was saying trailed off into significant incoherence as Krause went to the T.B.S. Dawson knew something about the ways of communications officers, and about the ways of commanding officers, too; and so did Krause. The Admiralty message was addressed to Comescort, but *Dodge* and *James* were likely to have taken it in. And they were likely to have decoded it as well, even though to do so would be a mild infraction of orders. It would be hard for discipline to withstand the assaults of curiosity at this moment and in these circumstances.

When Krause began speaking to the two ships the replies he received echoed Dawson's apologetic tone comically, despite the way that the T.B.S. took most of the expression out of the voices.

'Yes, sir,' said Dicky; and after a moment's hesitation. 'We took that signal in too.'

'I guessed so,' said Krause. 'You have the challenge and reply?'

'Yes, sir.'

'Did you unscramble those numerals?'

'It wasn't a numeral, sir,' answered Dicky. 'It was "point T." We made that bit out to be "Anticipate point of contact point T." '

'We're nearly up to point T now,' said Krause.

'Yes, sir.'

Help, then, was very close at hand. And he had not appealed for it.

'And we got another bit, sir,' said Harry. ' "Report position if north of fifty-seven." '

They were well to the south of fifty-seven degrees North Latitude.

'Thank you,' said Krause. He would not take official notice of the venial sin. And in any case if he had been

268

killed in the night action they would have had to have decoded that message. They could not be sure. That started
another train of thought. It was hard to keep everything in
mind, even the unpleasant thing he was thinking about.

'Did you know,' he asked, 'that *Viktor* was lost last night?'

'No!' said a shocked voice over the T.B.S.

'Yes,' said Krause. 'She was hit just at dusk and went
down at midnight.'

'Anyone saved, sir?' asked the T.B.S., subdued.

'Everyone, I think, except those killed in the explosion.'

'Is old Tubby all right, sir?'

'The British liaison officer?'

'Yes, sir.'

'I think so.'

'I'm glad, sir,' said one voice, and the other said, 'It
would take more than that to drown old Tubby.'

Krause had imagined the owner of that lackadaisical
voice to be tall and lean; apparently he was nothing of the
sort.

'Well, you fellows,' said Krause; the tired mind had to
pick its words carefully again, for a formal moment was
approaching and he was dealing with allies. 'It won't be
long now.'

'No, sir.'

'I won't be in command much longer.' He had to say
that steadily and with every appearance of indifference.
The T.B.S. waited in sympathetic silence, and he went on,
'I have to thank you both for everything you've done.'

'Thank *you*, sir,' said one voice.

'Yes,' said the other, 'it's us that have to thank you, sir.'

'You're very welcome,' said Krause, banally and
idiotically. 'But that's all I have to say. Except good-bye
for now.'

'Good-bye, sir. Good-bye.'

He came away from the T.B.S. feeling sad.

'Now about you, sir,' said Cole. 'When did you eat last?'

Krause was taken completely by surprise by the question. At some time or other he had eaten cold cuts and salad, but to pin-point the time in his memory was absolutely beyond him. Watch had succeeded watch with, in retrospect, a rapidity that left him bewildered.

'I had some coffee,' he said, lamely.

'Nothing else since I ordered dinner for you, sir?'

'No,' said Krause. And he had no intention whatever of allowing his private life to be supervised by his executive officer, even though that officer was his lifetime friend. 'I'm not hungry.'

'Fourteen hours since you ate last, sir,' said Cole.

'What I want to do,' said Krause asserting his independence, 'is to get down to the head. I don't want to eat.'

He formed an irritating mental picture of himself as a fretful child and Charlie Cole as an imperturbable nurse. He had used a child's excuse.

'That's fine, sir. I'll get breakfast ordered for you while you're gone. I suppose there's no chance of your taking a rest until that plane shows up, sir?'

'Of course not,' said Krause.

This was Krause's first campaign; at least it would teach him the necessity of snatching every available minute later on in the war. But his indignant negative had salved his dignity.

'I was afraid not, sir,' said Cole. 'Messenger!'

Cole applied himself to giving orders for finding a mess attendant and having bacon and eggs prepared for the captain. And Krause found himself in the position of a man whose casual remark turns out to be true. Now that he had announced that he wanted to go to the head he was in a state of overwhelming anxiety to do so. It was shockingly urgent. He could not wait another minute. He found it was very difficult, nevertheless, to drag himself over to the ladder and start the descent. With his foot on the rung he remembered the red spectacles, and with relief decided they would not be necessary now that the light was increasing topside. He went on painfully down the ladder, into the cold light and bleak silence of the ship. His head was swimming and his whole body ached. There was a dull but distressing pain in the back of his head, and it was agony to transfer his weight from one foot to the other. He shambled into the head; he had no eyes for anything about him, and he shambled out again. The bridge seemed unbearably far away, until his tired mind recalled that before long touch would be gained with the mainland. The thought of it brought a little life back into his body. He actually mounted the ladder with a certain amount of verve. Cole saluted him as he came into the pilot-house.

'I'm going to take a look at the gun crews and look-outs, sir,' he said.

'Very well, Charlie. Thank you.'

He had to sit down. He simply had to sit. He made his way over to his stool and sank down on it. The relief, what with sitting and what with having been to the head, was considerable. All but his feet. They seemed to be red-hot with agony. A wicked thought came rising up into his mind; he had discarded it once, long before, but now it returned, repulsive and yet insistent, like an insufficiently weighted corpse rising with corruption from the depths. He could take off his shoes. He could defy convention. He could be bold. Important it might be for his crew always to see their captain correctly dressed, but it could not be at this moment more important than the misery of his feet. Nothing could be more important. He was being tortured like an Indian captive. He had to—he simply must. It might be the first step down the slippery path of complete moral disintegration, yet even so he could not hold back. He reached painfully down and undid a shoe-string. He loosened it in its eyelets. He took the mental plunge, and, hand on heel, tried to thrust off the shoe. It resisted stubbornly for a moment and then—and then—the blend of agony and paradise as it came off was something indescribable; only just for a moment did it remind him of Evelyn with whom he had experienced something similar. He forgot Evelyn at once as he worked his toes about, stretched out his foot, felt the returning life creeping back within the thick arctic sock. The necessary seconds to take off the other shoe were hardly bearable. Both feet were free now; all ten toes were squirming with joy. To put the freed soles down on the icy steel deck and feel the chill penetrate the thick socks was a sensuous pleasure so intense that Krause actually forgot to be suspicious of it. He stretched his legs and felt the relieved circulation welling through his muscles. He stretched luxuriously, and caught himself at that moment—or several moments later; he did not know how many—falling forward from the waist sound asleep. He would have been on his nose on the deck in another second.

It was the end of bliss. He was back in a world of war, a world of steel, swaying on a slate-grey sea; and this steel ship of his might at any moment be torn open in thunder and flame with that grey sea flooding in through the holes, exploding boilers and drowning the dazed survivors. There was the pinging of the sonar to remind him of the sleepless watch that was being maintained against the enemies deep below the surface. Far ahead of him he could see a row of dim shapes on the horizon which were the helpless ships he had to guard; he had only to turn on his stool to see behind him the three others he was trying to lead to safety.

'T.B.S., sir,' said Harbutt. 'Harry.'

He had already forgotten about taking his shoes off; it was a surprise to find himself walking in his stockinged feet. But there was nothing he could do about that at present.

'George to Harry. Go ahead.'

The careful precise tones of Lieutenant-Commander Rode spoke into his ear.

'We have an aircraft approaching on our screen, sir. Range sixty miles, bearing oh-nine-oh.'

'Thank you, Captain. It may be the plane we have to look out for.'

'It may be, sir.' The tone suggested that Rode had been bombed so often from the air that he took nothing for granted, and the next words went on to confirm the impression. 'I've seen Condors as far out as here, sir. But we'll know soon enough.'

'I don't doubt it.'

'I'll report again as soon as I'm sure, sir.'

'Very well, Captain, thank you.'

Krause's heart was beating perceptibly faster as he put down the hand-set. Friend or enemy, the report meant that he had achieved touch with the far side of the ocean.

'Cap'n, sir, yo' breffus.'

There was the tray with its white napkin cover raised into peaks by what lay under it. He eyed it without interest. If the plane were sixty miles from *James* it would be seventy-five miles from *Keeling*. In a quarter of an hour it would be in sight; in half an hour it might be overhead. Common-sense dictated that he should eat while he had time, and while the food was hot. But between fatigue and excitement he had no appetite.

'Oh, very well. Put it on the chart-table.'

He had forgotten again about being in his stockinged feet. And there were his shoes, lying disgracefully on the deck. He paid ten times over in that minute for the ecstasy he had felt when he had taken them off.

'Messenger! Take those shoes of mine to my cabin and bring me the slippers you'll find there.'

'Aye aye, sir.'

The messenger evinced no concern at being ordered on such a menial duty; it was Krause who felt the concern. He tasted all the bitterness of the pill he had to swallow; he was sensitive about the dignity of the men who served under him; and was quite unnecessarily worried about the messenger's feelings. He could order the messenger into mortal danger more easily than he could order him to pick up his shoes. Already, forgetting the agony that had forced him into taking off his shoes, he was taking a mental vow never to indulge himself in that fashion again. It lessened his appetite for food even farther. But he plodded over to the desk and lifted the covers indifferently. Fried eggs, golden and white, looked up at him; from strips of bacon a pleasant odour rose to his nostrils. And coffee! Coffee! The scent of that as he poured it was utterly enticing. He drank; he began to eat.

'Your slippers, sir,' said the messenger, putting them on the deck beside him.

'Thank you,' replied Krause with his mouth full.

Charlie Cole was just entering the pilot-house when he was called again to the T.B.S.

'Catalina in sight, sir,' said Harry.

'Good,' answered Krause. It was only then that he knew

he had been worrying in case it had been a Condor. 'Is her challenge correct?'

'Yes, sir. And I have made reply.'

'Plane in sight! Plane dead ahead!'

Keeling's look-outs were shouting wildly.

'Very well, thank you, Captain,' said Krause.

'PBY, sir,' said Cole, his binoculars to his eyes, looking at the bright eastern horizon, and then, loudly, 'Very well, you men. It's one of ours.'

The 20 mm. gun crews had already started training their weapons forward and upward. It was a black dot over the convoy, approaching fast. It was winking at him feverishly. Dot dot dash dot dash dash.

'Plane signals "U W," sir,' from the signal-bridge.

'Very well. Reply "B D." '

U W U W—that pilot had been shot at by so many friendly ships he wanted to make quite sure he was recognized. Now the plane was visible in detail, with all the clumsy comforting elephantine outlines of a PBY.

'One of ours, not British, sir,' commented Cole.

The stars were plain on the wings. It roared on overhead; at the 40 mm. guns the men raised a cheer and waved their arms. It passed on astern; Krause and Cole turned to watch it as it went nearly out of sight. Then they saw it swing leftwards, to the south.

'Checking up on how far we're scattered,' said Krause.

'I guess so, sir. It looks like that. And he'll scare down any sub. within thirty miles, too, sir.'

So he would. In this clear daylight no sub. would venture to remain on the surface with a plane circling overhead. And below the surface a sub. would be half-blind and slow, no danger to the convoy unless fortunately right in the convoy's path. The PBY swung on round, and settled on

275

an easterly course back past the right flank of the convoy. They watched it steadily dwindling in size.

'Isn't he going to cover us, sir?' asked Cole.

'I know what he's doing,' said Krause. 'He's homing the escort group on us.'

A bird of the air shall carry the voice, and that which hath wings shall tell the matter. The Earl of Banff and his escort group were already far out at sea, and the PBY was going to inform them of the bearing of the convoy.

'His course is not much south of east, sir,' said Cole, binoculars to his eyes. 'They must be nearly dead ahead of us.'

Nearly dead ahead, and probably making fourteen knots. Relief and convoy were heading towards each other at a combined speed of twenty-three knots at least. In an hour or two they would be in sight of each other. Less than that, perhaps. Krause looked forward; the rear line of the convoy was now hull-up; *Keeling* had brought the lost sheep back to the flock.

'Out of sight, sir,' said Cole taking the glasses from his eyes.

Now there was no knowing how much farther the PBY would be going.

'What about your breakfast, sir?' asked Cole.

Krause would not admit that he could not remember in what condition he had left his tray. He walked over to it. The large plate bore a cold egg and strips of congealed bacon.

'I'll send for some more, sir,' said Cole.

'No, thank you,' replied Krause. 'I've had all I want.'

'Surely you could use some coffee, sir. This is cold.'

'Well——'

'Messenger! Bring the captain another pot of coffee.'

276

'Thank you,' said Krause.

'Watch is just going to change, sir. I'll get down to the plot.'

'Very well, Charlie.'

When Cole had gone Krause looked down again at the tray. Automatically his hand went out and he picked up a piece of toast and started to eat it. It was cold and leathery, but it disappeared with remarkable rapidity. Krause spread the other piece thick with butter and jelly and ate that. Then he found himself picking up the strips of cold bacon and eating them too.

Friday. Forenoon Watch—0800-1200

Harbutt saluted and reported his relief.

'Very well, Mr Harbutt. Mr Carling! I want a fuel report from the engine room.'

'Aye aye, sir.'

Krause looked again at the convoy and back at the three ships aft. Was it sentimental to want to be at the head of his command when the reinforcements arrived?

'Pardon me, sir,' said the messenger, putting hot coffee on the tray in front of him.

'Get me a signal-pad and pencil,' said Krause.

He wrote out the message.

COMESCORT TO SHIPS ASTERN. RESUME STATIONS IN CONVOY.

'Signal bridge,' he ordered. 'And tell them to send slowly.'

'Aye aye, sir.'

'The T.B.S., sir,' said Carling.

It was *James*.

'The Catalina's crossing our course at thirty-five miles,

sir. Looks as if the escort group isn't far ahead. Thought you'd like to know, sir.'

'I sure would. Thanks a lot,' said Krause.

He was on the way back to his coffee when the messenger saluted him.

'Ships astern acknowledge message, sir.'

'Very well.'

Lieutenant-Commander Ipsen up from the engine room with his written fuel report. Enough for fifty-seven hours' steaming at economical speeds. Enough.

'Thank you, Chief. Very well.'

'Thank you, sir.'

Ahead of him the convoy was practically in good order. He could go ahead up a lane in safety.

'I'll take the conn, Mr Carling.'

'Aye aye, sir.'

Keeling drew away from the ships astern and entered the lane. Ships all round him. Battered ships and nearly new ships, with every colour of paintwork and every style of build. There had been thirty-seven ships when he had taken over escort duty. Now there were thirty; seven had been lost. Heavy losses, no doubt, but convoys had known even heavier than that. He had brought thirty ships through. Out of his escort force he had lost a destroyer; a very grave loss indeed. But he had sunk two probables and a possible. Thou art weighed in the balance—in the balance —he came to himself with a start. While having the conn, while actually in charge of the ship, he had gone to sleep on his feet, here in a convoy lane with danger all round. While I was musing the fire burned. He had never before known such fatigue.

Coffee might help. It was only then that he remembered the pot that had been brought him. It was nearly cold, but he drank it, draining the second cup as they emerged ahead of the convoy.

'Mr Carling! Take the conn.'

'Aye aye, sir.'

'Take station three miles ahead of the commodore.'

'Aye aye, sir.'

'Forward look-out reports plane dead ahead, sir.'

It was the PBY back again. Krause watched it alter course patrolling in long leisurely zig-zags far out on either side of the convoy's course. Oh, that I had wings like a dove. Visibility was excellent, the sea moderate.

'Forward look-out reports object dead ahead, sir.'

Krause raised his binoculars. There was nothing in view. Nothing? Nothing? The tiniest speck on the distant horizon.

'Forward look-out reports object is a ship.'

This was the moment. Wink-wink. Wink-wink-wink. Already a light was flashing there. Overhead he heard the clank of *Keeling*'s lamp answering. Wink-wink-wink. He could not keep his heart from beating fast. He could not keep his hands from trembling a little.

'Well, we've made it, sir,' said Cole beside him.

'We have,' answered Krause. He was aware of a dryness of the throat that affected his voice.

The messenger came running.

SNO TO COMESCORT. WELCOME. KINDLY MAKE VERBAL REPORT TO DIAMOND.

There followed a wave frequency. Krause handed the message pad to Cole and walked over to the T.B.S. It was not easy to walk so far.

'George to Diamond. Do you hear me?'

'Diamond to George. I hear you.' Another of those English voices. 'Afraid you've had a rough time.'

'Not so rough, sir. We've lost seven ships out of the convoy and two slightly damaged.'

'Only seven?'

'Yes, sir. *King's Langley, Henrietta*——'

'It doesn't matter about the names at present.'

It was a relief to hear that; it was only with an effort that he could recollect them.

'We've lost Eagle, too, sir.'

'Eagle? That's bad luck.'

'Yes, sir. She was hit in the engine-room last night.' Last night? It was almost impossible to believe it was only then. Krause steadied his reeling mind. 'And she sank at midnight. Everything was done to save her.'

'I don't doubt it, Captain. And what is the condition of your command?'

'In this ship we have fuel for fifty-six hours' steaming at economical speed, sir. We had one slight hit from a four-inch on our main-deck aft with unimportant damage. Three killed and two wounded, sir.'

'A four-inch?'

'A sub. fought it out on the surface, sir. We got him. I think we got two more. The conduct of the other ships of the escort was excellent, sir.'

'Three subs.? Well done! I don't expect you've a depth-charge left.'

'We have two, sir.'

'M'm.' It was a vague meditative remark over the T.B.S. 'And your other two ships? What are their code names?'

'Harry and Dicky, sir.'

'I'll ask them to report to me direct.'

Krause heard them reporting. *Dodge* with her gun out of action, with no depth-charges, serious damage forward,

280

adequately patched, and fuel for thirty-seven hours. *James* with three depth-charges and fuel for thirty-one hours.

'It'll be a tight squeeze for you to make it to 'Derry,' commented Diamond, who must be Captain the Earl of Banff.

'Might just do it, sir,' said *James*.

'Not too sure,' said Diamond.

Krause heard him say it while a wave of sleep broke over him again; like the waves of a rising tide the need for sleep was reaching higher and higher and submerging his faculties longer on each occasion. He steadied himself. The new force was hull up over the horizon now, four ships in rigid column, Diamond's destroyer in the lead, three escort vessels astern of her.

'I'm going to detach you three,' said Diamond. 'You can make the best of your way to 'Derry.'

'Sir,' said Krause, goading his mind to think of the right words. 'This is George. Submit I stay with the convoy. I've fuel to spare.'

'No, I'm afraid not,' said Diamond. 'I want you to see these two boys get home all right. They're not fit to be out by themselves.'

It was said lightly, but there was a positive quality about the words; Krause felt it in the same way as, when his blade slipped along an opponent's foil, his wrist would feel the transition from foible to forte.

'Aye aye, sir,' he said.

'Form on the left flank of the convoy,' said Diamond. 'I'll come in on the right.'

'Aye aye, sir.'

'You've done the hell of a good job, Captain,' said Diamond. 'We were all worried about you.'

'Thank you, sir,' said Krause.

'Good-bye and good luck,' said Diamond.

'Thank you, sir,' said Krause. 'Good-bye. George to Harry. George to Dicky. Form column astern of me. Speed thirteen knots. Course zero-eight-seven.'

Along with his fatigue the blackest depression was settling on him. Something was over, finished. Those last heartening words of Diamond's might be very gratifying. It was obvious that by bringing his charge within touch of England, and handing it over to the relieving force, he had completed the duty entrusted to him. I have fought a good fight, I have finished my course. Could he say that? Perhaps. Yet this unutterable sadness possessed him, even while he mechanically gave the orders that carried him away from the ships he had guarded so long. He looked back at them. There was a long, long war ahead of him, he knew. He would fight, he would know agony and danger, but even if he lived he would be unlikely ever to set eyes on those ships again. He had a last duty to fulfil, a final step to take for the sake of international accord.

'Messenger! Signal-pad and pencil.'

He hesitated over the first word. But he would use it once more during these last seconds. COMESCORT TO COM-CONVOY. GOOD-BYE. MOST GRATEFUL THANKS FOR YOUR SPLENDID CO-OPERATION. GOD SPEED AND GOOD LUCK.

'Signal bridge,' he said. 'Come right to course zero-eight-seven, Mr Carling.'

He heard the quartermaster repeat Carling's order.

'Right rudder to course zero-eight-seven, sir. Steady on course zero-eight-seven.'

Overhead the shutters of the lamp were clattering as his message went out. *James* and *Dodge* were wheeling round to take station astern of him. The relieving force was moving into screening positions, the White Ensigns flying.

Terrible as an army with banners. He was swaying again on his feet. The Canadian Ensign and the White Ensign were following along behind the Stars and Stripes, but there was no Polish Ensign. The commodore was winking back at him now. He fought back his fatigue again and waited.

The messenger brought the signal pad. COMCONVOY TO COMESCORT. IT IS FOR US TO THANK YOU FOR YOUR MAGNIFI-CENT WORK. DEEPEST GRATITUDE FROM US ALL. HEARTIEST GOOD WISHES.

That was all for now. It was finished.

'Very well,' he said to the messenger. 'Mr Carling, I'll be in the sea-cabin if you want me.'

'Aye aye, sir.'

Charlie Cole was standing, eyeing him closely, but he had not the strength even to exchange a word with him. A little sleep, a little slumber, a little folding of the hands to sleep. Blindly he found his way to the cabin.

3

I T was swaying round him. He fumbled at the hood
which had hung unbuttoned for so long round his face,
and a lucky tug dragged it off. He put his hands to the
buttons of the sheepskin coat but he did not succeed in
unfastening them. He wanted to sleep. He dropped to his
knees by the bunk and put his hands before his face.

'Dear Jesus.'

It was the attitude and the words he had used when he
was a child, when the beloved mother so shadowy in his
memory had told him about the gentle Christ-child, to
whom a little boy could take his troubles. The sunshine of
his childhood was round him. The sun had always shone
when he was little. He had been enfolded in love. When
the sweet mother had faded from his life the dear father
had loved him enough for two, the father whose desolate
mouth could always smile for him. The dear father; the
sun had shone when they went fishing together—the sun
had brightened their happiness and their excitement as they
took the train to Carquinez Straits to fish for bass and on the
very few, the memorable occasions when they had taken the
ferry across the bay and had places in a boat through the
Golden Gate out on to the tossing ocean under the golden

sun. He had learned his texts, he had read his Bible for that, because when he knew his texts they could go fishing, and only then; the father was sad when he did not know them.

Krause forgot the sunshine; his knees were uncomfortable on the steel deck and his face was buried in his hands on the bunk. In a second of returning consciousness he squirmed forward and upward on to the bunk, lying breast downward on it with his face turned to one side. He lay spreadeagled, the sprouting beard disfiguring his dirty face, his mouth a little open, as heavily asleep as if he were dead .

He had learned texts at home while he learned mathematics at high school. He had learned about duty and honour, too, the two inseparables. He had learned about charity, about being kind, to think well of everybody but impartially about himself even while the sun shone on him. The sunshine ceased when his father died, leaving him an orphan just graduating from high school when America was entering into a war. The Senator had nominated the much-loved pastor's orphan son to Annapolis, a nomination strange for those days as it brought no political benefit, strengthened no political alliance, even though the nomination was old-fashioned enough in that no attempt was made to select the most academically suitable candidate.

Three hundred dollars; that was the estate his father left him when he died, when his books and furniture had been sold. It paid Krause's fare to Annapolis; he could have managed without the balance, living on his pay as midshipman; the class of 1922 graduated in 1921 in the aftermath of war, and Krause graduated with it, half-way up the list not specially noted for anything except for the above average skill in fencing which he unexpectedly discovered. He had learned something of discipline and subordination and self-control to supplement his childhood training. The

Senator's nomination had directed a considerable potential into a channel that Krause would never have selected for himself. It was one of those freaks of chance that may change the fate of nations. Without his Annapolis training Krause would have grown up into a very similar man, but perhaps without the unrelenting realism that stiffened his humanity. Severe and logical discipline, grained into him, produced an odd effect when reinforcing an undeviating Christian spirit that already knew little of compromise.

The United States Navy was his home and he knew no other for so many years. He had no family, not a relation in the world, and when the chances of service brought him back to the scenes of his childhood the changes that had taken place there cut him off from that past as if with a knife. Oakland was noisy and different, and the Berkeley hills were built over. Carquinez Straits with so many happy memories were now crossed by a vast and terrible bridge of steel jammed with squawking traffic, and soon the ferries on the Bay were replaced by other bridges over which the traffic hurtled with a pitiless single-mindedness so unlike what he remembered. The sun did not shine as warmly; the kindness and the kindliness seemed to have disappeared.

The transition was abrupt; it seemed as if he had never lived here. Some other little boy, about whom he had heard in much detail, had lived here, had trotted to the grocery store holding his mother's hand, had sat enchanted at the circus, had walked to school round those corners which were now so different. It was not he; he had no past, no roots. What he knew as home was enclosed between four steel bulkheads; what he knew as family life went on in the wardroom and at captain's mast. Promotion came, to lieutenant junior grade, to lieutenant, to lieutenant-commander, responsibility expanding with his experience.

286

For seventeen years, from eighteen to thirty-five, he lived for nothing but his duty; that was why those hateful words 'fitted and retained' hit him so hard, even though he knew that in the service of which he was a part there could only be one commander for every ten lieutenant-commanders.

But that came after he had met Evelyn, which made it all the harder. He had loved her as only a single-minded man can love a woman; the first love of a man of thirty-five, and she was in her early twenties and both brilliant and beautiful—he thought so, which was all that mattered —but for all her brilliance she had failed to appreciate the tragic implications of 'fitted and retained.' He could not believe her to be unsympathetic, and still less could he believe her to be stupid, and so the deductions to be made regarding himself cut still more deeply. He had loved her so madly, so frantically. He had known an intoxication, an active happiness, quite unlike any other experience, and it had been so overwhelming that it had stilled completely the doubts he might have felt regarding his unworthiness of so much happiness and his uneasy feeling that no man should be so deficient in self-control. It had been a supreme moment. There was the house in Coronado; during those weeks roots began to sprout; Southern California with its sun-baked beaches and its barren hills began to be 'home.'

And then 'fitted and retained.' Evelyn's inability to understand. The unworthy, hideous suspicion that the idol had feet of clay; the suspicion strengthened by Evelyn's lack of sympathy towards his determination to do his duty —and that determination strengthened, contrariwise, by the service's opinion of him expressed in 'fitted and retained.' The quarrels had begun, the bitter, bitter quarrels, when everything combined to goad him into insane rages, and the rages were followed by black remorse that he could have ever said such things to Evelyn, that he could have said such things to any woman at all, and further that he could have lost his self-control to such a frightening extent, just as he had forgotten his self-control when he was in bed—uneasy thought.

Yet all this did little or nothing to lessen the pain when Evelyn told him about the black-haired lawyer. That was pain such that he did not know could ever be suffered by anyone. The dreadful pain when she told him; unrelieved unhappiness; not even pride could help him. The pain persisted as he went through the necessary formalities, rising to fresh peaks sometimes as he went on with them, when he was confronted afresh by the inability to retrace a single step—not to halt the legal proceedings, but to undo deeds that had been done, and to unsay words that had been said. Then there was the culminating peak of pain on the wedding day, and the wedding night.

There was still duty to be done and life to be lived; and it did not clash with duty to ask BuPers for assignment to the Atlantic seaboard, away from Southern California and the house in Coronado; to tear off the fragile roots that had begun to sprout; to face the rest of life with duty as his sole companion. Chance—the chance that elevated a paranoiac to supreme power in Germany and a military clique to power in Japan—dictated that when it was too late he should receive the coveted promotion to commander, if it can be called chance. Chance had made him an orphan; chance had brought about the Senator's nomination. Chance had put him in command of the convoy escort. Chance had made him the man he was and had given that man the duty he had to carry out.

Now he was asleep. He could be called happy now, lying spreadeagled and face downward on his bunk, utterly unconscious.

———————————— ★ ————————————